Reviews of Note
from colleagues and professionals

THIS GROUND-BREAKING, ONE-OF-A-KIND BOOK DEALS WITH THE SPECIAL REWARDS OF OUTDOOR ADVENTURE, RISK-TAKING, AND WILDERNESS EXPERIENCES FOR WOMEN.... As a licensed Adirondack wilderness guide, I have long recognized the boost to self-reliance, self-confidence, and general health that our excursions bring to women. Now, the authors present proof of the liberating and empowering value of wilderness therapy."

—Dr. Anne LaBastille, Wildlife Ecologist and Author, *Woodswoman, Beyond Black Bear Lake,* and *Women and Wilderness,* Lives at the edge of the Adirondack wilderness

Will be thoroughly enjoyed by professionals who work with women's groups in adventure programs. It is a heartfelt anthology of how wilderness activities provide transformational experiences for women.... REQUIRED READING FOR THOSE PROGRAMS AND STAFF WORKING WITH WOMEN SURVIVORS OF INCEST AND RAPE."

—Michael A. Gass, PhD, Coordinator, Outdoor Education Program, Chair, Department of Kinesiology, School of Health and Human Services, University of New Hampshire

ENJOYABLE.... IT IS PACKED WITH MUCH-NEEDED INFORMATION FOR THE PROFESSIONAL. ....Contains rich material to spark discussions among those planning to become involved in wilderness leadership/therapy.... Virtually all selections in the book present significant detail through narrative and statistics ... while holding one's interest through the use of action images.... A VITAL ADDITION TO YOUR LIBRARY."

—Carol F. Harley, BA, Editor, *Women Outdoors*

In my years of working as an Outward Bound instructor and teaching in the field of psychology, I always wished for some means of conveying the message that I so often observed among women who were seeking to discover their own strengths. I never expected to find it so clearly and powerfully related in a collection of writings by women, for women. But find it I did in this book. . . . Clearly offers a journey of healing through the 'power of adventure' and the therapeutic medium of wilderness experience. . . . A GUIDEBOOK FOR ALL WOMEN, PIONEERS, AND EXPLORERS OF THE MYRIAD BENEFITS OF WILDERNESS EXPERIENCE."

—Virginia Savage, PhD, Sport Psychologist, Faculty, Outdoor Action, Prescott College

Wilderness Therapy for Women: The Power of Adventure

Wilderness Therapy for Women: The Power of Adventure

Ellen Cole, PhD
Eve Erdman, MLS, MEd
Esther D. Rothblum, PhD
Editors

Wilderness Therapy for Women: The Power of Adventure, edited by Ellen Cole, Eve Erdman, and Esther D. Rothblum, was simultaneously issued by The Haworth Press, Inc., under the same title, as a special issue of the journal *Women & Therapy*, Volume 15, Numbers 3/4, 1994, Ellen Cole, and Esther D. Rothblum, Editors.

Harrington Park Press
An Imprint of
The Haworth Press, Inc.
New York · London · Norwood (Australia)

1-56023-058-4

Published by

Harrington Park Press, 10 Alice Street, Binghamton, NY 13904-1580

Harrington Park Press is an imprint of The Haworth Press, Inc., 10 Alice Street, Binghamton, NY 13904-1580 USA.

Wilderness Therapy for Women: The Power of Adventure has also been published as *Women & Therapy*, Volume 15, Numbers 3/4 1994.

The Haworth Press, Inc., 10 Alice Street, Binghamton, NY 13904-1580, USA

Library of Congress Cataloging-in-Publication Data

Wilderness therapy for women : the power of adventure / Ellen Cole, Eve Erdman, Esther D. Rothblum, editors.
    p. cm.
    Also published as: Women & therapy, v. 15, no. 3/4, 1994.
    Includes bibliographical references and index.
    ISBN 1-56024-682-0 (acid-free paper).–ISBN 1-56023-058-4 (acid-free paper)
    1. Adventure therapy. 2. Feminist therapy. 3. Wilderness survival. I. Cole, Ellen. II. Erdman, Eve. III. Rothblum, Editor D. IV. Women & therapy.
RC489.A38W55 1994
616.89'165–dc20

94-17240
CIP

INDEXING & ABSTRACTING

Contributions to this publication are selectively indexed or abstracted in print, electronic, online, or CD-ROM version(s) of the reference tools and information services listed below. This list is current as of the copyright date of this publication. See the end of this section for additional notes.

- *Abstracts of Research in Pastoral Care & Counseling*, Loyola College, 7135 Minstrel Way, Suite 101, Columbia, MD 21045

- *Academic Index (on-line)*, Information Access Company, 362 Lakeside Drive, Foster City, CA 94404

- *Alternative Press Index*, Alternative Press Center, Inc., P.O. Box 33109, Baltimore, MD 21218-0401

- *Digest of Neurology and Psychiatry*, The Institute of Living, 400 Washington Street, Hartford, CT 06106

- *Expanded Academic Index,* Information Access Company, 362 Lakeside Drive, Forest City, CA 94404

- *Family Violence & Sexual Assault Bulletin*, Family Violence & Sexual Assault Institute, 1310 Clinic Drive, Tyler, TX 75701

- *Feminist Periodicals: A Current Listing of Contents*, Women's Studies Librarian-at-Large, 728 State Street, 430 Memorial Library, Madison, WI 53706

- *Higher Education Abstracts*, Claremont Graduate School, 740 North College Avenue, Claremont, CA 91711

- *Index to Periodical Articles Related to Law*, University of Texas, 727 East 26th Street, Austin, TX 78705

- *Inventory of Marriage and Family Literature (online and hard copy),* National Council on Family Relations, 3989 Central Avenue NE, Suite 550, Minneapolis, MN 55421

(continued)

- *Mental Health Abstracts (online through DIALOG)*, IFI/Plenum Data Company, 3202 Kirkwood Highway, Wilmington, DE 19808

- *PASCAL International Bibliography T205: Sciences de l'information Documentation,* INIST/CNRS-Service Gestion des Documents Primaires, 2, allee du Parc de Brabois, F-54514 Vandoeuvre-les-Nancy, Cedex, France

- *Periodical Abstracts, Research I* (general & basic reference indexing & abstracting data-base from University Microfilms International (UMI), 300 North Zeeb Road, P.O. Box 1346, Ann Arbor, MI 48106-1346), UMI Data Courier, P.O. Box 32770, Louisville, KY 40232-2770

- *Periodical Abstracts, Research II* (broad coverage indexing & abstracting data-base from University Microfilms International (UMI) 300 North Zeeb Road, P.O. Box 1346, Ann Arbor, MI 48106-1346), UMI Data Courier, P.O. Box 32770, Louisville, KY 40232-2770

- *Psychological Abstracts (PsycINFO)*, American Psychological Association, P.O. Box 91600, Washington, DC 20090-1600

- *Sage Family Studies Abstracts (SFSA)*, Sage Publications, Inc., 2455 Teller Road, Newbury Park, CA 91320

- *Social Work Abstracts*, National Association of Social Workers, 750 First Street NW, 8th Floor, Washington, DC 20002

- *Studies on Women Abstracts*, Carfax Publishing Company, P.O. Box 25, Abingdon, Oxfordshire OX14 3UE, United Kingdom

- *Women Studies Abstracts*, Rush Publishing Company, P.O. Box 1, Rush, NY 14543

- *Women's Studies Index (indexed comprehensively)*, G.K. Hall & Co., 866 Third Avenue, New York, NY 10022

(continued)

SPECIAL BIBLIOGRAPHIC NOTES

related to special journal issues (separates)
and indexing/abstracting

- ☐ indexing/abstracting services in this list will also cover material in the "separate" that is co-published simultaneously with Haworth's special thematic journal issue or DocuSerial. Indexing/abstracting usually covers material at the article/chapter level.

- ☐ monographic co-editions are intended for either non-subscribers or libraries which intend to purchase a second copy for their circulating collections.

- ☐ monographic co-editions are reported to all jobbers/wholesalers/approval plans. The source journal is listed as the "series" to assist the prevention of duplicate purchasing in the same manner utilized for books-in-series.

- ☐ to facilitate user/access services all indexing/abstracting services are encouraged to utilize the co-indexing entry note indicated at the bottom of the first page of each article/chapter/contribution.

- ☐ this is intended to assist a library user of any reference tool (whether print, electronic, online, or CD-ROM) to locate the monographic version if the library has purchased this version but not a subscription to the source journal.

- ☐ individual articles/chapters in any Haworth publication are also available through the Haworth Document Delivery Services (HDDS).

CONTENTS

ABOUT THE EDITORS

Ellen Cole, PhD, is a psychologist and sex therapist and Dean of the Master of Arts Program at Prescott College in Arizona. Author and editor of a variety of books, articles, and book chapters about women's mental health, Ellen has developed a love of the outdoors since moving, five years ago, from the Northeast to the Southwest. Her current interest is in "eco-psychology," a collaboration between ecologists and psychologists to re-establish connections between human beings and the non-human natural world.

Eve Erdman, MLS, MEd, is Librarian and member of the faculty at Prescott College, where she specializes in outdoor action and education studies. A 14-year passion for climbing has led Eve up crags all over the Western U.S., Canada, and France, including multi-day solo climbs on the sandstone cliffs of Zion National Park.

Esther D. Rothblum, PhD, is Professor of Psychology at the University of Vermont. Her research, writing, athletic pursuits (racquetball), and even her hobby (juggling) are all performed indoors. Esther claims to dislike nature, but she has been known to escape to wild places. She travelled to the Antarctic aboard an icebreaker that sank one week after she got off.

Introduction

Ellen Cole
Eve Erdman
Esther D. Rothblum

We know now we have always been in danger
down in our separateness
and now up here together but till now
we had not touched our strength

−Adrienne Rich
from "Phantasia for Elvira Shatayev,"
The Dream of a Common Language

For too long, women have been isolated from nature. Whether because of social norms that do not reward women for adventure pursuits or because of a fear of the wilds, women have not been "at home" in the outdoors. Leslie Ryan (1992) writes about when she first realized women were *afraid* to go into the woods. She cites a deep-seated fear of being attacked or raped; probably every woman has been warned about this and considers it a primary deterrent to striking out into the wilds.

The editors would like to thank Alisa Butler for her willingness to share her computer wizardry in a pinch and Michelle Dereschuk for her editorial skills; Joan Clingan, Leslie Laird, Thom Shelby, and Gus Murray for their cheerful assistance; and Annette Maggitti, wilderness soloist, for sharing her ideas about the manuscript. They would also like to thank the authors for doing beautiful things in the woods and on the rivers; we hope we can all gather around a campfire together one day.

[Haworth co-indexing entry note]: "Introduction." Cole, Ellen, Eve Erdman, and Esther D. Rothblum. Co-published simultaneously in *Women & Therapy* (The Haworth Press, Inc.) Vol. 15, No. 3/4, 1994, pp. 1-8; and: *Wilderness Therapy for Women: The Power of Adventure* (ed: Ellen Cole, Eve Erdman, and Esther D. Rothblum) The Haworth Press, Inc., 1994, pp. 1-8. Multiple copies of this article/chapter may be purchased from The Haworth Document Delivery Center [1-800-3-HAWORTH; 9:00 a.m. - 5:00 p.m. (EST)].

Women together, in any circumstance, can create a powerful bond; yet, women together in the wilderness, taking risks, become empowered in a way that enables them to break through gender barriers–and therapeutic barriers–by facing the basic unforgiving state of nature together. The stark metaphors of uncertainty and daring allow women to rekindle their natural spirits in ways that cannot be achieved in a traditional therapeutic setting.

What is therapeutic about wilderness? How can risk and adventure enhance women's self-esteem? What are the ethical implications of taking women out of the offices where traditional therapy occurs? This collection of essays addresses these questions and others in an attempt to broaden the knowledge base and enliven the discussion about wilderness therapy for women. "Wilderness" in this book is generally considered a place where people are visitors and should leave the land in a natural state as it has been for all time. Some of the articles describe non-wilderness experiences that are nevertheless adventurous–ropes courses in the woods, for instance. What these experiences have in common is that they transpire in the outdoors and involve taking risks. That is what makes the adventure therapeutic.

This collection is intended for mental health professionals who already practice some form of wilderness therapy and for those who would like to know more about this approach. It is designed for professional outdoor leaders and outfitters who may benefit from the chapters on theory, applications, and special populations. It is also written for outdoor program administrators and educators whose positions demand that they remain on the cutting edge of their industry.

Wilderness and adventure therapies are relatively new, although there are approximately 250 organizations internationally that offer therapeutic "adventure and experiential activities," according to *The Directory of Experiential Therapy and Adventure-Based Counseling Programs* (1992). Despite this popularity, only one book is in print on the topic as we go to press. Michael Gass' *Adventure Therapy: Therapeutic Applications of Adventure Programming* (1993) does an excellent job of introducing the vast array of theoretical and programmatic concerns. H. L. Gillis (1993) has produced an annotated bibliography on the general subject of adventure therapy as well.

The inspiration for this collection, therefore, is based partly on an obvious gap in the literature: this is the first collection of writings to deal specifically with wilderness therapy for women and the symbolic value of wilderness accomplishments to women's mental health. While a fair number of articles on wilderness therapy for women have been indexed in recent years by Psychological Abstracts and the Educational Resources Information Center (ERIC), there are no books or anthologies that address this large body of work. We hope this collection will be another step toward the professional recognition the field deserves.

ELLEN'S STATEMENT

When residents of Prescott feel particularly disdainful of Prescott College and its students, one of their favorite sayings is, "Oh, that's where the men are men, and the women are, too." What they mean is that women at Prescott College tend to sport hairy legs and underarms, thick socks and hiking boots, and large backpacks. What they also mean is that Prescott College women give the appearance of being strong and independent, and of course, women aren't supposed to be that way. P. C. is a college known for its outdoor education and wilderness leadership programs, its environmental emphasis, and the three-week wilderness backpacking trip in which every entering student participates.

Before coming to this college, five years ago, I was definitely an indoor person. Winter in Vermont, my beautiful former home-state, was too cold for me. Spring and Summer were too buggy. In the Fall I had allergies. I appreciated the beauty from behind a window, as I sat at my computer screen. I played tennis indoors.

At Prescott College I soon realized that I envied those tightly muscled women with the hiking boots, and I was powerfully drawn to the Arizona landscape. I was also afraid. I'd donned a borrowed backpack only once in my life on a single overnight camping trip. I was afraid of heights and terrified of anything remotely resembling physical risk or challenge. I remembered how hard it was as a little girl to learn to ride a two-wheel bicycle in New York City; I remembered my life-long terror of skiing too fast and, instead, traversing back and forth in the widest possible arcs so I'd never have to point my skis down the hill.

In my recent life, as they are in this anthology, the themes of being outdoors, spending time in natural wilderness settings, and experiencing the adventure of physical challenges and risks are intertwined. I am not the woman I was. I am no longer terrified by physical challenges. I know my limits. I can decide what to do, what not to do, and how to determine acceptable risks.

My first year in Arizona I took a rockclimbing course from a Prescott College student and his mother (Maggie Kessell, one of the authors in this collection), hiked the Grand Canyon three times, and had the ultimate thrill of whitewater rafting down the Colorado River. Although I enjoy my weekday worklife immensely, there's a sense in which I live for weekends and vacations now when I can spend time in the woods. A few weeks ago my husband and I took a 19-mile day-hike in the Mazatzal Mountain Range, viewing, unbelievably, thousands of agave (century) plants in full bloom.

For me, these have all been therapeutic experiences. They make me feel good about myself and the world, in fact exhilarated. At first I began to wonder if there were applications for psychotherapy. As I learned more about Outward Bound and other adventure-based programs, I recognized that a great deal was already available, but it wasn't being called psychotherapy, and most office-based psychotherapists had no idea about any of it. These thoughts, then, inspired the gathering together of the articles that follow. Some of the authors, such as Denise Mitten and China Galland, are true pioneers. They took psychotherapy out of the office and into the woods and the mountains and the rivers long before I began to venture out of doors. Other authors are newer to wilderness therapy, and I'm pleased to say that they represent many others who recognize the important role that wilderness experiences and physical adventure can play in the mental health of women.

Finally, I have become increasingly certain that there is a side-benefit to wilderness therapy, and perhaps this is its most significant contribution to the betterment of the world. I believe it is not possible to spend any length of time "in nature" without developing a sense of wonderment and awe about its magnificence. It is a small step, then, from connection with the non-human natural world to an urgency about environmentalism. Ultimately, what nurtures and heals the individual, also nurtures and heals the planet.

EVE'S STATEMENT

Jean Angell, in her essay on the solo wilderness experience, wrote that she felt she must go to the woods to gather her thoughts to write about the solo. I took her advice and headed for the hills myself. My "solo" took the form of climbing a rock face in Zion National Park known as the Moonlight Buttress. I employed the techniques I have learned over a dozen years as a technical rock climber, and spent three days alone on that thousand-foot face "quieting my inner dialogue," as Angell puts it, and coming to terms with why I feel a need to be alone in such extreme conditions, while revisiting my appreciation of nature.

Risk is the key to adventure, and all of the essays presented here deal with risk either implicitly or explicitly. Bill Byrd, in his essay "Danger as a Way of Joy" (1977), defines danger as a liberating element that is absent from most day-to-day living. Risk-taking has become ingrained in my worldview, and although the rock face is enormous and ominous, the fragile, minute fractures allow me to wend my way up the cliff's weaknesses, as a forgiveness and a blessing. Even as I put myself in danger, I am glad to be beyond the reach of others, physically, emotionally, and intellectually. Why take the chance? Why not just camp in a tent? Leslie Ryan (1992) contends that, for women, the very nature of living provokes life-reserving precautions. When I reach a threshold that marks a point of living or dying, persisting or getting hurt, I make a conscious choice. Returning to the "real world" is a lot more real when I have risked it all to survive.

ESTHER'S STATEMENT

"I am two with nature" has been credited to Woody Allen (Gopnik, 1993). It is somewhat embarrassing to state in a feminist publication that I don't enjoy nature. (It is even more embarrassing to quote Woody Allen to a feminist audience.)

I live in Vermont, a rural and agricultural state. In fact, the small town in which I live has more cows than people. Nevertheless, my lifestyle probably has more in common with people who live in large, urban areas. I commute to work in an air-conditioned car with a car phone. Living in a condominium means not having to deal with snow removal or lawn mowing. I am mystified when my friends want to climb up and down mountains, bike on dirt roads, canoe in muddy rivers, or–worst of all–*camp* in the open. My experience with these ways of interacting with nature has been to feel cold, hot, damp, thirsty, and irritable.

Part of the problem is that when I hear accounts of wilderness experiences, they sound so full of action. Women tell me they saw a heron, or a moose, or rare wildflowers. When I'm out in nature, I expect a virtual parade of interesting animals and plants. Instead, they are slow to appear and quite hard to identify. Friends tell me that the wonders of camping include sleeping under the stars, close to beautiful views. This sounds intriguing, until it's time to sleep, and I realize that the tent meant for three is actually smaller than my bed and that crickets and frogs don't stop making noises at night. I feel like I've slept in my clothes because I *have* slept in my clothes. Friends respond that the secret to good camping is having the right equipment and bringing gourmet food. I, for one, find this spartan compared to a good hotel with a choice of restaurants.

Nevertheless, I have recently begun conducting research on risk-taking among women, after years of studying women's fear of failure. I decided to begin by interviewing a group of women that was very high on risk-taking and adventurousness, and chose women who had lived and worked in the Antarctic. Very few people live at the South Pole or the coastal Antarctic stations, and only a small percentage of these are women. Why would women want to travel thousands of miles away from their family and friends to live in small, crowded, isolated field stations in a frigid environment that has no sunlight during the winter?

The majority of these women stated that they did not consider the Antarctic a risk, because they had been in similar situations or because the Antarctic was tame when compared with other situations, like climbing Mount Everest or being in a war zone. Although most women did find the Antarctic stay to contain some risk or danger, the majority wanted to go back. Women went to the Antarctic for adventure or job opportunities, even when family members (particularly mothers) were hesitant to see them go. Many women loved the physical beauty of the Antarctic, coped with stress by being alone (when they could), and had a difficult time adjusting to the crowds, fast pace, and noise back home.

This research has taught me that what is extreme and unusual for some people is safe and commonplace for others. As many of the authors mention in the accounts that follow, women are not socialized to be alone, to leave the safety of their home environment, and to take risks. Yet most women report that risk-taking in the context of being in the wilderness resulted in an increased sense of self-reliance and self-esteem. As Ursula LeGuin stated in her "left-handed commencement address" at Mills College (1983, pp. 116-117):

> Because you are human beings, you are going to meet failure. You are going to meet disappointment, injustice, betrayal, and irreparable loss. You will find you're weak where you thought yourself strong. You'll work for possessions and then find they possess you. You will find yourself–as I know you already have–in dark places, alone, and afraid. . . .
>
> Well, we're already foreigners. Women as women are largely excluded from, alien to, the self-declared male norms of this society, where human beings are called Man, the only respectable god is male, and the only direction is up. So that's their country; let's explore our own. . . .
>
> If there is a day side to (our country), high sierras, prairies of bright grass, we only know the pioneers' tales about it, we haven't got there yet. We're never going to get there by imitating Machoman. We're only going to get there by going our own way, by living there, by living through the night in our own country.

REFERENCES

Byrd, Bill (1977). Danger as a way of joy. Unpublished manuscript, Northwest Outward Bound School, Eugene, OR.

Gass, Michael A. (1993). *Adventure therapy: Therapeutic applications of adventure programming.* Dubuque, IA: Kendall/Hunt.

Gerstein, Jackie (1993). *Directory of experiential therapy and adventure-based counseling programs.* Boulder, CO: Association for Experiential Education.

Gillis, H. Lee (1993). *Annotated bibliography of adventure therapy and related programs, 1980-1992.* Boulder, CO: Association for Experiential Education.

Gopnik, Adam (October 25, 1993). The outsider. *The New Yorker*, pp. 86-93.
LeGuin, Ursula (1983). *Dancing at the edge of the world: Thoughts on words, women, places.* New York: Harper & Row.
Rich, Adrienne (1978). *The dream of a common language.* New York: Norton.
Ryan, Leslie (1992, Fall). The clearing in the clearing. *Northern Lights 8* (3), 27-30.

Nuestra Hermana

Sister River
eternal winding lover of ancestral canyon cliffs
the Trickster visited you and built the mammoth concrete barrier
which stands guard like a pack of hungry gargoyles
regulating your dance of energy, strength, power, tranquility

Sister River
your eternal Spirit moves with the patience of a loving Mother
creating pulsing life beneath
an ever changing surface
wavy ripples become a flock of birds taking flight
over emerald algae world below
hungry fish leap eagerly with open mouths to greet
insects skimming the watery tension of your skin

Sister River
your life offers unique balance
to the children of your Canyon lover
scrubby bushes overtaking once trodden paths
family of mountain sheep emerging from green labyrinth
older ram directing younger ones with blows from spiral horns
each animal kneeling at your shores to drink
graceful waterfowl flying in pairs
coming to rest on abandoned cable depth line
lizard awkwardly crossing rocky beach to become
the surefooted climber on vertical rock face
hawk navigating invisible rapids of sky and light

Sister River
each moment illuminates your transitory nature
current surging up and down river simultaneously
your hands molding rapids around jutting rocks
fierceness dissipating into tranquility
continually your breath rises and falls
causing disappearing shores and caves
and revealing the forgotten burial ground of canyon trees

Sister River
eternal winding lover of ancestral canyon cliffs
the Trickster visited you and built the mammoth concrete barrier
your wisdom permeates such transitory walls
your Spirit becomes the Shapeshifter baffling the Trickster
and beckoning respect

–Anjanette Estrellas

Anjanette Estrellas, BSW, is currently pursuing her MA in counseling psychology. Her focus is on utilizing multicultural feminist wilderness therapy and storytelling as treatment modalities with Latina adolescent trauma survivors. This poem reflects a women's adventure canoe outing down the Black Canyon Colorado River. "Nuestra Hermana" is Spanish for "Our Sister."

[Haworth co-indexing entry note]: "Nuestra Hermana." Estrellas, Anjanette. Co-published simultaneously in the *Women & Therapy* (The Haworth Press, Inc.) Vol. 15, No. 3/4, 1994, pp. 9-10; and: *Wilderness Therapy for Women: The Power of Adventure* (ed: Ellen Cole and Esther Rothblum) The Haworth Press, Inc., 1994, pp. 9-10. Multiple copies of this article/chapter may be purchased from The Haworth Document Delivery Center [1-800-3-HAWORTH; 9:00 a.m. - 5:00 p.m. (EST)].

THEORETICAL PERSPECTIVES

Wilderness Therapy:
What Makes It Empowering for Women?

Irene G. Powch

SUMMARY. Wilderness therapy is neither a newcomer nor a fringe therapy–it originates from wilderness challenge programs that were established in 1945, and it has been applied to clinical populations in the United States since the 1960s. Its efficacy, particularly in work with adolescent populations, is supported by a solid body of research. Its therapeutic application to survivors of incest, rape, and battering is, however, very recent (early 1980s), as is its specific application to empowerment for women (mid 1980s). After a brief review of the general wilderness therapy model, this paper turns to a

Irene G. Powch earned her Bachelor's degree in Biology from Brown University in 1986 and is currently a doctoral student in Clinical Psychology at the University of Kansas (KU), where she earned her Masters degree in 1991. Her clinical and research work has focused on violence against women and women's health. Her personal experiences in the wilderness have taken her from the Adirondacks to the Rockies, through the Sierras, up to Katmai and Denali in Alaska, down to the desert and canyons of the southwest, the Sierra Madre in Mexico and Guatemala, and to the Blue Mountains of Jamaica.

[Haworth co-indexing entry note]: "Wilderness Therapy: What Makes It Empowering for Women?" Powch, Irene G. Co-published simultaneously in *Women & Therapy* (The Haworth Press, Inc.) Vol. 15, No. 3/4, 1994, pp. 11-27; and: *Wilderness Therapy for Women: The Power of Adventure* (ed: Ellen Cole, Eve Erdman, and Esther D. Rothblum) The Haworth Press, Inc., 1994, pp. 11-27. Multiple copies of this article/chapter may be purchased from The Haworth Document Delivery Center [1-800-3-HAWORTH; 9:00 a.m. - 5:00 p.m. (EST)].

11

consideration of wilderness therapy in work with survivors of abuse and empowerment for women. The author draws on the voices of women who have experienced wilderness as healing and empowering, and includes her own voice, to explore two distinct components of wilderness therapy–the healing effects of specific therapeutic activities and challenges in a novel environment, and the more elusive spiritual healing effects of a newly found or renewed sense of connectedness with the power of the earth.

"Why are you always running in the woods?" my mother asked me with her thick Austrian accent when I was ten. "What is in Alaska? Why are you running to those mountains?" she asked again 13 years later when I was 23. Now, as I enter my third decade of life and begin writing this paper I am still striving to articulate the answers. I recall inching my way across the near vertical, sandy slope of a nameless mountain in Alaska and looking down a 2,000 foot drop–and out over an endless range of rock and volcanic sand. How can I describe the intoxicating feeling of realizing that leaning into that mountain is the only way anybody could cross it? How can I describe the feeling of merging with and becoming part of that mountain's strength and beauty, the simultaneous experience of connectedness and freedom? How can I describe the sense of connectedness with others who have shared in that experience? It is certainly empowering, although that word hardly conveys the profound richness of the experience.

My work on this paper took a serendipitous turn as I began talking with women who had experienced the wilderness as healing–survivors of sexual abuse, women who work with survivors, and women who, like myself, are "merely" survivors of the patriarchal context in which we were raised. We shared common perceptions about what was empowering, what was healing about our wilderness experiences. For all of us it seemed to include but go beyond the therapeutic components of wilderness therapy that are described in the research literature. This tremendous validation of my own sense that something was missing in the literature prompted me to articulate my perception that there are two distinct components of wilderness therapy–the healing effects of specific therapeutic activities in a novel environment, and the more elusive, spiritual healing effects of a newly found, or renewed sense of connectedness with the powers of the earth and the creative life cycle in the wilderness.

My goals for this paper are to develop the distinction I have drawn between the mechanistic components and the spiritual components of wilderness therapy and to highlight the relevance of this distinction to work with women. In doing so, I will focus on wilderness therapy that is empowering for women, including survivors of sexual abuse, rape, or battering. This will include discussion of issues of emotional safety and the appropriateness of variations of wilderness therapy to women with different personal histories and attributes. It has been important to me to include the voices of women of color and other marginalized groups of women.

WILDERNESS THERAPY AND ITS HISTORICAL ROOTS

Before considering specific components of wilderness therapy and their roles in empowering women, it is useful to briefly review the origins of wilderness therapy as it is generally conceptualized and practiced, and then to define the term as it will be used in this paper.

The historical roots of the common conception of wilderness therapy lie in the original Outward Bound model, which was not developed with women in mind. Indeed, the original purpose of the Outward Bound program, which was established in 1942, was "to prepare young British seamen to survive the rigors of sailing the North Atlantic during World War II" (Bacon & Kimball, 1989, p. 117). This original Outward Bound program had its roots in experiential education. It was developed in the 1920s by Kurt Hahn, a German educator who sought to create a learning environment in which students could discover through experience the validity and utility of values such as tenacity and compassion (Richards, 1981). Hahn identified wilderness training and rescue training as particularly conducive to his educational aims, and his program had wide appeal. Within ten years of Outward Bound's 1962 arrival in the United States, thousands of programs using aspects of the Outward Bound approach were established, a sizable number of which have been working successfully with a wide range of clinical populations (Bacon & Kimball, 1989).

Because they all share roots in the original Outward Bound model, terms such as "adventure-based therapy," "challenge courses," and "ropes courses" are often used synonymously with "wilderness therapy." It would be more accurate, however, to use these terms in a way that reflected their relationships to one another–namely that a ropes course can be one component of a challenge course, which can be one component of an adventure-based therapy, which in turn, can be one component of a wilderness therapy program. For example, a ropes course might involve having a person learn to rappel down a vertical wall and experience having to trust a belayer to hold the safety line. Such a course could be set up on a mountainside in the wilderness, on the side of a building, or in a gym. To merit the term "wilderness therapy," however, I contend that the experience must occur in a wilderness setting,[1] and that the wilderness must be approached with a therapeutic goal in mind. The role of the therapist is to facilitate the process by which a person engages the wilderness, either alone or with others, and derives healing from that interaction. To this end, the therapist may use, among other techniques, structured experiences, metaphors, or rituals that draw spiritual meaning from the natural environment.

The definition of wilderness therapy that I have set forth is more restrictive than the one that is implicitly or explicitly used in the psychological literature. My definition requires that wilderness therapy occur in a wilderness setting. The more common attitude regarding the role of the wilderness setting is represented in the words of Bacon and Kimball (1989, p. 118) ". . . the essential need is not so much for wilderness as it is for an unfamiliar environment. Hence wilderness therapy courses have sometimes been conducted in the 'wilderness' of an unfamiliar urban environment." I do not dispute that therapy can occur in settings other than the wilderness, but I would not call it wilderness therapy. For such a distinction to be justified, the wilderness setting must contribute something unique to the therapeutic experience. It is my contention that this is the case, that this "extra ingredient" is an important element in empowerment of women, and that, because of its historical roots, the traditional conceptualization of what constitutes wilderness therapy and related programs overlooks this more spiritual ingredient that I and others recognize as an important component of wilderness therapy.

MECHANISTIC COMPONENTS
OF WILDERNESS THERAPY

Mechanistic components refer to activities (sometimes called "challenges") that a wilderness therapist structures with specific goals in mind. To suggest that mechanistic components of wilderness therapy do not constitute the totality of the healing effects of this therapy should in no way diminish their importance. Because these components of wilderness therapy have enjoyed recognition by psychologists, they are fairly well developed and researched. Therefore, before proposing that there is an additional "ingredient" in wilderness therapy that is empowering for women, it is important to consider what constitutes the mechanistic components and what effects these components have been shown to have that may be empowering and healing for women, and in particular for survivors of abuse.

The reader should be aware that the review which follows is not intended to be an exhaustive review of particular activities; for such a review, see Schoel (1988). The reader should also be aware that as I describe common mechanistic components of wilderness therapy, I am assuming that they are carried out within the context of programs such as the collaboration of the Colorado-based Ending Violence Effectively (EVE) and Outward Bound program for survivors of domestic violence and sexual assault, the program for sexual assault survivors at the Santa Fe Mountain Center, or the "Looking Up" program based in Maine for survivors of incest.[2]

One example of a mechanistic component of wilderness therapy is an activity that is structured to connect participants with fear–the most dreaded emotion of survivors of abuse, and possibly of all women, given that women are socialized to internalize a deep-seated fear of rape (Griffin, 1971)–and to restructure their automatic reactions to this emotion (Ewert, 1988). Crossing a raging river by walking across a narrow log might be a specific activity designed to elicit the fear. Successful resolution of this fear depends on the collaborative work of a skillful outdoor recreation specialist, and a skillful therapist. The outdoor specialist would have to insure the physical safety of the participant in case she did lose her footing, yet do so in an unobtrusive way that does not diminish the participant's perception of being exposed and in control rather than part of a "Disneyland-like charade." The therapist's task is a complex one that includes monitoring the participant's psychological preparedness for the activity. If the participant is a survivor of rape or other abuse the therapist must be familiar with the stages of recovery and know where the participant is in her recovery.[3] The therapist must create an environment that feels psychologically safe to each participant, and the therapist must provide a psychological "road map" for the participant so that she both understands the purpose of the challenge she is about to undertake, and at some level can "see" herself coming to resolution. The wilderness therapist working with survivors must also be skilled in working with dissociative states because the capacity for induced trance and dissociation is high among survivors, particularly survivors of childhood abuse (Chu & Dill, 1990).

When done well, the therapeutic effects of a challenge of the type described are tremendously empowering, as is richly captured in the words of Mary McHugh, a rape survivor and one of the founders of Ending Violence Effectively: "I can do things even when I'm frightened. My body's shaking, and I can still trust my body. It still works" (Obereigner, 1986). Herman (1992, p. 198) compares the effects of this component of wilderness therapy to the effects of self-defense exercises in which survivors "put themselves in a position to reconstruct the normal physiological responses to danger, to rebuild the 'action system' that was shattered and fragmented by the trauma" (p. 198). She describes the survivor in a wilderness therapy situation as placing herself

> . . . in a position to experience the 'fight or flight' response to danger, knowing that she will elect to fight. In so doing, she establishes a degree of control over her own bodily and emotional responses that reaffirms a sense of power. (p. 199)

Another example of a mechanistic component might be a "trust fall" where a participant might be asked to stand in a tree six or seven feet above the ground and fall backwards into a group's waiting arms. Depending on the participant's stage of recovery from abuse, the goal of this exercise might be to break through denial and bring to the surface powerful feelings related to the shattering of trust that results from abuse so that these emotions can then be worked through in individual therapy. Or the goal of the exercise may be to offer an experience whereby the participant can build a bond of trust with the women who do not let her down and do catch her in repeated falls. It is common for women who have shared a wilderness therapy experience to remain in close contact long after the trip is over. Rock climbing experiences can also be designed to elicit trust issues for a therapeutic purpose. At some point the climber must place her life in the hands of a belayer, a person who holds the safety rope which is tied to the climber. The belayer is there to prevent the climber from falling should she slip. Having to trust a partner in this concrete way can bring deeper feelings to awareness that can then be addressed in therapy (Mason, 1987).

I would like to turn now to two characteristics of wilderness experience that are inherent in the wilderness environment and contribute to a sense of empowerment regardless of what activities a therapist might or might not structure. The first is the immediacy and concreteness of feedback from the wilderness environment. In Mason's words:

> Feedback from one's actions and deliberate inaction is very clear-cut . . . on the rock, for example, we know clearly when we are on top, when we are stuck, and when we are frozen at the bottom, looking up. The metaphor of rock climbing can thus allow us to become more honest with ourselves. (p. 93)

Herman (1992) cites a wilderness therapist who works with survivors of childhood abuse as saying,

> Magical or neurotic means of ensuring safety do not work in this setting. Being "sweet," not making demands, "disappearing," making excessive and narcissistic demands, waiting for a rescuer; none of these maneuvers puts breakfast on the table. On the other hand, victims are surprised and delighted at the effectiveness of their realistic coping. In reality, they are

able to learn to rappel down a cliff; their adult skills . . . outweigh the fears and low estimation of themselves that initially made them judge this impossible. (p. 198)

The second characteristic of wilderness experience that is a function of the environment itself, and is also inherently empowering for women–as well as other marginalized groups–is the even-handedness of consequences. In the words of Ki, an African-American recreational therapist who also serves as an Inner City Outings (ICO) volunteer introducing ethnically and racially diverse groups of underprivileged youth from Oakland to the wilderness:

In dealing with mother nature there's no favoritism . . . if it's going to rain it's not just going to rain on me. I'm not going to run into 'isms' . . . and I have a sense of me getting to take care of myself . . . I can prepare myself and wear the right clothes and so on . . . in cities I feel more subjected to racism and sexism . . . I feel it's a place that I can deal and not expect curve balls (this is especially true about solos) or run up against macho-ism.[4]

In the words of 16-year old Naomi, who was once a participant of ICO, and now co-leads ICO wilderness trips:

There's just more acceptance in the wilderness . . . you have to depend on people and it's no time to be afraid or prejudiced for any reason (racism, sexism, homophobia . . .). Nature's blind to everything . . . all it cares about is that you're a person and that you want to be there and respect it.

These anecdotal effects of wilderness therapy and wilderness experience are corroborated by empirical process and outcome studies, including well-designed studies with matched control groups and large samples. Among the effects of wilderness therapy that such studies have demonstrated are significant and sustained increases in self-esteem, assertiveness, expectations that powerful others and chance would have less control in their lives (survivors of sexual assault and battering), as well as significant reductions in trait anxiety (Ewert, 1988; Marsh, Richards, & Barnes, 1986). An

Outward Bound study by Marsh and Richards (1989) that used 23 reasonably distinct groups of participants in different locations and tested them before, at the beginning, at the end, and at 18 month follow-up, concluded that "Outward Bound produced significant changes in well-established personality traits, a demonstration that is rare in the personality literature" (p. 133).

SPIRITUAL COMPONENTS OF WILDERNESS THERAPY

There is something inherent in wilderness experience that goes beyond the benefits that can result from a self-defense class or a climbing class, beyond the benefits of overcoming one's fears, experiencing fair and equal treatment, or becoming more self-reliant. It cannot be explained entirely by the quality of the immediacy and concreteness of cause and effect in the wilderness. It goes beyond that. The first time I recall vividly experiencing this transformation was a few weeks into my first experience in the southwest, where I spent a summer as a naturalist in Zion National Park. I had scrambled up a red rock monolith that was away from the heavily visited canyon drive. After making a large flat boulder at the top my home for five or six hours, I looked out over the horizon at an endless stretch of red rock, white rock, sage–and suddenly everything was different. I no longer just felt the warmth of the sun, smelled the scents of earth and sage, saw the rock and sky–these were no longer just sensory experiences–a moment had crept upon me where everything transformed. I was enveloped by a sense of belonging and being "in place" that I had never known before. There is no comparable experience with which I can describe this except, perhaps, to ask the reader to call up a memory of a person suddenly "opening up" and allowing a deep intimacy to develop. Magnify this a thousand times. Imagine this emanating not from one focus, one person, but from every rock, every breath of air, every pore of earth. Imagine strongly feeling the power of the universe, and taking your place in it, knowing it is within you. Some might call this touching the Earth Mother, the Goddess.

I found this experience with wilderness echoed by all of the women with whom I spoke about their wilderness experiences. For example, in the words of Debora, a 42-year old graduate student in the history of science who also led high school students on wilderness trips:

> ... that connection with nature had a very profound impact on me. The sense of connection of the earth as mother, and the power of that kind of image helped me to expand beyond my own struggle for survival in a world where I felt like I didn't really fit in . . . as a woman . . . I think that the sense of belonging I feel in the wilderness was tied into that–what some people call the earth-based spirituality . . .

The wilderness strikes a deep chord in a woman's soul (although this is not unique to women, and in fact, to me represents the greatest and most beautiful area of union and healing between women and men), it is a chord that a woman recognizes as vital to her essence as a woman, as the woman she is, not the woman she is forced to be. At some level, we must be aware of the core of our womanly power and yearn to reconnect with it, gravitating to the wilderness where that reconnection becomes possible. To me these words ring true:

> A healthy woman is much like a wolf: robust, chock-full, strong life force, life-giving, territorially aware, inventive, loyal, roving. Yet, separation from the wildish nature causes a woman's personality to become meager, thin, ghosty, spectral . . . it is . . . time for the wildish woman to emerge; it is time for the creating function of the psyche to flood the delta. (Pinkola Estes, 1992, p. 12)

When this happens, what results is change like that described by a 30-year old survivor of incest, who told me of her first wilderness experience simply: "I learned to like my body again . . . it's not just for abuse, it's for other things, good things . . . I'm learning that it could be strong and that I can go hiking with it and do things that I love doing."

There are women who draw on the natural environment to enhance therapy in ways that do not merely use the wilderness setting as a novel environment, but that actively engage the spiritual healing inherent in wilderness. The practitioners of this kind of wilderness therapy usually come from the feminist spirituality perspective, which has its roots in ancient and indigenous religions, viewing Goddess as being within all life, and hence viewing all of nature as sacred (Stone, 1979). An example of this was described by Debora, the history of science graduate student mentioned earlier. She described her work with a group that does ceremony for women who have been sexually abused. This is a year-long program, which uses ceremonies that draw on a variety of traditions, including Native American and Sufi teachings, to help participants connect with the power of the feminine. Its name is symbolic of the butterfly emerging from the cocoon; its staff are called grandmothers or elders, and the participants are called granddaughters, drawing on the images of a time when women were revered as goddesses and priestesses. This kind of feminist spirituality wilderness therapy is growing independently from the Outward Bound-derived programs, and has not been described in any of the research literature that I have encountered. I will thus convey its effects on the survivors of sexual abuse in Debora's words:

> . . . it was like they were blossoming from having gone through years of having been held down and stifled from the ways they grew up . . . letting go of old patterns and releasing them in symbolic ways . . . the natural setting is important . . . there was one ceremony in which they ran into the ocean for cleansing and purification . . . there is a sense of empowering women, and a part of it is the connection with nature.

The significance of including a spiritual connection with nature as part of a wilderness therapy experience that is empowering for women is articulated very clearly by Merlin Stone, a feminist involved in Goddess reclamation:

> I began to believe that sharing what I knew about the historical existence of Goddess reverence . . . that people had regarded the Goddess as the creator of the entire world, might help to provide other women with the inner strength I had gained from this knowledge . . . I began to dream of a time when a knowledge of ancient Goddess history might become a familiar part of general education, and thus expose and refute many of the

simplistic stereotypes and views of womanhood that had come to be accepted by both women and men. (Stone, 1979, p. x)

Susan Griffin captures the healing power of this image:

As I go into the Earth, she pierces my heart. As I penetrate further, she unveils me. When I have reached her center, I am weeping openly. I have known her all my life, yet she reveals stories to me, and these stories are revelations and I am transformed. Each time I go to her I am born like this. Her renewal washes over me endlessly, her wounds caress me; I become aware of all that has come between us, of the noise between us, the blindness, of something sleeping between us. Now my body reaches out to her. They speak effortlessly, and I learn at no instant does she fail me in her presence. She is as delicate as I am; I know her sentience; I feel her pain and my own pain comes into me, and my own pain grows large and I grasp this pain with my hands, and I open my mouth to this pain, I taste, I know, and I know why she goes on, under great weight, with this great thirst, in drought, in starvation, with intelligence in every act does she survive disaster. This earth is my sister; I love her daily grace, her silent daring, and how loved I am, how we admire this strength in each other, all that we have lost, all that we have suffered, all that we know: We are stunned by this beauty, and I do not forget what she is to me, what I am to her. (Griffin, 1991, p. 380)

ISSUES OF EMOTIONAL SAFETY AND MARGINALIZED WOMEN

Before coming to closure, I must address a contradiction that took me by surprise as I was finishing this paper. Lost in my own experience, and in the experience of other wilderness women, I took for granted that wilderness is the safest place on earth–until a friend pointed out that she and most women she knows think of wilderness as a terrifying place. Do women experience the wilderness as a "safe place"? A woman's answer to this question may be the single most important factor that will affect the quality of her wilderness experience, or whether she ventures out into the wilderness or a wilderness therapy program at all. Countless women are probably denied the healing benefits of wilderness because of the fear of rape behind every bush, around every corner–a fear that every woman in this culture has been taught along with Little Red Riding Hood and the big, bad wolf (Griffin, 1971). Marge Piercy's Rape Poem captures this pervasive fear of rape:

> . . . Fear of rape is a cold wind blowing
> all of the time on a woman's hunched back.
> Never to stroll alone on a sand road through pine woods . . .
> (1982, p. 164)

The fact that the vast majority of sexual abuse, rape, and battering occurs behind closed doors does little to introduce women to the healing powers of wilderness. Most women who go to the wilderness for healing have at some point been introduced to the wilderness in a nonthreatening way–sometimes through friends, sometimes through organizations such as the Girl Scouts. The failure of these social networks to reach out to marginalized groups of women may be one reason why there are few women of color in the outdoor movement (that has been my observation and the observation of women with whom I have spoken; LaBastille (1984) also notes in her book that out of over 200 responses from outdoors women to her call for women to interview, not one was a woman of color). Ki, the African-American recreational therapist I interviewed, offered the following insights:

> When I go out I don't see a lot of other women or people of color out . . . and I think there's a lot of things that are connected to that. I think that historically we as a people–speaking inclusively of people of color–have not had those opportunities in that we've been in the cities . . . and there's actually been some survival connected to it . . . I know as an African American going out in the woods at night was not a place that you'd want to trust because there's lots of things that would happen in terms of safety issues and harm, and being lynched and what not. And I think going out in the woods didn't get the association of being a safe place–we just don't go.

Majority group members often are oblivious to the impact this situation has on emotional safety considerations for a member of a marginalized group. In Ki's own experience:

> When I think about those activities that I want to get involved with, I kind of am looking at how safe am I going to feel emotionally . . . who else is doing the activity . . . and if I go in a group and I'm the only woman per se or I'm the only person of color, I tend to be a little bit more hesitant about jumping in.

Ki shared her personal perception about wilderness as a "safe place" for her, that she finds very empowering as a woman of color:

> Part of the way I feel really taken care of is just by being in nature and immersing myself in it. Another part of it for me is if I'm in a group, the sharing . . . the interconnectedness I feel with other people because we strip away a lot of things we carry around with us in the city . . . it's warm and healing . . . it's the greatest thing with people to share and do this.

She concluded, drawing on her experience with "Out and About," an outdoor club on the East coast for women of color, which she founded and ran for several years:

> What I thought by the time I was leaving the East coast and "Out and About" which probably had 80 women of color on the mailing list at that point, was that there is a real need to offer this environment as a safe place that could be healing for us as women of color. And I remember that culturally through ancestral lineages, we have had a connection to the earth and that a lot of indigenous people have that deep connection to the earth. . . .

When their emotional safety needs are met, the wilderness experience is much the same for women of color as for white women. The safety needs of women of color, lesbian women, older women, women with different body builds and weights, or women with disabilities or diseases, do not set them apart. Safety needs are universal and individual; one cannot even assume that all young, thin, white survivors of sexual abuse would approach the wilderness with the same safety issues. For example, one survivor of incest with whom I spoke felt inherently safe in the wilderness:

> I feel safe if I'm in a tree or up high, on a roof somewhere . . . I can see all around me . . . feeling closed in doesn't feel safe . . . I was abused in my home . . . I think a lot of survivors feel drawn to and safe in nature and really love animals, maybe because they love you unconditionally and they don't hurt you.

Ki pointed out that in her experience in the Southwest, many survivors were abused outside, and for them the wilderness evokes entirely different safety issues. This, of course, does not mean that the person who was abused outdoors could not benefit from wilderness therapy, but that person's history and safety issues must be taken into consideration lest she be retraumatized by what should be therapy. Wilderness therapy, like any therapy, cannot be universally and monolithically applied; it is not for everyone–but the judgement is a complex one to be made by each individual woman in collaboration with a wilderness therapist in the program which she is considering. Wilderness therapy can be tailored to meet the needs of the woman who is seeking healing; Outward Bound has developed a wilderness therapy program for MS and cancer patients (Foote, 1990). Wilderness therapy programs have also been successfully used with sufferers of juvenile rheumatoid arthritis, and with blind persons and their families–wilderness therapy can undoubtedly be creatively adapted to meet other needs.

CONCLUDING THOUGHTS

Wilderness therapy appears to be a promising vehicle for empowerment of women. Its promise is not limited to being a vehicle by which women can master skills that enhance self-esteem and a sense of control. Its promise is much greater and goes beyond the personal when it is connected with the feminist spirituality movement and reclamation of the earth as a woman's place, woman as creator and part of the spirit of the earth. A partnership between the environmental movement and feminist spirituality is growing. As

Stone points out, "Many ecology groups draw upon women's spirituality and images of the Goddess in the effort to preserve planet Earth . . . regarding pollution as blasphemy might be just what we need to do today" (Stone, 1979, p. xiv). On a very practical level, environmental groups such as the Sierra Club are providing insurance for fledgling groups such as ICO, groups which could not otherwise afford insurance coverage for wilderness trips or wilderness therapy. On a higher plane, wilderness is returning to women their souls and their rightful place on this planet–as Goddesses.

NOTES

1. I refer to wilderness with David Brower's definition in mind, as quoted by LaBastille (1980, p. 288): Wilderness is a place wherein the flow of life, in its myriad forms, has gone on since the beginning of life, essentially uninterrupted by people and their technology. It is a place where people respect what that life force built in the old eternity and what that same force can probably keep building well in the new eternity, and without human help–except in the willingness of people to come, see and not conquer. (I have replaced "man" with gender-neutral pronouns; otherwise this is a direct quote.)

2. Programs such as these make deeper levels of healing work possible because of their extended time frame of three, four, or seven days, and their small group size–usually fewer than eight women. The therapy involved in these programs also extends beyond the duration of the time spent in the wilderness; indeed, many of these programs require that participants be in ongoing therapy that is integrated with the wilderness therapy experience. Most participants have several months of therapeutic preparation before their wilderness therapy experience and will have several months more of follow-up therapy. Thus, these are not "encounter groups." Typically, participants do, however, make significant strides during this concentrated and intensive therapeutic experience; EVE staff members and participants have been cited as comparing the effects of a three-day wilderness therapy experience to six months of therapy (Obereigner, 1986).

3. For an excellent resource on trauma and recovery, see Herman (1992).

4. Quotes from Ki, Naomi, and Debora are taken from transcripts of my telephone interviews.

REFERENCES

Bacon, S., & Kimball, R. (1989). The wilderness challenge model. In R. D. Lyman, S. Prentice-Dunn, & S. Gabel (Eds.). *Residential inpatient treatment of children and adolescents.* New York: Plenum.

Chu, A., & Dill, D. L. (1990). Dissociative symptoms in relation to childhood physical and sexual abuse. *American Journal of Psychiatry, 147,* 887-892.

Ewert, A. (1988). Reduction of trait anxiety through participation in Outward Bound. *Leisure Sciences, 10,* 107-117.

Foote, M. (1990). HES research–Results from several projects. *Ascend!*: Denver: Colorado Outward Bound Health and Education Services.

Griffin, S. (1971, September). Rape: The all-American crime. *Ramparts,* pp. 26-35.

Griffin, S. (1991). In E. Roberts, & E. Amidon (Eds.). *Earth Prayers* (p. 380). San Francisco: Harper Collins.

Herman, J. L. (1992). *Trauma and recovery.* New York: Harper Collins.

LaBastille, A. (1984). *Women and wilderness.* San Francisco: Sierra Club Books.

Marsh, H. W., & Richards, G. E. (1989). A test of bipolar and androgyny perspectives of masculinity and femininity: The effect of participation in an Outward Bound program. *Journal of Personality, 57,* 115-137.

Marsh, H. W., Richards, G. E., & Barnes, J. (1986). Multidimensional self-concepts: A long-term follow-up of the effect of participation in an Outward Bound program. *Personality and Social Psychology Bulletin, 12,* 475-492.

Mason, M. J. (1987). Wilderness family therapy: Experiential dimensions. *Contemporary Family Therapy, 9,* 90-105.

Obereigner, D. (1986, June 15). Wilderness therapy aids victims: Participants find they have to learn trust. *The Coloradoan,* p. B4.

Piercy, M. (1982). *Circles on the water.* New York: Alfred A. Knopf, pp. 164-165.

Pinkola Estes, Clarissa. (1992). *Women who run with the wolves: Myths and stories of the wild woman archetype.* New York: Ballantine Books.

Richards, A. (1981). *Kurt Hahn: The midwife of educational ideas.* Unpublished doctoral dissertation, University of Colorado, Boulder, CO.

Schoel, J. (1988). *Islands of healing: A guide to adventure based counseling.* Hamilton, MA: Project Adventure Inc.

Stone, M. (1979). *Ancient mirrors of womanhood.* Boston: Beacon Press.

Self-Control:
The Key to Adventure?
Towards a Model
of the Adventure Experience

Jackie Kiewa

SUMMARY. Adventure always provides a powerful learning experience, but not always a positive one. Four components are identified which create the powerful learning situation: an experiential learning base; a simple yet meaningful reality; cooperation; and intensity of feeling. To optimize the chances of creating a positive experience, four other components should be present: a means of processing the experience; success; choice; and a humane climate.

These eight components are located within three existing models of the adventure experience: The Outward Bound Model (Walsh & Colins, 1976); The Outdoor-Adventure Education Process (Luckner, 1986); and the Benefits of Leisure: Mediating Processes Between Situational Triggers and Outcomes (Scherl, 1988). Strengths and weaknesses of these models are discussed before a final model (Personal Growth Through Adventure), which encapsulates those features most salient in the adventure process, is presented.

Jackie Kiewa is a Lecturer in outdoor education at Griffith University, Brisbane, Australia, teaching in the skill areas of rock climbing and whitewater kayaking, as well as in the areas of interpersonal skills and the use of adventure as a medium for personal development. Her Masters Degree in Education included a study of the application of adventure activities to a school counseling program. Present research is focused upon a study of women involved in adventure pursuits throughout Australia and New Zealand.

[Haworth co-indexing entry note]: "Self-Control: The Key to Adventure? Towards a Model of the Adventure Experience." Kiewa, Jackie. Co-published simultaneously in *Women & Therapy* (The Haworth Press, Inc.) Vol. 15, No. 3/4, 1994, pp. 29-41; and: *Wilderness Therapy for Women: The Power of Adventure* (ed: Ellen Cole, Eve Erdman, and Esther D. Rothblum) The Haworth Press, Inc., 1994, pp. 29-41. Multiple copies of this article/chapter may be purchased from The Haworth Document Delivery Center [1-800-3-HAWORTH; 9:00 a.m. - 5:00 p.m. (EST)].

29

It is suggested that a major outcome of the adventure process is the development of self-control. The nature of control forms the basis of a discussion which examines traditional approaches to control of the environment and self-denial, before focusing on the empowering nature of self-control for women in reducing self- and other-imposed limitations.

INTRODUCTION

I am involved in Adventure Education because I believe that it offers tremendous potential for personal development. I speak from personal experience (climbing certainly helped me make the transformation from wife to Woman), and vicarious experience: the heady excitement of my students feeling the effect of exposure to adventure. This power, however, is not always so positive; I have seen children and adults in tears of frustration, anger, or fear; who have returned from their outdoor experience with confirmed feelings of failure or resentment. There are no guarantees with adventure; it can disempower as well as empower.

In my role as outdoor educator, I have wanted to create the most positive learning situation possible. I began to study the adventure experience more closely. Why is adventure such a powerful medium? And what are the ingredients of a positive adventure? Is it a happy accident, or can it be planned? Through study and observation, I developed a list of eight components: four are necessary components of an adventure program, and, in themselves, create a powerful learning situation. The other four are not necessary, but have tremendous importance in shaping this potential for positive effect.

COMPONENTS OF THE ADVENTURE EXPERIENCE

(a) The Necessary Components

1. An Experiential Approach

An experiential approach is an essential ingredient of adventure education. Experiential learning requires the learner to first *do* or *experience* something. Later, reflection upon this experience will bring about a personal realization and in-depth understanding of certain underlying concepts or guiding principles. Experience, followed by reflection, offers opportunities for the individual to understand and learn from her or his behavior.

2. A Simple and Meaningful Reality

A second component of an outdoor experience that contributes to its effectiveness lies within the nature of the microcosm of reality which is created by the program. A group involved in the outdoors, whether for a few hours or a few weeks, finds itself in a world in which tasks are clear, and meaningful in terms of consequences.

The simplicity of the outdoors is important. Reality, which can appear to be quite complex, pares itself down to simple basic needs: to eat, to be warm and dry, to have shelter. Within this essentially manageable world, tasks are quite clear. Simplicity, however, does not imply a "soft" option: actions in the outdoors have an immediacy of consequence which is often absent in the real world. Results of poor planning (being lost, tired, hungry, thirsty) are immediate and understandable, and force the participants to reassess their situation continuously. In addition, these consequences are *situationally* dependent: they are forced upon a group by the objective characteristics of their present situation, rather than by an angry leader. No one is saying to the group: "You did not consult the map, nor did you carry sufficient water, therefore I decree that you shall be lost and thirsty." In this situation, individuals are encouraged to be situationally dependent rather than leader dominated (Royce, 1987, p. 27), which encourages the development of personal responsibility.

3. Need for Cooperation

The need for cooperation is a further strength of outdoor/adventure activities. Participants find that they need each other in order to successfully meet many of the challenges with which they are confronted. At times survival can, in fact, depend on other participants. In this situation, participants need to identify and utilize the strengths of all other group members. Royce (1987, p. 27) observes:

The need to physically stay within a group for reasons of safety and/or survival, and to pool resources and talents in response to situational demands, provides a potent scenario for group interaction. Such interaction is not necessarily available in more normal situations where it may be avoided, for example, by leaving the group, ignoring situational demands, or downgrading them as unimportant.

The need to physically trust another with one's life, and the bond that develops when the other proves trustworthy, can be a vital growth experience which is seldom encountered in the competitive milieu of today's society. The outdoor program structures a society based on cooperative effort; to succeed, all must succeed.

4. Intensity of Feeling

The perceived and real dangers which are a vital part of an adventure activity are a source of fear for participants. The release from tension which accompanies a successful confrontation of the challenge engenders an intense feeling of elation. To feel *safe*, free from physical harm, brings with it a sense of relief which does much to restore a sense of balance and proportion in our lives. This intensity of feeling, when shared in the group, also promotes a deep bonding, a sense of shared experience.

These conditions create a potentially powerful learning situation. However, they do not, in themselves, guarantee success or a positive result. Four other elements should be present in order to develop this potential.

(b) Other Requirements

1. Processing the Experience

Principles of experiential education state that learning takes place through reflection on experience. While it is true that everyone will engage in some degree of reflection, it is also true that, at times, this reflection may be limited or distorted by certain biases, blind spots, or misunderstandings. To optimize personal growth, participants in the experience should take part in some form of "debriefing" or processing of the experience. With the help of a skilled facilitator, individuals in the group can discuss happenings, share feelings and discoveries, evaluate contributions, and apply learnings. Failures can be talked through and used to develop a fresh plan of action. The structured nature of this review is what transforms these activities into true educational experiences; a means to an end rather than an end in themselves.

2. Success

In describing the components of an outdoor program, emphasis is placed on the reality of consequences: of the real possibility of becoming lost, thirsty, cold. While there is much to be learned from such situations, this experience may not be conducive to growth, particularly for groups accustomed to, and expecting, failure. Far more constructive would be to carefully plan a series of challenges which would "create tension without being overwhelming" (Kimball, 1986, p. 45). Success will contribute significantly to the development of individual self esteem and enhance feelings of personal efficacy and empowerment as well as group bonding.

3. Choice

While facilitators carefully introduce challenges which at the time appear appropriate, success cannot be guaranteed, for two reasons. The first is that participants must make their own decisions about how they will respond to this challenge. If all goes well, group members will make some positive and growth-oriented decisions, resulting in success. But such a scenario cannot be guaranteed. Participants may choose to engage in verbal abuse; they may refuse to cooperate or show lack of commitment. Such behavior may greatly reduce chances of success.

The second reason is based on a principle which is perhaps more contentious, and that is whether participants should be allowed to choose their level of challenge; that is, whether they should be free to refuse to rappel (or descend a rope) over a cliff, or climb a mountain. Royce (1987, p. 28) states that the key to growth in any situation is that participants should *choose* to confront fear, rather than being forced to engage in fearful activities. Allowing freedom of choice encourages individuals to take control of their lives instead of remaining other-directed. Not every program adheres to this principle, and peer pressure also reduces real choice. The notion of "challenge by choice," however, is becoming a central tenet in many programs.

4. A Humane Climate

The humane climate is dealt with at length by Knapp (1988), who developed the notion of a greenhouse, providing optimal conditions for growth, into a metaphor for the creation of a "humane climate" which is optimal for the growth and realization of human potential. A humane climate "includes factors such as respect, trust, high morale, opportunities for input, growth and renewal, cohesiveness and caring" (Knapp, 1988, p. 17). Such a climate is very much a product of group norms. It is a key role on the part of the facilitator to play an active part in the creation of these norms, such that the factors listed above come to be accepted as "what happens in this group." This is easiest to manage during the structured debriefing activity, which is engineered by the facilitator to become a time of sharing and growth. It is hoped that standards of behavior developed within debriefing sessions might spill over to the wider activities of the group.

MODELS OF THE ADVENTURE EXPERIENCE

Identification of key components is an important aid to the provision of positive adventure experiences, but this is only the beginning. We need to develop links between the components, and identify sequences and causality, in order to fully understand and explain what is happening. In attempting this task, I have developed a model of the adventure experience, which is discussed below. First, however, I need to briefly describe three models which preceded my own, and on which I drew heavily.

1. The Outward Bound Process

First to be described is the model developed by Outward Bound (Bertolami, 1981; Walsh & Colins, 1976). The process begins with the learner, who is placed into a unique physical and social environment. Within this environment, the learner is given a set of problem-solving tasks which place the learner in a state of dissonance. In this idealistic framework, it is assumed that the individual masters the problem. This successful experience results in increased self-awareness, self-esteem and sense of belonging, as well as increased motivation to repeat this problem-solving behavior.

This model does not mention the notion of "choice," but skates around the problem by stating at the beginning that the learner is "motivationally ready." Other components which are not articulated include the need for reflection, and for a "humane climate."

2. The Outdoor-Adventure Process

Luckner (1986) has developed a model which closely parallels the Outward Bound process, but has added a number of conditions. In the Outdoor-Adventure Process, the student does not have to be motivated or able to share sentiments, but once again experiences disequilibrium through the combination of environment and problems to be solved. The social environment is above all *cooperative* and includes the elements of group cohesiveness, altruism, universality, and imitative behavior (on coping models). Success in the problem-solving tasks will lead to feelings of accomplishment, manifested through enhanced self-esteem and an internal locus of control. These feelings are augmented by processing the experience through reflection, which promotes generalizability and transfer. The experience thus becomes a metaphor for personal growth and development.

Luckner's model represents a substantial development on the basic Outward Bound process in that considerable emphasis is placed on group climate, as well as on the need for processing. The role played by the student in *choosing* to be challenged, however, is still ignored.

3. The Benefits of Leisure: Mediating Processes
Between Situational Triggers and Outcomes

The third model presented here begins with an altered perspective. Scherl (1988) reminds us that any outcome is the result of an individual-environment transaction, and is dependent upon the individual's subjective perception of the situation. Scherl's model begins with what she calls "situational triggers," which include such contextual cues as a person's expectations and definitions of the situation, a person's perceived capabilities and demands, the activities and their sequencing, the social group, the wilderness setting, and motivation for participation. It concludes with "outcomes and self insights," which include self-insight and self-definition, modified perceptions and expectations, enjoyment, appreciation of the environment, and motivation for future involvement. Between these triggers and outcomes, Scherl suggests that there occur two specific "mediating processes": the first being the nature of the transaction, which is challenging and commands the utmost in involvement and attention from the participant; and the second being the nature of the feedback, which is clear and unambiguous, providing ongoing information about the self (through physiological arousal) to the participant.

The direct, unambiguous nature of the feedback is an important element in the development of *self-control*. Much has been written about the ability of the adventure experience to enhance one's sense of personal efficacy and internal locus of control. Scherl, however, shifts the focus to self-control. She suggests that the individual, involved in a transaction with the environment, is faced with a situation in which she or he cannot exert control over external factors. Nothing can be done about the fact of gravity, or the weather, or the force of the current. The only control which the individual can exert in this situation is over one's self–to master the anxiety, to control the physical body, to push one's self that little bit more–beyond what one thought was possible. Thus, Scherl develops the idea that the participant, placed in a stressful situation within an impartial and uncontrollable environment, must exert self-control; and it is the development of self-control which leads to personal growth. Self-control will:

- focus attention on the self which enhances the intensity of the emotions;
- increase awareness of one's inner capabilities and resources;
- increase confidence; and
- increase personal freedom through breaking the constraints of previous barriers and fears. (Scherl, 1988, p. 312-317)

4. Personal Growth Through Adventure

The final model presented (Diagram 1) represents my attempt to combine the most salient features of the previous models. In so doing, I hope to provide both a structure and an explanation for the notion of "personal growth through adventure."

In this model, an individual is placed in an environment which is perceived as being strange and somewhat frightening–but also holds the potential for enjoyment–with a small group of other individuals and a skilled facilitator who is responsible for structuring the experience. This structuring includes the establishment of group norms which are supportive and cooperative. Within this situation, certain problem-solving tasks are created which are meaningful, concrete and holistic, have uncertainty of outcome, but contain the definite possibility of success. At this point, a choice element is created. Participants may choose to engage in the challenge, or to "opt out." Freedom to choose is perceived as vital to personal growth. The problem-solving tasks demand a high degree of cooperation and self-control. Individual response elicits feedback which is quite clear and unambiguous, as well as meaningful. If all goes well, the feedback will be positive, and the combination of achievement with cooperation and self-control will lead to enhancement of self-insight, self-esteem, confidence, and a sense of personal power and freedom. Failure may not increase self-esteem, but should lead to fresh insights which can be just as positive in facilitating future success.

To illustrate this model, let me describe "Fiona," a woman in her forties, divorced, returning to full-time study. Fiona had many doubts about her ability to cope–she felt inadequate intellectually and physically. Part of the coursework involved a rock climbing experience. Fiona's expectations were grim, but she decided to give it her best shot. Her classmates rallied around, and I gave her as much advice as I thought she needed. I think we all experienced a

Diagram 1: Personal Growth Through Adventure:

A Model for the Adventure Experience

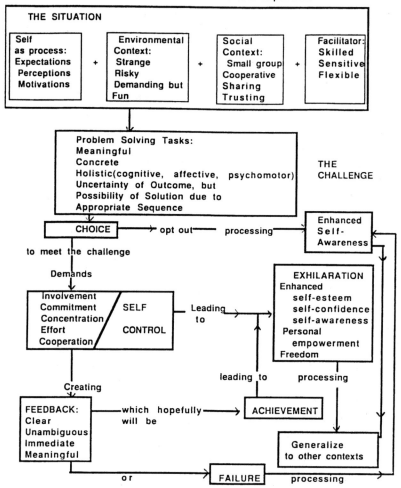

"high" when Fiona made it to the top. She left that afternoon exclaiming, "Just wait till I tell my daughter what I've been doing!" Through this experience, Fiona discovered that she could exercise control over her emotional and physical fears and, in so doing, achieve more than she believed possible. In subsequent classes, Fiona was a vibrant and committed member, making many valuable contributions.

CONTROL

The "Personal Growth Through Adventure" model focuses upon self-control as a major component in realizing our potential. This is particularly relevant to women, who often have mixed feelings about the notion of control.

The idea of control as mastery over the environment is not of great importance to women in the outdoors. Women are more interested in the "inner journey" than any outward "quest" or "conquest" (Warren, 1985). The notion of "conquering" a mountain or a river seems be the height of arrogance (and illusion). How could we imagine that our climbing a mountain made the least amount of difference to its being? Far from the notion of "conquest," the self-control that I am talking about is based on the fact that the wonderful wilderness environment is essentially uncontrollable, and we like it that way.

Another kind of control is that rigid self-control that denies access to any kind of feelings, that insists on a "stiff upper lip" and discounts the need to cry. The self-control that I am advocating, however, arises from an understanding and acceptance of one's self and one's needs. At any given point, a host of needs and desires are clamoring for recognition. Our job is to prioritize these and fulfill them accordingly. Often we give in to short-term desires such as immediate gratification or relaxation, running away from problems, or disengagement. The immediate feedback that we receive in an adventurous environment teaches us that such short-sightedness can be disastrous. So we learn to push these desires aside and attend to our real needs, developing self-control in the process.

In every situation, balance is required. There may be times when we feel exhausted and discouraged. To carry on regardless in the face of such emotions may be to invite disaster. We need to stop, recuperate, and consolidate, before continuing with renewed vigor. Self-control involves insight into ourselves, including a realistic understanding of when to stop and when to push forward.

Women are often only too familiar with that kind of self-control which is a denial of self, having been taught from girlhood to ignore their own needs and serve others. Adventuring, however, is a glorious celebration of self and the nurturing group. Self-control engenders the freedom to fulfill one's needs. Women are also taught helplessness in the face of physical and technical demands. Self-control teaches that many of these limitations are illusory. Learning skills in the outdoors, and how to use one's body (in whatever shape) to achieve one's objectives encourages an ecstatic dumping of these limitations as we realize that we can do (almost) anything! Thus the self-control of which I am writing is both a fulfillment and a liberation.

CONCLUSION

In this paper I have attempted to clarify the adventurous process through identifying some key components and incorporating them into a model which can be used by therapists as both a guide and an explanation for what should be happening. It is my hope that enhanced understanding of practitioners will increase the likelihood of positive adventure experiences; these ideas are so much "pie in the sky" if they cannot be translated into practice!

A final note: I am aware that the "Personal Growth Through Adventure" model neglects an area of importance: the effects of the wilderness environment on the participant. Living and journeying in natural surroundings has in itself a profound significance which lies beyond the scope of this paper.

REFERENCES

Bertolami, C. (1981). *Effects of a wilderness program on self-esteem and locus of control orientations of young adults.* Summary of thesis. Paper presented at the Annual Canadian Conference on the Application of Curriculum Research. (ERIC Document Reproduction Service No. ED 266928)

Kimball, R.O. (1986). Experiential therapy for youths: The adventure model. In M. Gass and L. Buell (Eds). The season of ingenuity: Ethics in experiential education. *Proceedings of the Annual Conference of the Association for Experiential Education* (pp 42-46). (ERIC Document Reproduction Service No. ED 274487)

Knapp, C. (1988). *Creating humane climates outdoors: A people skills primer.* Washington: Office of Educational Research and Improvement. (ERIC Document Reproduction Service No. 294706)

Langer, E.J. (1975). The illusion of control. *Journal of Personality and Social Psychology, 32*: 311-28.

Luckner, J.L. (1986). *Outdoor adventure education as an ancillary component in rehabilitation programs for the hearing impaired: A pilot study.* (ERIC Document Reproduction Service No. ED 289270)

Royce, D. (1987). Why outdoors? *Journal of Adventure Education and Outdoor Leadership, 4* (4): 24-29.

Scherl, L.M. (1988). *The wilderness experience: Psychological and motivational considerations of a structured experience in a wilderness setting.* Unpublished Thesis, James Cook University, Queensland.

Walsh, V. & Colins, C. (1976). *The exploration of the outward bound process.* Denver: Colorado Outward Bound Publications.

Warren, K. (1985). Women's outdoor adventures: Myth and reality. *Journal of Experiential Education, 8* (2): 10-14.

Transforming Body Image Through Women's Wilderness Experiences

S. Copland Arnold

SUMMARY. This paper explores the possibilities for transforming body image through women's wilderness trips. The author proposes that through the metaphor of reconnecting with the Earth body, a woman is given the opportunity to reconnect with her individual physical body. However, the wilderness experience alone is not sufficient to create a major transformation. Other critical elements are the therapeutic effect of the group process and risk-taking activities, such as hiking and team building exercises which contribute to breaking down the stereotypes concerning women and their bodies. Through this combination of experiences, women have the opportunity to reevaluate and reformulate their own norms for the female body.

As a graduate of the Pacific Crest Outward Bound school at 19 and now as an outdoor educator/instructor for the school at 26, I have matured into womanhood through my experiences in the wilderness. My experiences in Outward Bound as a young woman

S. Copland Arnold received her BA from Prescott College in Wilderness Leadership and Counseling. Currently, she is a graduate student in Counseling Psychology and Dance Therapy at Prescott College, and Senior Instructor for the Pacific Crest Outward Bound School where she has been employed since 1990.

[Haworth co-indexing entry note]: "Transforming Body Image Through Women's Wilderness Experiences." Arnold, S. Copland. Co-published simultaneously in *Women & Therapy* (The Haworth Press, Inc.) Vol. 15, No. 3/4, 1994, pp. 43-54; and: *Wilderness Therapy for Women: The Power of Adventure* (ed: Ellen Cole, Eve Erdman, and Esther D. Rothblum) The Haworth Press, Inc., 1994, pp. 43-54. Multiple copies of this article/chapter may be purchased from The Haworth Document Delivery Center [1-800-3-HAWORTH; 9:00 a.m. - 5:00 p.m. (EST)].

43

deeply affected my self-acceptance, self-esteem, and body image. I gained an appreciation for my strength and agility as I climbed, hiked, and became competent in back country camping. Rather than an object to be adorned and perfected, my body became an ally.

I began to feel personal satisfaction and a sense of being complete and whole. For the first time in my life, muscular and athletic women who didn't fit the cultural norm of thinness were my role models and the mother Earth was my teacher. My perception of beauty changed as I began to appreciate the diversity in sizes and shapes of the female body. After working my first all-women's course, I recognized that these courses, in particular, can provide a safe environment for growth and transformation. It is my belief that the combination of wilderness experience, the therapeutic effect of an all-women's group process, and challenging physical activities such as hiking and rock-climbing, offer an opportunity for women to reevaluate and reformulate their own norms for the female body. The wilderness setting allows for a conscious use of the Earth body metaphor as it relates to women's physical bodies. The technical skills and physical activities allow women to experience their body in an active, functional arena rather than an aesthetic one. The all-women's group provides a safe place for women to explore their body image and self-esteem. The structure of the group process allows instructors to use a cognitive approach, consciously focusing on body image and self-esteem issues for women.

Despite the fact that there has been substantial research and writing on the subject of women and body image and on the general therapeutic benefits of wilderness courses, no studies yet published examine the impact of all-women's wilderness courses on the participant's body image. It is the purpose of this article to examine this issue.

REVIEW OF THE LITERATURE

Women and Body Image

The concept of body image has changed over the course of the century. Freud defined body image as the mental image one has of one's body. Secord and Jourard (1953) included the feelings one has about one's body when defining body image (Powers & Erickson, 1986, p. 37). For the purposes of this article, body image is the relationship one has with one's own body sensations, mental images, and feelings. Positive body image includes, but is not limited to, being "embodied," connected with and present in one's body.

Disturbances in body image have become increasingly important to educators and mental health professionals as the number of girls and women with eating disorders and/or poor body image has risen dramatically. Ben-Tovim and Walker (1991) studied methods for measuring women's attitudes about their bodies. They found that in the basic silhouette method, where subjects are asked to choose a silhouette (ranging from very slim to very fat) that represents themselves now and one that represents their ideal, normal women of all ages choose an average or overweight silhouette as their present shape and an underweight silhouette as their ideal (p. 162).

Not only are women's visual and mental images distorted but their feelings about their bodies are negative as well (Dworkin & Kerr, 1987, p. 136). Magraw (1984) used a *Glamour* magazine survey of how women felt about their bodies to illustrate the immensity of this issue. Out of the 33,000 female readers surveyed, 6% of the women were "very happy" with their bodies. In a culture that perpetuates an anorexically thin ideal for the female body, the standards are so high, very few women can include themselves and there is no acknowledgement of the diversity in normal sizes and shapes (McBride, 1985, p. 18).

The 1984 *Glamour* survey found that women's feelings about their bodies affected almost every aspect of their lives–especially their feelings about themselves. This association between self-esteem and body image has been confirmed by many studies (Dworkin & Kerr, 1987; Ben-Tovim & Walker, 1991) and is important information for anyone who is concerned with women's issues.

As a feminist, outdoor educator, and mental health professional working with women, I am particularly concerned with the connection between self-esteem and body image. I want to empower women to reach their fullest human potential, which is a goal shared by many feminists. "In order to achieve this goal it is essential that women feel good about themselves and an integral part of that is feeling good about their bodies" (Magraw, 1984, p. 1). If programs like Outward Bound propose to help individuals realize their potential and increase self-esteem, then courses for women need to address the issue of body image.

Women and Wilderness

The link between Outward Bound-type courses and improved self-esteem has also been confirmed (Ketchin, 1981). The four pillars of Outward Bound are: physical fitness, self-reliance, compassion, and craftsmanship. The combination of these four elements empowers students to feel good about themselves and their accomplishments. Although Outward Bound is often recognized for its work with troubled youth, the school offers programs for many different populations, including all-women's courses. Henderson and Bialeschki (1987), who have researched all-women's courses, suggest "that the outdoors may be a metaphor for the lives of women. As women gain strength and confidence in the outdoors, they are able to experience strength and confidence in other areas of their lives" (p. 25).

I found only one study on women and wilderness experiences which mentioned body image. Pfirman (1988) conducted a study that examined the effects of a three-day wilderness course, Wilderness Challenge, as an adjunctive treatment for victims of rape. Pfirman evaluated 16 women before and after the course using the Modified Fear Survey, the Tennessee Self-Concept, and the Levenson Locus of Control. Pfirman's study found that women reported more positive feelings towards their bodies after the three-day course.

Exercise alone probably does not improve body image. It is well-known that anorexics typically engage in rigorous exercise programs and claim to feel fat even when emaciated. Skrinar, Bullen, Cheek, McArthur and Vaughan's (1986) research indicates positive changes in body image and the perception of one's physical abilities only occur when the exercise produces either increased levels of fitness or improvement in skill levels. I also believe that when exercise is initiated from a desire to honor and develop the body rather than in a quest for the cultural ideal, body awareness and appreciation is enhanced and body image subsequently improves.

My belief is that women do not automatically experience increases in self-esteem and a more positive body image as a result of participating in a wilderness course. Nor do I believe that increased physical activity automatically improves body image. I am convinced that by focusing on the needs of women, Outward Bound-type women's courses can provide the tools for transformation. Group process in an all-women's group, increased body awareness through skilled movement in risk-taking activities, and the wilderness setting are all necessary elements for a transformative experience.

GROUP PROCESS

In both my review of the literature and my interactions with Outward Bound participants, several common themes emerged from all-women's groups. The group provides a safe environment for personal growth and transformation. The group also provides a community free from the typical gender roles of a mixed group. Finally, the group provides universality, what Yalom (1985) describes as a "welcome to the human race" experience. The sharing of experiences, concerns and information provides a sense of relief to group members and an opportunity "for frank and consensual validation" in an intimate setting (Yalom, 1985, p. 8).

Universality

An all-women's course provides universality in nightly de-briefs and group processing. From the first evening "circle" where women share their reasons for coming on the course, common themes and experiences emerge: participants realize they are not alone, that many women are struggling with the same issues. They begin to realize that even the women who fit the cultural norm of thinness feel inadequate. An important aspect of universality is consensual validation and affirmation. It is important for women to feel supported and encouraged by their fellow group members and their instructors if they are going to take new risks and meet new challenges. This notion of external validation is confirmed by Dworkin and Kerr (1987), who compared several interventions applied to women with body image problems. They concluded that cognitive therapy as opposed to cognitive behavior therapy or reflective therapy is the most effective intervention because of the external reinforcement provided by the counselor. This implies that affirmation from another is needed as well as self-affirmation.

Safe Environment

Henderson and Bialeschki (1987) gathered participant observations of a week-long women's wilderness experience. They concluded that the women-only experience was an important aspect of the course. A frequently mentioned reason women prefer to be with women is the lack of competition with men and with each other for men's attention. The women's courses offer a non-competitive or safe environment. McBride (1985) found that "often young women consider having an ultra-thin figure as the best means of competing for male attention and popularity" (p. 21). Does the absence of men allow women to relax into their bodies? One Outward Bound participant said:

> I personally wanted an experience where I was freed of male influence. . . . I often feel more self-conscious, judged, less secure when a male is present. I believe that group dynamics can be significantly different with male presence for other women as well. This often takes the form of increased competitiveness amongst women, more evident insecurities about appearance and body image.
>
> Therefore, all-women's experiences allow women to relax and explore themselves further in a female chosen way without fear of judgement that it will not fit with male expectations.

Another commented:

> I am a very competitive person, particularly when I am in the company of men, or when I feel threatened which provokes

insecurity. Being in a women's group, when I didn't have to worry about my physical capabilities, I was allowed to get in touch with a core problem that I had been harboring since childhood . . . I am a survivor of incest.

For survivors of incest, in particular, choosing an all-women's group is a matter of safety and an opportunity for healing and connecting with their bodies in a positive way. It is my belief that all-women's groups allow women to avoid a negative, noxious element in the men's presence. What is this element? What exactly happens when men are in the group? Obviously, competition is an issue. I would also speculate that when men are absent, so are their projections of the ideal woman and their projections of their own internal feminine aspects.

If they [women] find their self-esteem in the approval of men, they need to realize that what most men are projecting onto them is their own disembodied soul or their own Earth Mother. Neither projection recognizes the mature embodied woman who has the courage to be who she is. (Woodman, 1993, p. 154)

Perhaps, all-women's groups allow women to explore what a mature embodied woman is without the influence of the patriarchal ideal.

Gender Roles

All female groups provide a supportive environment where women can engage in activities that are not generally ascribed to women (Yerkes & Miranda, 1982). In a survey of women participating in outdoor adventure programs, Yerkes and Miranda (1985) found women often fear that skill attainment will be more difficult in a mixed group because of imposed gender roles. In the same survey, women were less inhibited by gender roles in their everyday lives after returning from their all-women's wilderness experience (p. 50). One Outward Bound participant agreed:

I chose an all-women's group because I did not want the feeling of competing with or being protected by men in the group. I sometimes feel that men feel the need to protect and instruct women in physical situations. We as women often defer to male physical strength.

Another said:

Nothing was assumed. And no one 'knew' how to do things, I mean, no one was telling people how to do things . . . it felt very equal. I was never made to feel dumb.

ROCK CLIMBING, RAPELLING AND PEAK CLIMBS

My research confirms the traditionally acknowledged benefits and goals of risk taking activities within an Outward Bound framework. I will briefly summarize these benefits. I will also expand on several other ways of using these activities specifically for an all-women's course.

Outward Bound uses risk-taking activities such as rock climbing and rapelling as metaphoric experiences. This is based on the assumption that the way you climb the rock may tell you something about the way you live life. Instructors consciously explore with students the ways in which Outward Bound activities apply in the "real" world and at home. Many students reflect back on these challenging activities when faced with challenging events at home.

Rock climbing and rapelling require the student to learn new skilled movements and mountaineering techniques. These activities create confidence and increased self-esteem as students surpass their self-imposed limits through successful mastery of a new and often stressful experience. One woman commented:

The trip reinforced, at a time when I really needed it, what I've always thought. I am not a quitter. I try hard. I can do new things and succeed.

Climbing and rapelling also require teamwork, cooperation, and communication. I have found that women, in particular, work well in this situation, encouraging and supporting each other emotionally as well as literally supporting each other with ropes. This reflects an emphasis on relationship rather than competition.

I would like to suggest two other ways of using climbing specifically for an all-women's course. Rock climbing is the one sport I have participated in where men and women are performing equally in competitions across the world. Climbing is a sport that proves Sukie Magraw's (1984) assertion that "women are closing the performance gap that still exists between themselves and their male counterparts" (p. 9). Climbing depends on balance and flexibility, female attributes, rather than strength and speed, male attributes. Women's legs and hips give them the strength and balance to be good climbers, strong hikers and stable rapellers. Ironically, women who are dissatisfied with their bodies seem to be "especially negative about their waist, hips and thighs" (Ben-Tovim & Walker, 1991, p. 157). Climbing, hiking, and rapelling give women a chance to experience their bodies as allies rather than imperfect objects. I believe that an all-women's course should consciously focus on the student's connection with her body through increasing an awareness of its existence. Developing a greater awareness of our bodies' capabilities often leads to a greater appreciation of our bodies.

As an instructor, my greatest joy in teaching climbing is to create a success experience for women and to demonstrate how graceful and capable our bodies are. I believe we instructors can deepen this body awareness by initiating discussions with students. How do we feel about our bodies? What do we like/dislike about our bodies? How have our bodies changed over time? What messages have we received about our bodies? Our capabilities in sports? How have climbing and hiking challenged those messages? What other ways can we enhance body awareness on these courses?

I have used aikido centering exercises, yoga, and breathwork in the mornings to bring women into their bodies. I remind them to find their center and breathe as they reach a difficult spot in climbing or hiking. I also think it is important for instructors to role model body awareness and acceptance throughout all of the course activities.

WILDERNESS AS METAPHOR

Throughout spiritual history, the wilderness has been a place of transformation. Jesus struggled through 40 days and nights in the desolate wilderness, yet emerged revitalized. The Buddha sat underneath a tree until he gained enlightenment. In ancient matriarchal cultures, women left their community during the dark moon, going into the wilderness to bleed and receive visions together. It is this dualistic quality of wilderness that Outward Bound emphasizes: the wilderness may be filled with hardship and suffering but it offers refuge and transformation as well. Thus, the wilderness is a consciously used metaphor for life within the Outward Bound experience. In order to transform body image, I believe instructors for all-women's courses should consciously use the Earth as a metaphor for women's bodies. Eco-feminists compare the cultural disrespect and degradation of the Earth with that of the female body, claiming that the two are inextricably connected. On an Outward Bound course, students begin to have a relationship with the Earth, learning how to camp without impacting her, learning to read and travel her terrain, gaining an awareness and appreciation of her diverse plants and animals. What if participants began to see the Earth as a symbol and a reflection of their bodies? What if all-women's courses encouraged women to develop a relationship with their bodies? What if learning how to travel and live in our bodies in "non-impactful" ways and gaining an appreciation of the beauty and diversity of the female body were objectives for an all-women's course? My answer to these questions is that by seeing the opportunity provided by the Earth/body metaphor, we instructors would come closer to our goal of helping participants reach their human potential. In my experience, as an instructor, the issue of body image has always arisen in all-women's groups. Instead of letting the issue arise by chance, instructors should use it as a theme for the course, basing course activities, conscious use of metaphor, and group discussions on the theme of body image.

CONCLUSION

Outdoor education programs need to acknowledge that all-women's courses are different from standard courses composed of all women participants. In order to transform body image, which is an integral part of women's self-esteem, several factors should be considered:

1. Rather than being based on the heroic quest theme, which involves conquering the mountain, women's courses are more relationship oriented. Relationships with body, self, and others are processes which need to be honored and given time within the course structure.
2. As women outdoor educators ... "we must work to physically educate women to feel good about their bodies, to claim them as their own, to feel their own strength" (Magraw, 1984, p. 5). Enhancing body awareness during the physical activities of the course is a priority. By augmenting traditional risk taking activities with a focus on balance, flexibility, cooperation and caring, we bring our female strengths to the sport.
3. In order for all-women's wilderness courses to affect body image positively, the course must consciously address this goal through the use of metaphor, group process and structured body awareness activities.

Finally, I would like to offer the possibility that although the wilderness is a wonderful place for transformation, brief Outward Bound-type courses provide a place to begin, not a place to end. I have spent several years on my quest for wholeness and embodied womanhood and I often feel I have just begun. As I discuss my ideas with other instructors, they, too, feel their experiences with women and wilderness have been transformative. Yet we instructors spend months at a time communing with the Mother Earth and other women. How long does this transformative process take? Are there stages in transforming body image? What are the stages? Is this an age specific issue? These are all questions that need to be addressed in future studies and writing on this topic. I hope more research will be done on outdoor education programs for women. However, my greatest hope is that the wilderness becomes a place of solace and healing for women and their relationship with their bodies.

REFERENCES

Ben-Tovim, D.I., & Walker, M.K. (1991). Women's body attitudes: A review of measurement techniques. *International Journal of Eating Disorders, 10*(2), 155-167.

Dworkin, S.H., & Kerr, B.A. (1987). Comparison of interventions for women experiencing body image problems. *Journal of Counseling Psychology, 34*(2), 136-140.

Henderson, K.A., & Bialeschki, M.D. (1987, Summer). A qualitative evaluation of a women's week experience. *Journal of Experimental Education,* 25-28.

Ketchin, A.F. (1981). Women out of bounds: An ethnograph of outward bound as symbolic experience (Doctoral Dissertation, University of Colorado at Boulder, 1981). *Dissertation Abstracts International, 42,* 3653A.

Magraw, S. (1984). *Women's bodies in a man's world.* (Viewpoints (120)) Wellesley, MA: Wellesley College, Center for Research on Women.

McBride, L.G. (1985, Fall). The slender imbalance: Women and body image. *Journal of NAWDAC,* 16-22.

Pfirman, E.S. (1988). The effects of a wilderness challenge course on victims of rape in locus of control, self-concept, and fear (Doctoral Dissertation, University of Northern Colorado, 1988). *Dissertation Abstracts International, 49107-B,* 2870.

Powers, P.D., & Erickson, M.T. (1986). Body-image in women and its relationship to self-image and body satisfaction. *Journal of Obesity and Weight Regulation, 5*(1), 37-50.

Secord, P.F., & Jourard, S.M. (1953). The appraisal of body-cathexis and the self. *Journal of Consulting Psychology, 17,* 343-347.

Skrinar, G.S., Bullen, B.A., Cheek, J.M., McArthur, J.W., & Vaughan, L.K. (1986). Effects of endurance training on body-consciousness in women. *Perceptual and Motor Skills, 62,* 483-490.

Warren, K. (1985). Women's outdoor adventures: Myth and reality. *Association for Experimental Education Journal,* 10-14.

Woodman, M. (1993). *Conscious femininity* (pp. 150-5). Toronto: Inner City Books.

Yalom, I. (1985). *The theory and practice of group psychotherapy.* New York: Basic Books, Inc.

Yerkes, R., & Miranda, W. (1982). The need for research in outdoor education programs for women. *Journal of Physical Education, Recreation, and Dance, 37*(4), 82-85.

Yerkes, R., & Miranda, W. (1985, March). Women outdoors: Who are they? *Parks & Recreation,* 48-51, 95.

Ethical Considerations
in Adventure Therapy:
A Feminist Critique

Denise Mitten

SUMMARY. The author addresses two major questions: (1) What ethical dilemmas exist in providing adventure therapy for women as it is commonly practiced? and, (2) Given what we know, how can adventure therapy be of the most therapeutic value to women? Research regarding the effectiveness of adventure therapy is mixed and inconclusive. A competing hypothesis for causation of the global changes people experience after a therapeutic experience is the impact of the natural environment. Adventure therapy has its roots in a patriarchal society and was developed for boys and men. The same principles and practices now are being applied to women, thus creating a challenge for feminists in the field of adventure therapy to selectively employ those aspects of adventure therapy which increase women's mental and emotional health, and to discard or modify those aspects which are ineffective or harmful. The author presents a model she believes recognizes women's strengths as well as needs. This model respects individual differences, recognizes and

For the past 20 years Denise Mitten has worked in adventure, outdoor, and environmental education. She has had opportunities to work with women, women offenders, women survivors of sexual abuse, nuns in emotional recovery, homeless people, men, and youth from a variety of ethnic and social backgrounds. Ms. Mitten developed and refined Woodswomen's acclaimed leadership program both through Woodswomen programs and as a faculty member at Metropolitan State University.

[Haworth co-indexing entry note]: "Ethical Considerations in Adventure Therapy: A Feminist Critique." Mitten, Denise. Co-published simultaneously in *Women & Therapy* (The Haworth Press, Inc.) Vol. 15, No. 3/4, 1994, pp. 55-84; and: *Wilderness Therapy for Women: The Power of Adventure* (ed: Ellen Cole, Eve Erdman, and Esther D. Rothblum) The Haworth Press, Inc., 1994, pp. 55-84. Multiple copies of this article/chapter may be purchased from The Haworth Document Delivery Center [1-800-3-HAWORTH; 9:00 a.m. - 5:00 p.m. (EST)].

55

addresses the power difference between the leader/therapist and client, and respects the natural environment.

INTRODUCTION

Adventure therapy began in the United States in the early 1960s. Since that time, its benefits have been extolled and the field has grown considerably. Just as the traditional field of psychotherapy has its roots in Freudian analysis and grew through other "fathers" of psychotherapy, adventure therapy has its roots in "fathers" such as Kurt Hahn (Gass, 1993). And just as women have examined and redefined clinical psychotherapy, I believe we need to examine traditional adventure psychotherapeutic practices before embracing current practices and applying them to women.

In this paper, I use Gass' (1993, p. 5) definition of adventure therapy* as a therapy that places the client in activities that challenge dysfunctional behaviors and reward functional change. This is done in small groups in the wilderness, in small groups at or near the therapeutic facility of the client, or in long-term residential camps that may last up to a year. It often includes the use of physical structures built by adventure programmers specifically for the adventure therapy experience. Low and high ropes courses and indoor or outdoor rock-climbing walls are examples.

Women participate in adventure therapy as survivors of sexual or other physical abuse, as troubled youths or adults, as family members in family therapy, and as clients of therapists who recommend a program. There are all-women's programs, programs for specific issues such as eating disorders, and coed programs.

In this paper, I address two questions: (1) What ethical dilemmas exist in providing adventure therapy for women as it is commonly practiced? and, (2) Given what we know, how can adventure therapy be of the most therapeutic value to women? Admittedly, these are hard questions and many professionals may shy away from such

---

*Other names such as adventure-based counseling, experiential-challenge, outdoor-adventure pursuits, therapeutic camping, and wilderness-adventure therapy are also labeled as psychotherapy. This field suffers from definitional problems and the plethora of terms contributes to the confusion.

deep self-examination. However, as a profession, it is important to look at these issues.

In addressing the first question, we need to determine if adventure therapy is effective. To this end, I discuss the information and research results used to support the notion that adventure therapy increases a client's emotional health. I then explore some of the ethical issues that arise in the context of adventure therapy including:

- the power difference between group leaders/therapists and the clients in an adventure-based or wilderness therapy situation and how that relationship impacts the therapeutic goals;
- the problem of a client self-prescribing a high risk activity for herself after having experienced its use in a supervised setting; and
- the impact of our patriarchal society on the application of adventure-based or wilderness therapy.

The second part of this paper focuses on ethical adventure therapy programs for women, including these facets:

- the value and impact of the outdoors in the therapeutic process;
- the place of eco-feminism in adventure therapy; and finally,
- a model that outlines ways to provide adventure therapy for women in a conservative and safe manner.

ADVENTURE THERAPY RESEARCH

Many people have reported global beneficial effects of adventure-based experiences for dysfunctional populations (Ewert, 1989; Kimball & Bacon, 1993). However, there is a great deal of ambiguity regarding this effectiveness. Gillis (1992) points out that there is not conclusive research that adventure challenge and outdoor wilderness programming are beneficial to therapeutic populations. Gillis shows that researchers in adventure challenge and outdoor wilderness therapeutic programming, as in psychotherapy, have used widely diverse measures such as self-report and behavioral methods, assorted environments and activities, and different levels of clients' functioning such as varying physical abilities and inpatient and outpatient status, and have assessed people at different lengths of treatment, making it difficult to have enough data to decide what indeed does work. Additionally, there is not sufficient consistency among programs to allow for replication of research. Therefore, it is hard to quantitatively or qualitatively assess programs for their effectiveness. In addition, general lack of randomization, the use of non-equivalent control groups, "in-house" evaluations, and the lack of adequate follow-up plague research in this field (Gillis, 1992; Kimball & Bacon, 1993). There have also been contradictory results reported, such as changes in self-report measures, but no difference in behavioral measures (Bandoroff, 1990; Ewert, 1989). Further complicating is Ewert's (1990) paper in which he noted that rock climbers' feelings of self-esteem related to rock climbing skills did not transfer to more global feelings of valuing themselves. Gillis (1992) uses this information also to question whether global changes in self-esteem or other commonly measured outcomes can translate to a specific therapeutic context of persons in various diagnostic categories, who also may be different in gender, race, class, or national origin than people who have been the norm for clients in the adventure therapy field.

Just as there are no set standards for what the process of adventure therapy involves, there are no set standards for who practices adventure therapy. In the adventure therapy field there are clinically trained therapists as well as on-the-job trained therapists. Staff need a particular combination of specialized skills to be able to competently handle the technical aspects as well as the clinical aspects. Kimball and Bacon (1993) note that there is a scarcity of qualified staff in the adventure therapy field.

Still, leaders and psychotherapists believe there are global changes in client's behaviors and attitudes. This may be true. However, there is not a body of research that specifically identifies *how* these changes are made, *what* specifically causes these changes, for *whom* these changes can be predicted, or the *duration* of these changes. Therefore, it is unknown what part of the adventure-therapeutic process, if any, contributes to these global changes. Akin to having unnecessary surgery, if we can't ethically say that adventure-therapy is the cause of the changes, then perhaps we shouldn't advise people to participate. Both qualitative and quantitative research methods should be employed to answer the how, what, by whom, for whom, and duration questions. A competing hypothesis for causation of the global changes that are seen may be the impact of the natural environment. This is discussed in a later section.

THE LEADER/THERAPIST
AND CLIENT POWER DIFFERENCE

In mainstream U. S. culture, we are conditioned as children to accept professionals' power and superiority as normal (Peterson, 1992). As we grow older, most of us have a more realistic view and acceptance of who we are as people, and there is more room for give and take between clients and professionals. The maturity of people's responses, however, often disintegrates during times of crisis. When clients are in positions of extreme need, helplessness, or dependency, they can revert to childlike postures based on the degree of trauma they experience. At these moments, clients often believe that cooperation and compliance with professionals' directives are essential for a positive outcome (Peterson, 1992). Adventure therapy professionals often work with clients who have experienced trauma or clients who at this time in their lives may not have the capacity to reach an adult level of maturity. This gives leaders a great deal of power and responsibility.

An often desired outcome of adventure therapy is personal empowerment for the client. This empowerment can be expressed as increased self-esteem, increased self-efficiency, and increased personal responsibility. However, using adventure-based activities to aid in this therapeutic process presents a conundrum. In adventure therapy settings, professionals take clients outside their comfort zone. For some clients, participating in a wilderness experience seems very scary and very challenging. Being in the outdoors is a new experience for many clients. Most clients coming to a wilderness or adventure therapy situation will come with increased feelings of insecurity. Again, this results in accentuating the power difference already there between leaders and clients and may be disempowering for clients.

This power difference is complicated by the fact that the living conditions and wilderness settings encourage leader and client relationships to have an informal aspect. While there may be benefits in eating with and carrying the same load as one's leader, there is also the temptation to blur the professional boundary.

Initially, clients gain a sense of security by establishing a connection with the leaders. This may also help exaggerate the power difference. Because of the client's feeling of dependence, the client may want to be "good." This can translate into the client attempting to figure out what the leaders want of her and doing that. This behavior can make it appear that positive long-term global changes have occurred when they have not.

In addition, the client who was dependent on the therapist for emotional guidance in a clinical setting is now also dependent on the therapist for basic needs such as food, shelter, and protection, as well as the skills needed to complete the program. The higher the risk or perceived risk of the program, the higher the client's initial dependency on the leaders. This sense of dependency gives leaders even more power over the client than in a traditional indoor therapeutic setting.

Young and Ewert (1992) write that women report higher levels of fear in outdoor programs than do males. This higher level of fear can translate into an even greater power difference for women. This means it will be more difficult for women to state their rights and believe that they can control their environment. This makes it difficult for women to own their accomplishments and leads to boundary confusion.

Thus, there is an imperative need for the generational boundary. A generational boundary is necessary whenever there is a power difference. This power difference is the result of one person having more experience, expertise, status, or a professional obligation (Peterson, 1992). Examples are parents, legislators, judicial officials, employers, and professionals such as doctors, lawyers, mental health practitioners, therapeutic recreation specialists, and adventure educators. The concept originated in the family system where the parents are literally in a different generation. What one learns about generational boundaries growing up usually constitutes the expectations about boundaries that one will have as a group member or client later.

In the family there is a need for clear generational boundaries in order for children to have the opportunity to develop healthy personal boundaries. Lewis, Beavers, Gossett, and Phillips (1976) revealed that firm parental coalitions contribute to family health. This means that in households with two parents, parents each individually have appropriate personal boundaries, and that parents maintain a generational boundary between their dyad and their children. In single parent households the same generational boundary is important for the children's well-being. It is the parents' responsibility to maintain this generational boundary. This boundary is neither completely rigid nor completely permeable. Information passes across the boundary. The generational boundary provides the security the children or clients need in order to learn, develop, and grow. In leader and client relationships, it is the leaders' responsibility to maintain this boundary.

In order for leader and client relationships to be therapeutic, there also needs to be trust. Many clients transfer the trust they had in their parents to professionals. However, before clients can have this faith they must believe that leaders place the clients' needs above their own. Clients are literally trusting that leaders will structure and maintain a generational boundary. In addition, clients are trusting that if they test the generational boundary, the leaders will continue to maintain it.

This trust and testing brings up a special concern when high-risk activities are used in adventure therapy. For example, a leader may need to tell group members that it is unsafe to swim in a certain area or that, when rock climbing, group members must be tied into a safety rope. If a group member decides to test these restrictions an accident or injury may occur.

Norms are the practiced, seldom verbalized, rules of conduct to which group members conform. These are group life guidelines and are positive when they serve as anchors to inhibit chaos, clarify expectations, and signal group membership and acceptance.

However, if a group member's personal boundaries conflict with group norms, that group member can become isolated, a fringe member, or a scapegoat. For example, if it is a norm to gossip about the leaders and a group member does not gossip, this member can become isolated. If it is a norm to talk about past relationships and a group member feels that is too private or fears that the group might reject her relationship choice, the member can become isolated. Cultural boundaries for people in the minority can often conflict with group norms. Defenses are what we do to protect or avoid the boundary. Anger and accommodation are both defenses. Defenses are not good or bad; however, clients with different cultural or personal boundaries than the group norm may appear uncooperative.

If a client is not clear about her boundaries or has low self-esteem, a potential loss of "place" in the group, or rejection from the group, can modify her behavior, and for the price of being accepted, a client may give up a core value, a piece of herself, or a boundary. For example, if a leader makes a sexual advance to a client and the client sees this as a way to be accepted into the group, then the client will give up that piece of herself. The client will yield because the expected loss is less than the expected loss in the case of resistance. A more subtle example would be a leader asking a client for some of her special dark chocolate candy stash that the client brought as a personal snack.

Norms have a big influence on group members in the wilderness. The experience is new, the place unfamiliar, and the distance (physical and emotional) from familiar objects and support people is great. In adventure therapy situations it takes more energy, skill, and courage than most clients have to challenge, ask questions, doubt authoritative statements, refuse to go along, and openly criticize what everyone else is doing, and defend their rights and boundaries.

Leader and client relationships are built on the leaders' expert authority and their obligation to serve (Peterson, 1992). For clients, compliance with a leader's advice is the means to achieving their common purpose, and it is clients' faith in the professional's abilities to respond to their needs that enables them to comply. To a certain extent, the client has to 'turn over' managing the outcome, leaving the client vulnerable. The client's trust is grounded in the assumption that professionals will operate within the context of the client's needs. This inherent ethos of care is profound. For clients to follow leaders into unknown territory assumes, and therefore requires, a depth of care and commitment from professionals that raises the relationship to a sacred covenant of fidelity and obligation (Peterson, 1992). For leaders to complete this challenging commitment, training, practice, and supervision are necessary. Leaders need not only appropriate personal boundary judgment but also to have the technical skills necessary for adventure-based activities. As mentioned previously, qualified staff is not available for the number of programs offered (Kimball & Bacon, 1993).

SELF-PRESCRIBING A HIGH-RISK ACTIVITY

High-risk activities are often used in adventure therapy programs. Rock climbing, for example, is used as a way to work on therapeutic issues or as a way to feel better about oneself during a time of depression or emotional stress. This author believes we need to examine the ethics of using high-risk outdoor activities for therapy.

Rock climbing is a risky sport. It needs to be undertaken with a clear head. Yosemite National Park Search and Rescue director John Dill (1992) has written that three states of mind frequently contribute to accidents: ignorance, casualness, and distraction. In his interviews of survivors of climbing accidents, he reports that survivors say that they lost their good judgment long enough to get hurt.

Rock climbers know that, because of safety details that need to be continuously monitored, having a "bad" day, feeling "off-center," or being emotionally stressed are distractions to rock climbing and are all reasons to cancel an excursion. However, when therapists and outdoor leaders use rock climbing for therapeutic purposes, they are in fact encouraging women to participate in a high-risk activity when they are depressed, suicidal, or in another compromised emotional state.

After a positive therapeutic experience using a high risk activity, there is a temptation for clients to self-prescribe such activities. For example, a woman suffering from depression is encouraged to participate in a therapeutic rock climbing excursion. If this woman perceives that she has received benefits from this experience and/or enjoys the activity, she may take up rock climbing as a sport. From her adventure therapy experience she has learned that when she is depressed or emotionally stressed, rock climbing can help her feel better. Unfortunately, stretching beyond one's physical limits to feel better or participating in a high-risk sport when depression or other emotional states might lead to poor judgment can, literally, be deadly.

THE IMPACT OF OUR PATRIARCHAL SOCIETY ON ADVENTURE THERAPY

A common practice in adventure therapy is to contrive a situation where the perceived risks are greater than the objective risks (Gass, 1993). This is done to give the client a feeling of success at overcoming fear, or of accepting a risk, while at the same time maintaining enough control over the situation to ensure physical safety. "The intentional use of stress is central to the change process of wilderness therapy. Stress is often magnified by the students' tendencies to exaggerate the level of risk inherent in adventurous activities. Certainly rock climbing, rappelling on vertical cliffs, exploring deep caves, and traversing steep snowfields entail some genuine danger; however, these potential risks can be managed much more simply than the novice imagines. Regardless, students often feel as if they are in a genuinely life-threatening situation" (Kimball & Bacon, 1993, p. 21). Here we need to examine if the means justify the ends. The goal is to have the client be successful and feel like a hero. However, this manipulation is reminiscent of the untruths women have been told over time. A respectful teaching opportunity is to explain the difference between perceived and objective risks and teach the client how to use her own judgment as to which risks to undertake. This allows the client to be proactive in her healing.

Many adventure therapy activities employ a great deal of equipment. For example, high and low ropes courses have many ropes connected by knots and platforms built on other structures. Only an expert or trained individual can construct a ropes course. Consequently, when a client participates on a ropes course she has to trust that the construction is safe. While participating in ropes courses is great fun–like a playground for adults–one has to question their use for therapy. In a ropes course situation, the client has to trust the judgment of the leaders. A leader says that riding the zip-line will produce feelings of competence and success. Comments such as "just jump and you'll see how wonderful it is" can remind the woman of being raped or coerced against her will. Yet now she is to do it here at the request of another person without enough information to determine, herself, whether the action is safe.

Trust is another area that adventure therapy is supposed to enhance. Many programs use a trust fall. A client stands on a stump, table, or other platform and falls back into the arms of other group members. The exercise is supposed to build trust among group members. However, this is a narrow definition of trust. For many men, trust has a physical basis. For example, Fred knows Tom will be there for him when he throws the ball to first base, or when climbing that Tom will safely hold the belay rope in order to catch him if he falls. For many women, trust also has an emotional component. Sue trusts Maria will listen to her feelings and problem-solve with her. Therefore, many men will learn about trust through doing physical activities with each other, while many women learn about trust by being with each other and relying on each other for emotional support.

It is important for women who have been physically or sexually abused to learn to judge who they can trust and who they cannot trust, both physically and emotionally. In an adventure-therapy setting the clients are told who to trust. An example is the trust fall. The client is told that the other clients will catch her. While she learns that leaders can decide whom to trust, she in fact has not learned to listen to her inner-self and decide when and whom to trust.

One purpose of the adventure therapy movement in the United States has been to provide an "educational process where adolescents [this includes young women] are initiated into the prosocial values that form the basis of the western culture" (Kimball & Bacon, 1993, p. 19). Kimball and Bacon (1993) see most troubled youth as "needing a reinitiation into cultural norms" (p. 19). As a feminist, I find this disconcerting. Our cultural norms are set for a dominant white, male, heterosexual, middle class population.

"The group decides what needs to be done and carries out their decision. Guided group discussion is used to settle problems, to give individuals feedback, and to evaluate performances" (Kimball & Bacon, 1993, p. 22). This helps maintain the status quo in our patriarchal society and gives both the leaders and the group a great deal of control over behavior. Given the power that leaders have in this situation, clients are undoubtedly, to a certain extent, compliant. This leaves little room for individual needs. These are the very needs that were overlooked that helped the clients become dysfunctional.

Kimball and Bacon continue, "Being in the wilderness also facilitates the breaking down of inappropriate defenses and denial. The level of physical and social stress and the pressure to succeed at concrete tasks tend to minimize an adolescent's ability to maintain a false front. It is difficult to hide one's true feelings when one is wet or hungry, and almost impossible to repress an emotion when one learns that it is necessary to hike three more miles before making camp" (p. 26). The impact of this stress needs to be assessed.

Assessing the Impact of Stress

The emotions and behaviors that come out under the stress described above, and the way they are dealt with, do not teach clients responsibility (Mitten, 1986a). In addition, people do not develop self-esteem under stress. People tend to resort to the defensive and protective behaviors they need to get through the situation and the situation can become a survival test. People can feel pitted against the environment, especially if they are trying to heal from past traumas.

I have been told by women that when under stress–from lack of sleep, hunger, exhaustion, or having external standards to meet– they feel alone, tense, child-like, irritable, defensive, frustrated, depressed, agitated, immobilized, weepy, and like they want to scream, and often want others to feel bad, too.

Once the stress, such as that described above, is relieved, women have told me they feel relieved, drained, guilty for outbursts, at a loss, depressed, and foolish. Most women agreed that they did not like themselves when their behavior changed under stress and felt that they resorted to old, often childlike, behavior patterns out of fear and desperation.

In the above example, people are being taught to push through the stress rather than manage the stress. People's judgment is often impaired under stress, which may lead to an unsafe situation or injury. In respect for women's safety, women need to be taught to stop participating in risky activities when they are under a great deal of stress.

At the same time, women say that they enjoy a challenge. I have been told that when they can freely choose a challenge, and they complete it, the exhilaration is high. When they don't complete the challenge, they can also take responsibility for that and work through their disappointment.

Bonding Through Stress and Fear

For some people, bonding or feeling closer under stress feels familiar and even comfortable. This is especially true for people from families where bonding took place during or after a conflict. In the mainstream U.S. culture this is exemplified by team sports where team members bond to win or beat another team. Another example is in war where men have historically bonded when fighting others.

Some women wonder if the bonding or sharing that occurred during their experience was real, or if the only way to connect with those people again would be under stress. These individuals may leave a program confused or believing that they have had a positive, honest connection with other members of the group. As exemplified in the Kimball and Bacon (1993, p. 26) quote, some people believe that under stress their true selves come out. However, this type of bonding does not lead to community building nor does it, in the long run, increase self-esteem. In fact, it may teach individuals to create a stressful environment when they want to feel close. It also teaches them that the emotions and feelings they have when under stress reveal the "real them."

Researchers disagree about all the reasons that people join groups, but they do agree that they join groups when scared. Schachter (1959) said individuals will affiliate when their opinions, attitudes, or beliefs are shaken. They then search for information that will define social reality and affiliation will successfully satisfy this need for information. He undertook a series of studies where he placed subjects in an anxiety-producing situation and then assessed their desire to affiliate with other people. They wanted to affiliate, but only with people in the same misery. He concluded that individuals under stress form groups both to gain information and to reduce anxiety levels. Therefore, putting people in unfamiliar, stressful, and scary situations will produce high group cohesion (Wills, 1981; Gerard, 1963). However, this does not necessarily help people learn to be part of a group when there isn't an external compelling situation.

Other research that supports this notion that group bonding in an adventure therapy situation may be due to the individuals' fear level includes the following:

- Human groups tend to become more cohesive when facing a threatening, rather than nonthreatening, situation (Kleiner, 1960; Pepitone & Kleiner, 1957).
- Many animals, including humans, prefer to join with others when fearful (Latané & Glass, 1968; Schachter, 1959).
- Individuals awaiting a negative event, such as receiving a series of painful electric shocks, prefer to wait with others rather than by themselves (Schachter, 1959).
- Joining a group is an effective way for people to reduce fear (Kissel, 1965).

ETHICAL ADVENTURE THERAPY PROGRAMS FOR WOMEN

The Value of and Impact of the Outdoors in the Therapeutic Process

A competing hypothesis for causing the global changes that clients experience after a wilderness therapeutic experience is the impact of the natural environment. Bardwell (1992) summarized the research to date on the restorative impacts of the natural environment. She asserts that the natural environment plays an invaluable role in enhancing our everyday well-being, our receptiveness to other people, our learning, as well as our overall quality of life.

Bardwell relates an important study. One of the most researched therapeutic programs has been Outward Bound. The elements of stress and challenge are integral to its programming. A program called Outdoor Challenge models itself after the Outward Bound program, with one distinct difference. The Outdoor Challenge program does not include many of the stresses and challenges of a traditional Outward Bound course. The results from the study of this program showed that the same global changes in behaviors and attitudes were found through pre- and post-testing of the clients that the research reports from programs that have more stress and challenge involved. This is evidence that merely being in the outdoor, natural environment can influence these global changes.

Bardwell continues by saying that four components are necessary for a restorative experience and while many environments can provide these components, natural settings are especially effective at providing opportunities for mental recovery. These components have been summarized by Kaplan and Kaplan (1989):

- Being away: The setting is removed from the everyday environment;
- Extent: The setting is big enough to feel like a different environment;
- Fascination: The setting has inherently interesting things going on;
- Compatibility: One feels a sense of belonging and it facilitates pursuing one's purposes.

Miles (1993) also cites Kaplan's work in suggesting that the outdoors has intrinsic healing capabilities. It could be that being outdoors without an intensive program can be enough to promote healing from sexual abuse or other traumas that may have caused a client's dysfunctional behavior. More research is recommended in this area. In addition, the client could more safely self-prescribe a relaxing outing for rejuvenation or healing.

While there is little specific research in this area, Cimprich (1990) has reported that breast cancer patients who engaged in outdoor restorative activities reported quality of life improvement and tended to initiate more projects, than those who did not. Canin (1991) found that in a study of AIDS caregivers, those who passed time in quiet activities, especially nature activities, which seemed particularly conducive to reflection, appeared to have less burnout and functioned more competently than those who passed time by watching TV or by playing or watching organized sports.

The Place of Eco-Feminism in Considerations of Adventure Therapy

Eco-feminism is the merging of feminist and ecological principles for the purpose of mediating humanity's relationship with nature (Kelly, 1988). To meet this end we need to understand the connections between the domination of women and other persons and the domination of nonhuman nature.

In 1974, Sheila Collins wrote: "Racism, sexism, class exploitation, and ecological destruction are four interlocking pillars upon which the structure of the patriarchy rests" (p. 161). Susan Griffin (1978) in *Woman and Nature*, wrote about the connections women have with the earth and how these connections have been eroded over the years. She says that our reconnection to the earth will heal and increase our capacity to love ourselves.

The following quote was used by Kimball and Bacon (1993) to show what they believe are positive gains of power through an adventure therapy experience. However, this young man learned to increase his domination over nature in order to feel more powerful.

> *When this trip starts, and all through it right on up to the last day before the truck is loaded and headed towards home base, you will despise the weight of the pack, curse every rock and every dirt mound, condemn every speck of dust, spit at every dirty mud puddle, and snarl at every ridge. You will push yourself, and be pushed, both mentally and physically further than you ever imagined possible, you will endure the seemingly unendurable. And as mad as it may sound, when it's all over and you've already loaded the truck and start to roll out on the roads, you will think back over those things, all of them, and you will feel this incredible surge of power over yourself, and all of those things will add up to the most fantastic and*

cherished adventurous memory you will ever know. You will feel the power overcome you, and you will know without doubt that you have done something that will irrevocably remain in your mind forever. You will feel the limitation of all the things you once thought impossible for you to do slip away from your mind and you will reach the ultimate realization that there are no limits to the things you are capable of accomplishing. That will be the supreme rush. (Tommy C., age 17) (p. 40)

Adventure therapy, traditionally, takes place in an outdoor environment. The environment is "used" in order for the client to have a feeling of success. When clients return from a wilderness experience feeling good about having conquered the environment or having seen their process as a survival experience, we are continuing the destruction and domination of nature.

In contrast, a woman returning from a trip that emphasized a connection with the environment wrote:

As I was driving home, I became a little sad that the trip was over and that I was heading back to the city . . . despite the rain and moments of irritability. I was ready for the comforts of home but did not want to go back to the city. I have a new appreciation of nature, the different kinds of fungus and plants, water, birds. On Monday I walked down to the river down by my house and was so disgusted with how little nature is respected. I walked back up to my car and got a trash bag and started collecting trash as I walked . . . It made me think about actually being a leader and bringing kids or groups out to the woods to learn and appreciate nature, to teach them that it needs to be respected if we are ever going to enjoy it.

A Model that Outlines Ways to Provide Adventure Therapy for Women in a Conservative and Safe Manner

Ingredients for Empowerment

Many clients enter adventure therapy programs because they are unable to form healthy relationships or they have a specific relationship issue. For example, they may be unable to establish trust, unable to shed the memories of a trauma, or lack basic social skills. Fedele and Harrington (1990) outline four interrelated curative factors in women's therapy groups that help address these situations. They include validation of one's experience, empowerment to act in relationships, development of self-empathy, and mutuality (Fedele & Harrington, 1990). In order for a program to provide a climate that facilitates these factors, it is necessary to have a program philosophy that respects women and the diversity of women, recognizes women's strengths, respects the environment, and includes allowing clients choices about their experience. Leaders who have an understanding of the professional relationship and are skilled in implementing the program philosophy, as well as technically competent, are necessary. In addition, women's self-assessment issues and the impact of natural elements on women's emotional states need to be considered in program design. The need for these two considerations is often heightened for women survivors of sexual abuse (Mitten & Dutton, 1993). This population is used as an example when further discussing the following two aspects.

Issues of Self-Assessment

Survivors often inaccurately assess their physical abilities, their stamina, what is dangerous, and how to be safe. The leaders' understanding of a survivor's experience will influence the survivor's safety as well as the group's. In general, survivors tend to either over-extend or under-challenge themselves. This may stem directly from the effects of the sexual abuse. In order to survive, women had to tune out the pain their bodies were experiencing, to discount what they were feeling, and act as if they were fine. This is known as disassociating or disconnecting from the experience. This can become a lifelong pattern (Mitten & Dutton, 1993). Therefore, some women learn to tolerate high levels of pain without seeming to notice. For example, a woman may overextend herself physically by hiking to complete exhaustion, become dangerously cold before adding clothing, or hike with blisters until they become infected. Conversely, a woman may paddle with minor exertion and feel she is overextending herself.

Accurately assessing whether an activity or situation is merely fear-producing, or truly dangerous and determining what can be done to be safe, is another problematic area for survivors. If a survivor doesn't see whitewater as dangerous, she may unwittingly canoe in rapids beyond her ability. On a day-trip to practice rock climbing, Kim became panicky about climbing down the rocks even with rope support. She was convinced it was dangerous. When her leaders helped her understand that it was scary but not dangerous, she was able to choose to descend. On another trip, Juanita was in a mountaineering group learning to slide down ice and snow using an ice axe for guidance and braking. Her leaders were struck by her absence of fear. She did not appear to enjoy the thrill of the activity; realistically, she simply did not comprehend the dangers.

This impaired ability to trust one's perceptions and act on them also extends to setting appropriate boundaries. The essence of sexual abuse is having one's most intimate boundary–the skin on one's body–violated. Survivors, therefore, may feel extremely sensitive about nudity. A survivor may be reluctant or embarrassed to undress or change clothes in the presence of other people or participate in nude swimming or saunas. Some women may feel uncomfortable around women, women and men, or just men.

This lack of clear boundaries extends to emotional and sexual boundaries as well. For example, survivors may say more about themselves than they are truly comfortable revealing to others, or they may engage in sexual activity with which they are uncomfortable. Leaders need to honor the survivor's own sense of boundaries and to help her use them as a guide. In certain instances, it is very important for outdoor leaders to set the example for boundaries rather than following a client's lead. For example, many survivors have used sex as a way to connect with people or as a way to gain protection. Some survivors habitually sexualize relationships (Blume, 1990).

The Impact of Natural Elements

Interaction with certain natural elements such as flies and mosquitoes, rain and lightning, dirt, and darkness can trigger sexual abuse memories and feelings, or panic. Invasive insects, such as flies and mosquitoes, can remind survivors of their lack of control over their bodies (Mitten & Dutton, 1993). The following example illustrates this concept:

> Sarah, on a two week canoe trip, would sometimes have to retire to her tent to get away from the bugs. Even though insect repellent kept most of the insects off her body, the buzzing around her was too much. Once while she was rock climbing, large flies landed all over her legs. She felt an immense lack of control and felt the flies were invading her while she was helpless. This incident brought back memories of her sexual abuse experience. She told the leaders how uncomfortable she was and then was able to continue. She said it took all of her self control not to scream, fall off the rock, and jump around.

Rain and lightning can also stimulate out-of-control feelings. Rain, like insects, can feel invasive and uncontrollable. Lightning can remind a survivor of "the jolt" her body received in response to being sexually aroused during the abuse or of her world being taken over by a larger force (Mitten & Dutton, 1993).

Cleanliness is another issue stemming from sexual abuse which is exacerbated on an outdoor trip. Generally, one expects to get dirtier in the wilderness than at home. But for a survivor, this inability to get "really clean" can trigger feelings of shame, feeling dirty, or feeling like "damaged goods," reminiscent of her response to the abuse as a child. Without being able to sustain a certain level of cleanliness, a woman's self-esteem can plummet. This can affect her ability to participate safely on a trip.

Coping with natural elements which are out of a person's control can trigger emotional, physical, visual, or other sensual flashbacks. Having a flashback means just that—in a flash, something in the environment catapults a survivor back to another time and she acts and feels as though the past is the present (Mitten & Dutton, 1993). Flashbacks can cause anxiety for a survivor. She may never have experienced them before. Resulting nightmares or uncontrolled screaming can cause embarrassment or terror that lingers into the day.

Program Philosophy

For a woman to develop self-esteem as an infant, youth, or adult, the woman needs to be in a nurturing and structured environment (Clarke, 1979). The woman needs to feel included and that she belongs there. Thus, the program atmosphere must feel and be safe and comfortable. In a supportive and nurturing program environment, clients will often respond by relaxing and having fun, which makes it possible to take the initiative to try new activities and skills, reach out to others, cooperate as individuals to accomplish group tasks and goals, and allow themselves to recognize and fulfill their wants and goals.

When women feel that they belong, they are more likely to feel confident and have a "can do" attitude. Conversely, when women do not feel safe, levels of performance can go down and the safety of the program can be compromised. This consideration of safety includes teaching women to practice stress management. Women first learn to recognize when stress is affecting them and then learn to take measures to lessen the stress or, if that is not possible, to cope with the stress. The outdoor environment is conducive to learning these skills. Then when women participate in challenging situations, the positive aspects of risk taking are enhanced and the negative aspects of stress are lessened.

In this supportive environment, women more easily choose to challenge themselves and take risks. This includes learning new activity skills as well as new behaviors that the leaders model. Learning new skills increases one's self concept because it increases competence (Iso-Ahola, 1980). Women take their accomplishments with them through increased self-esteem and pride, often realizing that this trip need not be an isolated event in their lives. In addition, they can more easily and safely replicate the activity later.

Being accepted for who they are, for many women, means feeling trusted and respected and having their differences acknowledged and affirmed. It also means feeling safe to state feelings. It takes time to develop trust and respect, which are necessary for healthy relationships. Because in outdoor situations women tend, as soon as the experience begins, to establish connections with each other, relationships can be based on dependency rather than on trust and respect. If relationships are based on dependency, for example, if a client establishes a relationship to ensure that she will have food, shelter, and protection and that she will be liked and not be left behind, this may be at the expense of her emotional or spiritual safety. A client may feel that she may not talk about certain things about herself or show any weakness or perhaps strength in order to be accepted. If she compromises her integrity in order to be accepted, then by definition she can't feel emotionally and spiritually safe and she won't develop self-esteem.

Setting a trip pace that includes time for leisurely chatting provides the time and space for healthy relationships to form. Women need relaxed time by themselves and with others to reflect and to process personal changes. Women tend to form trusting relationships by sharing personal information so there needs to be relaxed days with time for talking. This may also include special day trips for those who wish to continue a more active pace and choose to connect around an activity. People want to accomplish goals, see new territory, and try new skills. All these expectations are compatible with a program structure that also accommodates a flexible trip pace. However, a program schedule of always-on-the-move will impede the formation of trusting relationships. A pace that constantly pushes people to their limits can cause resentment. Relationships may be built around these resentments rather than around mutuality.

Suggested principles of program design for women's adventure therapy are:

- creating an atmosphere that is safe emotionally, spiritually, and physically;
- travelling in the wilderness for its own sake, not using it as a means to an end, not creating situations to take risks or prove competency;
- respecting and caring for the environment during trips;
- being aware that having fun is essential to many people's growth and learning process and that it helps in developing self-esteem;
- creating a trip environment supportive of differences in clients and their specific needs and of the belief that individual needs vary and are valid and possible to meet;

- being flexible about goals and understanding that there are many workable ways to learn skills and be outdoors;
- recognizing that individual accomplishments are different and special to each woman and encouraging women to have their own standards;
- recognizing that women do not need to be changed to fit into adventure programs or taught in order to be good enough to participate on outdoor trips;
- emphasizing that women's strengths are an asset to outdoor groups;
- understanding that leadership is a relationship, not a personality type, and believing that constructive safe leadership can take many forms;
- avoiding a success/failure approach to challenges;
- teaching outdoor traveling and living skills in order to increase self sufficiency. (Mitten, 1986b)

Participation Philosophy

In order for a person to internalize an experience as her own, she has to choose it and acknowledge to herself that she chose it. A woman's choices need to be informed choices, rather than "I'll do it because you say I should." It is not unusual for women to feel coerced into participating in programs by their husbands and boyfriends who want them to learn skills but don't want to teach them, by their employers, who want women to use their experiences for the benefit of the corporation, or by therapists or family members who want them to be healed or different. Unless a woman makes a free choice to participate, she may struggle the entire time with feelings that keep her from being fully present in the group.

Those who choose to participate in a program also need to choose each step thereafter, from whether to eat granola to whether to climb that day. A go-for-it attitude is compatible with women having a choice. A client needs to feel that the leaders and the group are supportive of her trying and want her to succeed.

At the same time, it is not useful to foster an attitude of "pushing through" one's feelings to get to a "better" place. Having this attitude as a norm would take away choice. It would reinforce women not listening to their bodies and minds. For survivors, the meaning of being sexually abused is to be pushed physically and emotionally, against one's will, beyond what a person can manage. This attitude can reinforce trauma and cause unnecessary stress. An example of the positive benefits of choice in a setting where leaving the group was both safe and appropriate is illustrated below:

> One-half hour into a day rock climbing clinic, Pat told a leader she was going home. The leader, of course, had a pang of disappointment. However, she said to Pat, "I'll walk you to your car." En route they chatted about the morning, and Pat told the leader that she was in therapy for sexual abuse and felt too exposed during the clinic. The leader said she understood, asked Pat if she could call her later that week, and bid her goodbye. That week the leader called Pat, and invited her to join the group on a clinic the next weekend that would have less people. Pat accepted and participated. The following week Pat attended an intermediate climbing clinic. Again, after a half-hour she needed to leave. She returned a few weeks later to complete an intermediate clinic. She shared with the leader that being able to say she felt exposed and needed to leave, then leaving without criticism, and being welcomed upon her return, supported her healing process. Women survivors are often afraid to say they need to leave, or to say no. They are afraid their "no" will be interpreted hostilely and they will be abandoned. When they were small children this would have threatened their survival. In this case the value for Pat of saying "no," leaving, and returning was substantial. The leader gave Pat a gift of knowing that she could set her own limits without being abandoned. In many other instances it is appropriate for leaders to hear and honor a woman's choice to say "no" or that she needs to stop. This "no" can be "no for now," "no, I'd rather do only this part," or "I'll watch for now."

Webb (1993) agrees. In her assessment of a program for survivors of violence she says that "for some clients, it may be therapeutically appropriate for them to take a firm stand in saying 'no' to an activity." This choice and personal decision making leads to empowerment and allows an individual to better take responsibility for her actions. By respecting individual differences, we allow and encourage clients to take responsibility for their own health, safety, and well-being.

A way to encourage informed choice is to consider a graduated approach when designing a wilderness experience program for women. For example, the staff at Woodswomen, a service organization in Minnesota, decided on a graduated approach when designing a wilderness experience program for women offenders. Most of the clients in the program were survivors of abuse. Their first trip was a short trip of three days. The location was a cabin with an outhouse and a pump for water. This allowed the women the opportunity to ease gently into rugged living. In fact, at the center where the cabin was located, there were also buildings with full baths. During the three days, they made one trip to these facilities for bathing. The women's next trip was a nine-day wilderness canoe trip. When the women participated on that trip, they were more mentally prepared for the challenge and could make a more informed choice about their participation. In addition, they had time to plan cleanliness and other coping strategies.

Leadership and the Professional Relationship

As in other professional relationships, leaders and clients enter into relationships with defined roles, goals, and objectives that are laid out at the start, and the relationships are time limited. This contractual relationship is a mutual partnership of trust and professional self-restraint. This contract is a direct reflection of the generational boundary implicit in the relationship (Peterson, 1992).

Hardin (1979) found that because clients look to leaders for direction and protection, the role of a leader is a powerful one. This huge power difference between leaders and clients, accentuated in an outdoor environment, needs to be recognized and respected. In Hardin's doctoral dissertation, *"Outdoor/Wilderness Approaches to Psychological Education for Women: A Descriptive Study,"* she described the goals and assumptions of outdoor leaders and their impact on clients. Her research supported the idea that leaders' goals and assumptions influence the experiences of the course clients, including their outcomes.

Therefore, the contract leaders must make is to maintain constant vigilance with respect to what is best for the client. For example, leaders may have wonderful ideas that they think will transform the client's life, but they have to keep asking, "Is Jackie's getting to the top of the climb for me or is it really in her best interest?" Being professional and establishing a contract to work in a therapeutic context with a client means not just exercising a skill; rather there is a contractual responsibility to the woman with whom the professional is dealing. Being responsible to clients means that leaders monitor their self interests while operating in the context of the relationship (Peterson, 1992). Leaders need to enter the process with care and shape what they have to offer to fit the individual client. In this contract leaders encourage the client to be active and assertive (the form of communication will be different depending on the client's capabilities) regarding her wants and needs.

To provide a healing environment in an adventure therapy setting, as described by Fedele and Harrington, leaders create a program environment supportive of the strengths and attitudes that women bring to a group. They help create a positive atmosphere for relationships to develop by creating a program setting that feels emotionally, spiritually, and physically safe. The needs of the individual group's members as well as the more general needs of the group inform leaders' responses and actions (Lehman, 1991).

At the beginning of the trip, leaders need to offer a great deal of structure. Having adequate initial structure facilitates people starting to form relationships by giving them access to the group and each other. Leaders need to be directive and dispense information that clients need to be safe. This increases their trust in the leaders and enables clients to be more comfortable trying new activities. For example, women new to the wilderness cannot accept nurturing or develop trust until they know where they are going to sleep. Especially in the beginning, women want details about safety, meals, and how general trip logistics are to be organized and taken care of. The greater the perceived risk or challenge, the more structure that is necessary. A wilderness trip involves a great deal of task focus, especially in the beginning, including packing gear, traveling to a destination, setting up initial campsites. Many of the early connections between clients are made at this task level. When clients can channel their nervous energy into tasks, tension is eased, fears subside, and some people find it easier to talk as they work together.

One of the primary things that unites a group immediately in a wilderness setting is the survival aspect. Some groups seem initially to view this as uniting against a common difficulty (for instance, high winds while canoeing, constant rain, or a mountain pass). During the course of the trip, leaders try to redefine this as working as harmoniously as possible with the wilderness and not spending energy fighting it. This redefining of working with nature instead of fighting it, for the client, carries over into self-appreciation as well.

CONCLUSION

Adventure therapy, as a field, can make important contributions to the health of individual women as well as the health of our society. Through a positive outdoor experience a woman can learn to manage herself in an environment that can feel out of control. She can find ways to feel safe, set clear limits and boundaries, and experience a oneness with nature. Most concretely, she can experience her traumatized body as powerful, supportive, and full of vital information (Mitten & Dutton, 1993).

Leaders have the outdoor and technical skills on which the client is dependent for her very survival. This power difference needs constant respect and maintenance. Sensitive, aware, and respectful professionally trained leaders are key elements in the quality of the outdoor experience. More emphasis needs to be placed on leader training and supervision.

We have a wealth of information from the eco-feminist literature explaining that women feel healed when in a nurturing outdoor environment. Given this, I recommend that we provide opportunities for women to go into the outdoors for healing. It is important for the program to complement and not to interfere with the powerful restorative effect of the natural environment.

However, a question that needs to be answered is whether the therapeutic benefits of participating in a high-risk outdoor activity are well documented enough to use this form of therapy with clients. We need to realize that we may be encouraging women to put themselves in risky situations at inappropriate times. In addition, if in fact therapeutic benefits are realized, it is not known if it is the accomplishment of a high risk activity, being in the outdoor environment, the group experience, the leadership, or some combination of the above that contributes to the therapeutic benefits. These are important ethical considerations that need to be addressed before jumping on a band wagon that may hurt other women. Until this research is completed, we need to weigh carefully the risks associated with using high risk activities as therapeutic tools and proceed conservatively. Because of the lack of conclusive information about how, what, or for whom adventure therapy works, leaders will want to be sure that the experience doesn't get in the way of a woman's own process. As in all therapy, what comes up for people in an adventure therapy situation is personal and person specific.

REFERENCES

Bandoroff, S. (1990). *Wilderness-adventure therapy for delinquent and pre-delinquent youth: A review of the literature.* Unpublished manuscript, University of South Carolina, Columbia, SC.

Bardwell, L. (1992). A bigger piece of the puzzle: The restorative experience and outdoor education. In Henderson (Ed.), *Coalition for education in the outdoors: Research symposium proceeding* (pp. 15-20). Bradford Woods, IN: Coalition for Education in the Outdoors.

Blume, E.S. (1990). *Secret survivors.* New York: Wiley.

Canin, L.H. (1991). *Psychological restoration among AIDS caregivers: Maintaining self care.* Unpublished Doctoral Dissertation, University of Michigan.

Cimprich, B.E. (1990). Attentional fatigue and restoration in individuals with cancer. (Doctoral Dissertation, University of Michigan.) *Dissertation Abstracts International, 51*(4), 1740B.

Clarke, J.I. (1979). *Self-esteem: A family affair.* Minneapolis: Winston Press.

Collins, S.D. (1974). *A different heaven and earth.* Valley Forge, PA: Judson Press.

Dill, J. (1992). Staying alive. *Mountain Bulletin, 5*(3), 4-6.

Ewert, A. (1989). *Outdoor adventure pursuits: Foundations, models, and theories.* Worthington, OH: Publishing Horizons.

Ewert, A. (1990). Risking it on wildlands: The evolution of adventure education. *Journal of Environmental Education, 21*(3), 29-35.

Fedele, N. & Harrington, E. (1990). *Women's groups: How connections heal.* Wellesley, MA: The Stone Center.

Gass, M.A. (1993). *Adventure therapy: Therapeutic applications of adventure programming.* Dubuque, IA: Kendall/Hunt.

Gerard, H.B. (1963). Emotional uncertainty and social comparison. *Journal of Abnormal Social Psychology, 66*(6), 568-573. Murray Hill, NJ: Bell Telephone Lab.

Gerard, H.B. (1961). Emotional uncertainty and social comparison. *Journal of Abnormal and Social Psychology, 62*, 586-592.

Gillis, H.L. (1992). Therapeutic uses of adventure-challenge-outdoor-wilderness: Theory and research. In Henderson (Ed.), *Coalition for education in the outdoors: Research symposium proceeding* (pp. 35-47). Bradford Woods, IN: Coalition for Education in the Outdoors.

Griffin, S. (1978). *Woman and nature.* New York: Harper & Row.

Hardin, J. (1979). Outdoor/wilderness approaches to psychological education for women: A descriptive study. (Doctoral Dissertation, University of Massachusetts.) *Dissertation Abstracts International, 40*(8), 4466-A.

Iso-Ahola, S. (1980). The Social Psychology of Leisure and Recreation. Dubuque, IA: Wm. C. Brown Co.

Kaplan, R. & Kaplan, S. (1989). *The experience of nature: A psychological perspective.* New York: Cambridge University Press.

Kelly, P. (1988). Linking arms, dear sisters, brings hope! In J. Plant (Ed.), *Healing the wounds* (pp. ix-xi). Philadelphia: New Society Publishers.

Kimball, R. & Bacon, S. (1993). The wilderness challenge model. In M.A. Gass (Ed.), *Adventure therapy: Therapeutic applications of adventure programming.* Dubuque, IA: Kendall.

Kissel, S. (1965). Stress-reducing properties of social stimuli. *Journal of Personality and Social Psychology, 2*(3), 378-384. Rochester, NY: Child Guidance Clinic.

Kleiner, R.J. (1960). The effects of threat reduction upon interpersonal attractiveness. *Journal of Personality, 28*, 145-155.

Latané, B. & Glass, D.C. (1968). Social and nonsocial attraction in rats. *Journal of Personality and Social Psychology, 9*, 142-146.

Lehman, K. (1991). *Integrating ethics and leadership: A journey with woodswomen.* Unpublished, College of St. Catherine, St. Paul, MN.

Lewis, J.M., Beavers, W.R., Gossett, J.T., & Phillips, V.A. (1976). *No single thread: Psychological health in family systems.* New York: Brunner/Mazel.

Miles, J. (1993). Wilderness as healing place. In M.A. Gass (Ed.), *Adventure therapy: Therapeutic applications of adventure programming.* Dubuque, IA: Kendall/Hunt.

Mitten, D. (1986a). Stress management and wilderness activities. In *Association of Experiential Education Conference Proceedings Journal* (pp. 29-34). Boulder, CO: Association of Experiential Education.

Mitten, D. (1986b). Women's outdoor programs need a different philosophy. *The Bulletin of the Association of College Unions-International, 54* (5).

Mitten, D. (1989). Healthy expressions of diversity lead to positive group experiences. *Journal of Experiential Education, 12*(3), 17-22.

Mitten, D. & Dutton, R. (1993). Outdoor leadership considerations with women survivors of sexual abuse. *Journal of Experiential Education, 16* (in press).

Pepitone, A. & Kleiner, R. (1957). The effects of threat and frustration on group cohesiveness. *Journal of Abnormal and Social Psychology, 54*, 192-199.

Peterson, M. (1992). *At personal risk.* New York: W.W. Norton & Company.

Schachter, S. (1959). *The psychology of affiliation.* Palo Alto, CA: Stanford University Press.

Webb, B.J. (1993). The use of a three-day therapeutic wilderness adjunct by the Colorado Outward Bound School with survivors of violence. In M.A. Gass (Ed.), *Adventure therapy: Therapeutic applications of adventure programming.* Dubuque, IA: Kendall/Hunt.

Wills, T.A. (1981). Downward comparison principles in social psychology. *Psychological Bulletin, 90*(2), 245-271.

Young, A. & Ewert, A. (1992). Fear in outdoor education: The influence of gender and program. In Henderson (Ed.), *Coalition for education in the outdoors: Research symposium proceeding* (pp. 83-89). Bradford Woods, IN: Coalition for Education in the Outdoors.

The Wilderness Solo:
An Empowering Growth Experience
for Women

Jean Angell

SUMMARY. How does solo wilderness adventure facilitate female empowerment? In this article, several types of solos are defined and described. The solo is a wilderness rite of passage which is currently rising in popularity as an opportunity for personal transformation being offered by outdoor experiential education groups and personal growth institutes. A return to the wilderness during times of personal transition, for guidance and growth and to reconnect with Spirit, has long been a part of most religions and cultures.

Jean Angell received her BA in Education in 1973 and is currently completing Master's level training as a wilderness psychospiritual guide and educator. She has over twenty years of experience back-packing, horse-packing, and llama-packing in the Southwest, and within recent years has co-facilitated and led groups in adventure travel, solo experiences, and nature awareness skills.

[Haworth co-indexing entry note]: "The Wilderness Solo: An Empowering Growth Experience for Women." Angell, Jean. Co-published simultaneously in *Women & Therapy* (The Haworth Press, Inc.) Vol. 15, No. 3/4, 1994, pp. 85-99; and: *Wilderness Therapy for Women: The Power of Adventure* (ed: Ellen Cole, Eve Erdman, and Esther D. Rothblum) The Haworth Press, Inc., 1994, pp. 85-99. Multiple copies of this article/chapter may be purchased from The Haworth Document Delivery Center [1-800-3-HAWORTH; 9:00 a.m. - 5:00 p.m. (EST)].

Solos described and discussed in this article are the VisionQuest, the reflective solo, the survival skills solo, and a simple self-imposed period of time alone in the wilderness. This article also explains how the author's personal experiences have increased her feelings of self-worth. Trained as a wilderness psychospiritual guide and educator, the author tells of methods used with individuals to expand their awareness and enhance their personal growth. Described are some of the causes for women feeling disempowered within the current male-dominated cultural paradigm. How these wilderness solos serve to empower women by increasing their self-esteem, self-love, self-confidence, and self-reliance will be covered. These strategies are viable, and important, alternatives and additions to a client's personal growth outside the confines of the therapeutic office.

INTRODUCTION

From the very beginning, when I was first given the opportunity to write this article, I felt a strong urge to go on another wilderness solo to bring present experience to the page. My previous encounters with solo time have been like that: a seed of an idea planted in the mind which ultimately grows into a compulsion, as if someone has grabbed me by the front of the shirt saying, "You *must* do this thing!" There are always the obstacles of having to organize normal life around a four day solo, with the additional need for several days of travel time to get into the backcountry and then still more time for re-entry/reincorporation. Yet somehow I find, each time the urge arises, the time becomes available, and another wilderness solo can occur.

While pressing the deadline for my first draft, I was again in the grips of the feeling that more solo time was an absolute must. With major pieces of my first writing lost to a "computer virus," I piled up hard copies of the leftover parts and my resource documents, retreated into the wilderness for new inspiration, and wrote.

The majority of what you read has been put together atop a rock on a canyon hillside overlooking peaks and valleys in the Rocky Mountains, surrounded by young aspen leaves bursting from their spring casings, all to the tune of a rushing spring-snowmelt creek. For me, almost all confidence, relaxation, creativity, and well-being comes through connection (one to one) with the natural world. This has been the case in my life for at least the past 20 years; for me, it was simply an intuitive idea to seek clarity and empowerment through a solo experience. Now I am pleased to be able to present this concept with backing from others who have also experienced, guided, and written about the wilderness solo as a path to self-confidence, self-esteem, self-reliance, and self-realization.

The solo is a wilderness rite of passage which is currently rising in popularity as an opportunity for personal transformation now being offered by outdoor experiential education groups, individuals, and personal growth institutes. Taking time in the natural world for renewal and purification is not a new idea. A return to the wilderness during times of personal transition, for guidance and growth, and to reconnect with Spirit has been a part of most religions and cultures. Four types of solos discussed in the pages that follow are: the VisionQuest (VQ), the reflective solo, the survival skills solo, and a simple self-imposed period of alone-time in the wilderness.

FOUR TYPES OF WILDERNESS SOLOS

One type of wilderness solo is similar to the Native American "VisionQuest" ceremony. The term "VisionQuest" is actually an English term from the latin "visum" meaning to see and "quaesitum" meaning to seek or ask. Nineteenth century Euro-American anthropologists used this term to describe a certain rite of passage practiced by American Indians (Foster & Little, 1984). In actuality, the Lakota term for this ceremony is "hanblecheya" which means "crying for a vision." It entails going up on the hilltop and staying there without eating and drinking for four days and nights while praying for guidance and answers from the Supernaturals. Some prepare for as long as a year before going out. General Lakota guidelines for such a solo include: participating in Inipi (sweatlodge) with a medicine man for instructions, then going naked (or with very minimal clothing) to a natural spot where green things are growing, taking only a blanket and one's Chanunpa (sacred pipe). Once there, the quester is instructed to empty the mind, listen to the spirits of the winds and the clouds, try not to sleep, and wait for an answer or a vision regarding one's life purpose (Erdoes & Lame Deer, 1992).

Evelyn Eaton, a Euro-American woman initiated as a pipe carrier in the Arapahoe tradition, tells of a similar type of VQ. As she describes it, the fasting is not just from food but also from books, conversation, and conveniences we take for granted. The fasting also serves as a way of expanding consciousness and getting in touch with "Those Above." These quests are not done for oneself alone; the fasting goes beyond the personal concept of sacrifice, and is done for family, tribe, land, world, and all life. One is fasting also, in order to discover, as well as to dedicate, one's unique gifts to serve. It is a symbolic journey on a highly serene level through the quiet regions of inner worlds, wherein vigilance is the keynote (Eaton, 1978).

According to Black Elk (1990), in order to really understand "hanblecheya," you have to go up there and be isolated. Despite much of what I will try to communicate in this article about this rite of passage, the essence of what it is can only be realized and completely understood through actually having experienced some form of wilderness solo time. Black Elk suggests that although it may look simple, it is really tough because you have to have courage, patience, endurance, and alertness. With no food and no water, and only holding your pipe, it becomes, in other words, "In God we trust" (Black Elk & Lyon, 1990).

During the VQ time of deprivation, altered states of consciousness are entered into: A trance state of alpha brainwaves occurs, internal dialogue quiets, attention becomes fused or expanded, and the force of one's old life ceases to hold things together. "Bodily states of emptiness and weakness often give rise to emotions and fears concerning personal survival. The body responds to the challenge and furnishes the individual with unexpected sources of strength and vitality" (Foster & Little, 1984, p. 7).

Tom Brown (1988) describes VQ as a feeling of purity, a purging of the old self, a connection to the land where each natural being reaches out to touch and communicate. Thus, one experiences the flow of life. He suggests that one gains a sense of relief from knowledge of the answers to the questions "Who am I?" and "Where am I going?" Further, he believes that this knowledge leads to a commitment to living one's truth.

The VQ may be the strictest method of doing a wilderness solo, and can yield some profound results in personal realization and transformation. It is a ritual for seeking answers to the deepest questions of our being. It is a ceremony of initiation: for entering puberty, taking on a new career, getting married. It is a rite of passage for endings: graduation, divorce, someone's death. It is a ritual that in the past was part of many religions and cultures. Today we can follow the lead of these native traditions to create contemporary nature-based experiences for spiritual growth and increased personal awareness.

Another form of wilderness solo is what is termed the reflective solo. Within this format, a person retreats into a solitary wilderness place, usually with some assisted preparation time regarding purpose and goals. Individuals embarking upon a reflective solo do well if prepared in advance by a facilitator who helps them to focus their attention on their life's problems, assures them that they can be their own inner teachers, and presents various journal writing styles (McIntosh, 1989).

Generally, this type of solo does not include the severe physical challenge of deprivation from both food and water (although it may be a time of greatly reduced food intake), nor is it a time of complete deprivation of manufactured articles. On a reflective quest, one may take a small amount of food, a tent and sleeping gear, some sacred personal objects or ceremonial items, gifts from those at home, pens and paper, and first aid supplies. Herein, the challenge is not so much to survive without food, water, and material objects and go into a trance state through deprivation, but rather to take time away from all communications with other humans and to reflect totally on only the connection with nature or one's own inner world.

Going to this place apart allows one the time to reflect upon changes that have recently occurred and how one is affected by them, the chance to face one's fears and resistances about transitions, to decide what new behaviors and attitudes one may wish to incorporate, and to experience a rebirth from the constricted circle of one's own self-imposed limitations so as to move through and beyond them. A reflective solo may also be beneficial to review the past, to rid oneself of excess baggage, and to face one's inner demons. Mirrored within nature, the person sees a way to go forward past a particular guidepost and onto the next life chapter (Foster & Little, 1989). One may do journaling, or rituals, or one may be very still and open to answers coming from the natural world. We may learn and incorporate conceptual principles while attuning to and observing nature. For example, one may note persistence from observing roots taking hold along a riverbank and trees growing out of rocks; or view a stream rushing by with fresh water every moment as a way to see our "old" partners as new each morning; or see willows bending as lessons of fluidity and rigidity; or discern the massive solidarity of an oak as enduring strength. The point is that all these natural beings have messages for us if we are only still enough to open up to them.

A third type of wilderness solo is the survival skill solo. This type of solo is construction and activity oriented. During their allotted time alone in the wilderness (usually from 24 hours up to 4 days), individuals are challenged to meet basic survival needs making use of newly learned skills. The focus of this solo is not sitting quietly still in silent, prayerful reflection. Instead the soloist is assigned the task of meeting the basic needs of shelter, water, fire, and food while alone in the wilderness. A type of shelter constructed from natural materials, sometimes known as a debris hut, is built by the soloist. Fire is brought to life through the practice of bow drill, hand-drill, the action of flint and steel, or through other more primitive methods than the usual "flick of the Bic." The individual may gather wild plants or hunt or set traps for wilderness meals. If the survivalist solo person is not camped near a natural water source, perhaps she may have to create a solar still or use other methods to gain water.

Meeting the challenges of providing one's own shelter, water, fire, and food can be a wonderfully empowering experience for the soloist. Individuals who have been apathetic or closed to new learning before the solo, may quickly begin to pay careful attention to learning the skills that are necessary for their own survival needs. These people, who previously may have felt ineffective in their actions within society, may experience a transfer of learning from a successful survival solo, a new sense of personal power and an inner respect of self which transcends the need for approval from others. The concreteness of challenges posed by wilderness experience (to those who usually fail to meet abstract challenges) helps them to enjoy success and consequent enhancement of self-image and confidence. The metaphorical potential for learning in wilderness is great and may allow insight into the challenges of normal life back home and how they can be managed (Miles, 1987). High adventure activities frequently provide women with the discovery that they can take risks and do more than they thought they could do–not only in the wilderness, but at school, on the job, or in interpersonal relationships (Strenba, 1989).

The fourth type of wilderness solo is when the woman takes a short period of self-imposed time out alone in the natural world. This could include a few days of backpacking into an isolated place, or it may even be as simple as a car-camping trip going into remoter areas off of main roads and incorporating a few solitary day hikes. It might even be just some time alone taken from a group of people with whom one is camping, such as taking one's tent out of earshot from the circle of others, or going off alone for a few hours each day.

These times can be opportunities to detach from demands and responsibilities, to remove oneself for a bit from phone, family, friends, and other societal distractions, and to take the time just to BE rather than to DO.

This type of solo is useful when one just needs to get away quickly without having to make too many long-term advance plans, or when one is extremely stressed and just needs a break. This is also an important first step for those who have never been alone in the natural world and who want to begin to challenge themselves in small, gentle increments of time. There are great benefits from this type of solo which may include self-confidence in decision-making. For example, a woman who is extremely dependent upon someone else in her life to make choices for her, could perhaps spend time on a car-camping trip making each of the many daily decisions without anyone else's input.

Recently my 13-year-old daughter "accepted the challenge" of a short solo wilderness hike. I had some fears for her safety or that she might become disoriented; however, I empowered her by allowing her to go. Upon her return, she reported how much she appreciated the alone and independent time. She said she felt completely free out there with no one telling her what to do, totally able to be herself without having to accommodate anyone else. Yet she said she never felt lonely because she felt strongly protected by the Mother Earth spirit. Additionally, she said she simply felt happy and freed from the problems on her mind.

Personal healing of this type does occur during moments of activity such as walking along a creek and really watching and listening. This focus on the natural world may remove the intensity from one's anxieties and allow one to relax into the present. Often, opening up to nature allows the shift in focus necessary for the subconscious mind to take over and solve the problems that loom so powerfully over us and which logic has not shown us a clear way through. Nature may lead us to the answers that we had within us all along. Being in and with nature helps attune us to the fact that we are not separate selves, but are related to and at one with all things. This experience can reduce feelings of alienation and unacceptability and bring us back to feeling more connected with the world and even more relieved, loved, and accepted.

I have found VisionQuest to be the type of solo most useful in extreme times of questioning "Who am I?" and "What am I here for?"–during those times when I am very discouraged about my path and have no logical way of sorting out just what I should be doing next. I have found the reflective solo to be especially useful during life crises, transitional times, and when I have needed to gain clarity, courage, and confidence. I have found the survival solo to be helpful when I have been in a low state of self-esteem and feeling "less than myself"–weak, disempowered, overly dependent upon others, or generally incompetent in my abilities. I have found self-imposed wilderness time to be useful when there was just too much going on around me to be able to make reliable decisions.

WILDERNESS EXPERIENCES ENHANCE SELF-WORTH IN WOMEN

In our culture, both men and women suffer from anomie and alienation. Too often, women especially feel unsupported by others, without direction or purpose, and able to choose only from alternatives that are meaningless to them. Frequently they know what they will and must do in a given situation regardless of their own interests. These conditions often create a feeling of powerlessness, indifference, and estrangement from self and others. Such sufferers become lethargic and depressed and they need to learn to bring into balance their perceptions of their abilities, responsibilities, and possibilities. During wilderness solo time, women can put themselves in situations where they have opportunities to recognize their own abilities and apply them completely and meaningfully to meet a challenge. Having successfully done so, they would then be able to reassess themselves as qualified, fit, capable, and adequate. Wilderness can be a place where people experience competence and consequent enhancement of self-worth. Thus people can be helped to cope with the contrasting conditions of anomie and alienation (Miles, 1987).

EMPOWERING WOMEN THROUGH WILDERNESS SOLO

Clearly, the wilderness solo can be of great benefit to anyone. I believe that it can be of special value to women because of the types of situations they deal with simply attempting to cope in today's world.

For too long women have come to believe that it is necessary to validate their identity externally, through the culturally predominant Eurocentric patriarchal system, in order to survive and to thrive. What is this "white male system"? At its most basic level, it is one that believes in its superiority to all things, that it is possible to know and to understand things through logical rationalization and objective thinking. It is a belief system that imagines that humans have complete control over their external environment rather than being participants within the web of life.

Although often discounted by male-dominated society, women tend to know that there is a place for the value of intuitive, emotional, subjective thinking which is characteristic of women (Schaef, 1981). Nature is a place where the white male system does not dominate. In nature, women's receptive, intuitive powers bring connection, confidence, and empowerment. During wilderness solo time, a woman comes to have success with these skills, to know that they are of value, and that she is not insane and restricted by her abilities, but instead directly empowered by them. In nature is external proof that always having to be prepared, on guard, with each moment planned, does not truly rule within the natural scheme of things. Researchers in wilderness adventure have pointed out that it soon becomes obvious that one cannot control all things in wilderness and therefore one ceases these attempts to control because it is unnecessary and impossible (Miles, 1987).

Once women open to what nature has to teach them, they begin to believe in their natural receptivity and inherent gifts, which may not be honored by patriarchal society, but which do have a powerful place within the scheme of the universe. When women recognize their abilities to observe and receive, they then realize the remarkable power that lies within them which is often eroded by their inability to play according to the rules of the current male-oriented society. As a woman's intuition is validated, her self-esteem improves. Just by opening the gut (as Tom Brown teaches)–listening from that place within that tells us this is right, this is safe, this is appropriate–a woman can come to trust and value her inner knowing as she participates in a solo and continues to be safe.

Women, according to Schaef (1981), battle with the original sin of being born female–of never quite being good enough, of feeling imperfect because they were born women. Even women who always appear impeccably dressed, have successful careers, and have an apparent veneer of confidence, often ultimately reveal that they feel that without male approval there is something intrinsically wrong with them.

Women are taught that if they attach themselves to a male, then they can get validation and approval in this way and will then feel better, will feel absolved of their "original sin." Often this results in a woman not knowing how to support herself or not having developed the necessary skills of self-care to function in the world. Through this comes the message that she is weak, and cannot cope with the world without the male.

A woman must have the opportunity to discover herself–her own capabilities and skills–and this is what occurs during a wilderness solo. She becomes self-reliant in her total aloneness, making moment to moment decisions which affect her safety and her experience. Without anyone else to depend upon, the woman discovers that she can accomplish the task of, for example, creating fire in the rain, or building a shelter that keeps her warm and protected, or that she can move about despite physical deprivations and still be alright.

"It is not the number of experiences, but the quality of experience, that determines whether or not a person's self-esteem will be influenced through participating in an outdoor experiential activity." In his article, Ewert relates that according to the research of Iso-Ahola, LaVerde, and Graefe, ". . . improving perceptions of competence can lead directly to feelings of increased self-esteem" (Ewert, 1990, p. 56). The key appears to be a sense of self-competence. This kind of stretching beyond, in the kinesthetic sense, overlaps into the conscious reality of how to reach beyond the limits a woman may have set for herself, or go beyond the place that she has come to believe that she is capable of enduring emotionally.

Women need to be given the opportunity to develop their warrior energy (Stone & Winkelman, 1989). When this is suppressed, the vulnerable child within is left feeling unprotected and we move the responsibility for that protection to someone outside ourselves. Then we tend to feel disempowered and dependent.

Our society encourages women to remain in their "nice girl" personality: to be a support and comfort to all, to be easy to get along with, to always be considerate, gentle, and peaceful. This constant reinforcement to remain "nice" disempowers the warrior energy that women need to protect themselves, or, for example, to compete in the business world.

Solo time teaches a woman to stretch her limits, to breathe without fear, to depend upon her own "killer who protects" (which Tom Brown often refers to as "the animal within") to meet her survival needs.

Additionally, women tend to relate from their personal, feeling side, which is ever-sensitive, warm, and nurturing to others. The cool, objective, impersonal self (who maintains psychological boundaries without needing to please) is less developed and less frequently rewarded in women. Yet as a woman reclaims these more buried energies, she is empowered and her ability to protect herself emotionally increases. Instead of feeling responsible or victimized in her relationships, she can use the impersonal part as a navigator in difficult situations (Stone & Winkelman, 1989).

VQ helps a woman to practice stepping into the use of her impersonal voice. On her solo, a woman deals with what needs to be done without having to consider the needs and feelings of others; thus, she has an experience of taking care of herself. She sets her own boundaries as to what feels safe, and she practices making level-headed decisions that affect her survival needs.

Empowerment can be defined as becoming a leader of your own life (Galland, 1980). One learns empowerment by exercising one's personal power, and this personal power increases by being centered and in touch with one's body, emotions, and thoughts. Solos provide avenues to help participants reflect upon and internalize their learning (Kohn, 1991).

Woman's bodily skills are honed for physical success on the solo, and she is reminded of her physical power. Her body image is improved by her ability to reach the quest site and to remain fit throughout the ordeal. Woman's emotional image is healed by the realization of her connection to all things–by release of the "I'm not good enough" thoughts, into an "I am one with all things" awareness. Woman's mental image is improved with the balance of the innocent one with the alert, aware one. The thinking, feeling world opens up to the realm of Universal Spirit and woman's spirit is healed through an excursion into Sacred Space.

Jung describes Sacred Space as a place of power, awe, mystery, a special place not suitable for everyday living because it lacks the necessary resources and access to the everyday world. Sacred Space is understood as a space for transformation and change. "If the seeker comes to the Sacred Space with full respect and a clean spirit, (s)he may be empowered in a positive way" (Miles, 1987, p. 8).

Woman on a solo has learned to trust her perceptions of the outer world while she still remains open, vulnerable, and loving. With physical, mental, and emotional realizations and successes comes increased sense of self-worth. With increased connectedness to and experienced acceptance from the natural world comes self-acceptance and self-love, and with these come an immense awareness of personal power and a confidence to do anything.

Robyn Davidson (1983), one of my heroines, who trekked across the Australian outback alone with camels, wrote that little girls are viewed as delicate and are taught to be careful and to stay neat. Thus, their energies go towards watching out for threats. Women's creative energies and self-confidence have thereby been effectively eroded into imprisoning self-worthlessness.

Davidson's courageous solo wilderness journey brought her many insights. She discovered that her fear, rather than incapacitating her or interfering with her ability, took on the useful quality of a fear one needs for survival. She then learned to use that fear as a helpful stepping stone rather than a stumbling block. She also reveals her belief that learning to be free involves continuous testing of oneself and gambling by going beyond what is viewed as safe.

PSYCHOTHERAPY AND THE SOLO

The central principle of many psychotherapies is that a person doesn't change unless she wishes to change, and so for one to go willingly on a solo means that she accepts the possibility of change. A transformation occurs because the person who embarks upon the VQ or the reflective solo does so with the genuine intention of leaving something behind when she re-emerges.

When the solo quester becomes totally one with Nature in meditation, there is a transformation to the transpersonal level of awareness. The sense of self-identification enlarges beyond the narrow boundaries of ego and this process unifies the smaller self with the whole of Nature and the Cosmos. This allows one to extend love and compassion to all beings, to reconcile tension between self and community, to be in unconditional harmonious relationship, and to accept the world as It Is (Drengson, 1990).

Shame is an issue that affects our sense of self-love and self-worth. Roads (1987) claims that if we speak aloud the thoughts that shame us, to the natural world (as if to a loving friend), that this will cause those thoughts to be released. Then they can no longer bind us by their unspoken deceit.

The "medicine teacher" or solo facilitator is someone who lives at the psycho-symbolic interface of humans and Nature. Their teachings can be as effective as conventional psychotherapy. In this method, the teacher takes the client out into Mother Nature and "She" takes care of the problem. The patient finds her inner answers reflected in the mirror of nature (Foster & Little, 1989).

We may not be able to measure exactly, through quantitative

research, how or why nature has curative and restorative effects upon us; but we do know that as we are moved farther away from our connection with the natural world through modern technology, we consciously seek the succor of wild lands. We are only just beginning to understand how much we gain from time spent in wilderness places (Miles, 1987).

CONCLUSION

At the close of the reflective solo which I felt compelled to do during this writing, I realize much has happened for me. I entered the wilderness feeling hopeless and stuck in writer's block about the completion of this article. I felt a lack of trust in myself and for my own discriminatory abilities due to the upheaval in the ending of an intense relationship. I felt overwhelmed by having to find a new home, and my physical body ached.

I felt very little joy, very little self-love, and even less self-acceptance. Yet trusting in the healing power of the Earth Mother and past experience in the wild, I went out. Less than four days later, I found myself creatively inspired by the landscape's alluring views. I rediscovered trust in myself as a being connected with the Spirit-That-Moves-Within-All-Things by using my own intuition to help me find a healing spot where I remained safe. I became cured of all back pain simply by lying for long periods of time upon the ground out amidst the sun and the wind listening to the creek. And I emerged bursting with a love and acceptance that had been radiated to me from the trees, the birds, and the small four-legged ones. Thus I find myself obliged to tell others of this healing rite and to offer opportunities to people to experience their own empowerment and healing springing forth from this Earth connection.

Wilderness solo time truly empowers and heals.

REFERENCES

Black Elk, W. & Lyon, W.S. (1990). *Black Elk: The sacred ways of a Lakota.* San Francisco: Harper.
Brown, T., Jr. (1988). *The vision.* New York: Berkley.
Davidson, R. (1983). *Tracks.* New York: Pantheon.

Dregson, A. (1990). In praise of ecosophy. *Trumpeter, 7*(2), 101-103.

Eaton, E. (1978). *I send a voice*. Wheaton, IL: Quest Books.

Erdoes, R. & Lame Deer, A.F. (1992). *Gift of power*. Santa Fe, NM: Bear & Co.

Ewert, A. (1990). Revisiting the concept of self-esteem through outdoor experiential activities. *Journal of Experiential Education, 14*(2), 56.

Foster, S. & Little, M. (1984). *The sacred mountain: A visionquest handbook for adults*. Big Pine, CA: Rites of Passage Press.

Foster, S. & Little, M. (1989). *The roaring of the sacred river: The wilderness quest for vision and self-healing*. New York: Prentice Hall.

Galland, C. (1980). *Women in the Wilderness*. New York: Harper & Row.

Kohn, S. (1991). Specific programmatic strategies to increase empowerment. *Journal of Experiential Education, 14*(1), 6-12.

McIntosh, H. (1989). Re-thinking the solo experience. *Journal of Experiential Education, 12*(3), 28-32.

Miles, J. (1987). Wilderness as a healing place. *Journal of Experiential Education, 10*(3), 4-10.

Roads, M. (1987). *Talking with nature: Sharing the energies & spirit of trees, plants, birds, and earth*. Tiburon, CA: H.J. Kramer.

Shaef, A.W. (1981). *Woman's reality: An emerging female system in a white male society*. Minneapolis: Winston Press.

Stone, H. & Winkelman, S. (1989). *Embracing ourselves*. San Rafael, CA: New World Library.

Strenba, B. (1989). Reflection: A process to learn about self through outdoor adventure. *Journal of Experiential Education, 12*(2), 7-10.

Women on the Ropes:
Change Through Challenge

Ba Stopha

SUMMARY. Although the ropes course has been used for many "special populations" it can be used as a powerful tool for learning and increasing self-awareness and esteem for many women in our society. Sexism and oppression of women create internal and external fears and mistrust. Leadership development is stifled in some women while others feel the pressure of having to lead. The all-women's ropes course experience presents opportunities for women to explore these fears, build trust in themselves and others, and try out their leadership skills within a safe and supportive environment. Women gain a new sense of possibility through the experience of seeing other women do what society says we should not be doing.

The development of the challenge ropes course as a tool for change was introduced to the United States by Outward Bound in the early 1960s. An experiential learning program, Outward Bound originally was designed in England as a survival program for young sailors (Schoel, Proudy, & Radcliffe, 1988). The U.S. Outward Bound programs of the 1960s and 70s originally focused on ser-

Ba Stopha, CSW, is a lesbian/feminist therapist who has worked as a ropes course facilitator since 1986. She has a private practice and runs her *Journey Weavers* programs in Ithaca, NY, where she lives with her partner of 12 years.

The activities described within this paper should not be attempted without appropriate training.

[Haworth co-indexing entry note]: "Women on the Ropes: Change Through Challenge." Stopha, Ba. Co-published simultaneously in *Women & Therapy* (The Haworth Press, Inc.) Vol. 15, No. 3/4, 1994, pp. 101-109; and: *Wilderness Therapy for Women: The Power of Adventure* (ed: Ellen Cole, Eve Erdman, and Esther D. Rothblum) The Haworth Press, Inc., 1994, pp. 101-109. Multiple copies of this article/chapter may be purchased from The Haworth Document Delivery Center [1-800-3-HAWORTH; 9:00 a.m. - 5:00 p.m. (EST)].

vices for adolescents and young adults, and soon began work with "special populations" of young people in a variety of training and treatment centers (Gass, 1993). Across the U.S in the 1970s and 80s "wilderness therapy programs" developed that utilized the ropes course independent of, and in combination with, other forms of adventure activities such as rock climbing, canoeing, and backpacking expeditions. In more recent years the ropes course has become a major therapeutic tool in programs that provide services to drug and alcohol addicted people, prison populations, survivors of sexual and other forms of violence, and perpetrators of abuse.

In the early 1970s, a group of former Outward Bound instructors joined together and adapted Outward Bound activities to a high school setting with the ropes course being a major component of the program. "Project Adventure" eventually received federal funding for expansion of this program model to other schools around the country. According to Project Adventure, "a challenge ropes course is a series of individual and group physical challenges that require a combination of teamwork skills and individual commitment. Constructed of rope, cables, and wood, courses are built outdoors in trees (or using telephone poles) and indoors in gymnasiums" (Webster, 1989 preface). Some challenges built close to the ground are called "low ropes elements." Those built in trees or telephone poles are referred to as "high ropes elements." Some high ropes elements require the use of a safety system consisting of a belayer, belay rope, hard hat, harness, and an anchor. With a basic orientation toward safety, this system is characteristic in ropes course work.

Over the past three years, I have offered "Women on the Ropes" programs to women in a rural, up-state New York community. Program titles have included: "Women, Challenge and Self-Esteem," "Unlearning Oppression–Ropes and Power," "Women Therapists–Facing the Challenges Together," and "Women on the Ropes–Stretching the Limits." Programs offered in the spring/summer of 1993 included: "Mothers and Daughters–Building on the Connections," "Women Survivors of Sexual Abuse–Challenges and Choices," "Lesbians on the Ropes, in the Woods, Everywhere," "Women Over 40–The Changer/The Challenger," and "Bisexual Women–Claiming Space." Participants attending past programs have been primarily white, working women and students, from their early teens through their late 50s. In these programs I have combined a feminist perspective and a "challenge by choice" philosophy with non-competitive group games, problem solving, support, and trust-building activities, as well as the use of low and high ropes course elements. While the women who participated in these *Journey Weavers* programs were drawn from the general public rather than those who were intentionally seeking "therapy," the process itself was found to be healing and therapeutic. In this paper I will discuss how the "all-women's" group provides role models for women, supporting them to move past oppressive socialization and prescriptions of what is acceptable behavior for women. Additionally, I will discuss how these groups help women from the general population increase their ability to identify and/or move past fear, build trust and support, and gain a clearer understanding of their relationship to leadership.

Groups participating in a ropes course generally move through a progression of warm-up and "getting to know you" activities before beginning the low or high ropes elements. Time is included for individual and group goal-setting. A participant might decide that she wants to become a more active leader, or become more aware of her decisions to "choose" to participate, rather than participate because she's expected to. A group goal might be to utilize as many resources found within the group as possible: for example, finding out if any women have experience building human pyramids before attempting to solve a problem that requires the group to go over an obstacle. These activities encourage the participants to begin to develop trust in themselves, find their voices, and express their ideas about how to solve a problem or accomplish a task. A base of trust and support begins to develop through these games and activities. Time is also built in for "debriefing" the activities, that is, discussing and sharing what actually happened for each participant during the activity. Discussions can cover topics of leadership, following, styles of communication, how the group handles suggestions from participants, feelings about the end result, as well as topics specific to the concerns of a particular group (the impact of age, body size, etc.). Reflection on the implications of the activity to "real life" is also an important part of the debriefing process.

Once the group proceeds to the low and high ropes course activities, metaphors are used to enhance the learning experience. Metaphors specifically designed to have meaning to the lives and struggles of the group members are powerful tools for change and growth. For example, a group of women exploring issues of oppression are presented with the metaphor of a maze representing what it is like for oppressed people unable to "see" their way out of oppression–people who are restricted by societal myths, stereotypes, and rules of what can and cannot be done by certain groups. The participants are first briefed about the activity in an area away from the maze and then those who choose to participate are asked to put on blindfolds. They are led into the maze–an area that is enclosed by ropes that prevent the participants from exiting unless the facilitator opens one of the "gates." Each woman is taken into the maze individually and led to an area away from the others. The women are told that they cannot talk with each other and that each must find her own way out. The women attempt to move through the maze individually, but are not successful in finding their way out. One random participant (the token woman, person of color, or lesbian) is allowed to exit. This participant is then given the choice of returning to the maze to help others still caught in the maze of oppression or of staying out, removing her blindfold, and enjoying her new freedom. She is told that if she chooses to go back in she risks the possibility that the exit she previously used may not be available to her again. At some point participants realize that they can no longer "play by the rules" and begin to talk and have contact with each other. They realize they do not need to be "blinded" and they take off their blindfolds and help others find their way out of the maze.

In the debriefing that followed this experience, women recognized the connection between their own feelings of isolation and oppression, of not being able to find their way out alone, and the need for contact with others in order to understand their oppression and the oppression of other groups. They also recognized the randomness of the "token" woman allowed to exit, and how the system limits that woman's ability to take leadership and guide others out. The risk of taking leadership is often counter-balanced by the threat of harassment, the possible loss of job and income, and/or the threat to physical safety. Being able to move past these possible losses means facing tremendous fear and learning to make use of support systems, trusted friends, and family.

Another metaphor is used to assist women in dealing with issues of support and trust. After participating in a series of individual and group trust building activities, a group of women therapists was given the opportunity to take a step further toward a place of trust in and support of each other. The "trust fall" is introduced as a way of allowing themselves to physically let go and fall backwards, from a four-foot-high platform, into the arms of their group. Taking the risk that they will be supported by others they have just begun to trust had implications for relationships in society and the work world. After describing the activity to the group, a volunteer is asked to join the facilitator on the platform. The remainder of the group forms two lines facing each other on the ground, standing shoulder to shoulder with their arms bent at the elbows, hands flat, palms up. They create a flat bed of hands and arms that are braced by stable bodies, feet solidly placed one in front of the other on the ground. The volunteer has the opportunity to have eye contact with each participant and is encouraged to express any doubts or fears she might have. The group provides support and encouragement for her to take her next step and assure her that they hear her fears and are ready to support her. If she chooses to continue, she turns her back on the line of women and, following a series of communications between her and the group, falls flat backwards onto the arms of her supporters. She is gently rocked back and forth and then placed back on her feet. Others in the group then have the opportunity to move onto the platform and experience the trust fall. For some this is a very frightening yet empowering experience of "letting go" and trusting that others will "be there for them," that they are not alone and can communicate when they are in need of support. For others the experience of falling is a feeling of relief in letting go to this degree. For yet others, making the decision not to do or complete the trust fall can also bring up strong feelings. As one woman explained:

> I felt sadness, fear, disappointment . . . I was unable to complete [the trust fall] because of terror. It was a rich, powerful, welcome experience because it helped point out more of my

denial about myself. The feelings are hard but also welcome because usually it's too easy to function and stuff these feelings and go on at a limited level emotionally.

In my experience working with groups of women, these beginning activities enable the group to feel connected in a fairly short period of time. An atmosphere of acceptance, encouragement, and "an acknowledgement of each woman's presence" (Mitten, 1992, p. 57) adds to the ability of women to form connections with each other, to gain self-esteem, and trust in their abilities and those of the other women in their group.

Denise Mitten, Executive Director of Woodswomen, Inc., writes about her experiences and philosophy for working with women and girls in the out-of-doors. Mitten (1992, p. 56) states that "in order for women and girls to feel empowered [in the out-of-doors] several factors must exist. The program philosophy needs to be one that respects women, and adds to the building of self-esteem, with leaders who are skilled in implementing the philosophy, and participants who have choices about, and within the experience."

Mitten also states that "women perceive that they can meet certain emotional needs, such as unconditional support, attention, acceptance for who they are, and personal time more readily in an all-female environment" (Mitten, 1992, p. 57). I would add that women participate in all-women outdoor groups because of the need women have for powerful role models. Women gain strength, self-esteem, self-empowerment, and a sense of possibilities for moving beyond assumed limits, by seeing other women doing what society has taught them not to do. Participants have stated: "Having all-women felt safer; having women role models was important to me–it made it feel possible for me to do the activities." "I enjoyed it (the all-women's group). I like being in a physical environment without men there. I can relate to *my* strength when with *my* gender." "I felt safer being with women. I also felt empowered by watching all kinds of women with different physical abilities come together and do things that 'women aren't supposed to do.' " The all-women group also allowed women to be more honest with themselves and each other. One participant stated: "An all-women group was necessary in order for me to be a more open and honest participant."

Fear is a common concern for many women participating in the ropes course programs. Women are generally conditioned not to take risks, and not to see themselves as strong or able to deal with physical challenges. In addition, on a daily basis women are confronted with the threat of violence through films, reports of rapes, physical assaults, murders of women and children, and the continued presence of sexism in our culture.

Women attending the ropes course programs became more aware of their fear, and in some cases, found themselves relating to their fear in a different way. For example, the following responses came from a survey of participants in my *Journey Weavers* programs: "When I get afraid, I think of what I did and what the other women did. For weeks after I felt centered and less victimized by circumstances around me . . ." "Overcoming fear is the main impact of the ropes course that I use in addressing other fears both in myself and in clients." "I felt in my body the terror of fear. I now am more humble about the fears of others. I relate more directly to the experience of fear." "For a week following the ropes course I felt very emotionally strong. I think that I am more accepting of my fear—realizing that it doesn't have to immobilize me."

In an unfamiliar environment, most people get in touch with feelings of fear, anxiety, uncertainty, and a need to develop trust and support within the group. Women with different abilities coming together to experience the ropes course are on some level equalized by the unfamiliarity of the situation. Through the trust building process, participants were able to gain new understandings of their fear, more acceptance as well as more ability to name fears they had otherwise avoided. One woman explained it this way:

> I've been able to name my fears better and face them more. A
> lot of emotions came loose for me during the ropes course and
> now I'm exploring them further through therapy. My life has
> changed because I'm allowing myself to be more vulnerable
> and open myself up to emotions I didn't want to feel before.

Another woman shared the impact of her experience on her general life: "I have thought long and hard about the nature of trust and support in every area of my life."

The leadership style of the facilitators on the ropes course has the potential of bringing out leadership in many of the women participants. One of the advantages of this work is the flexibility of the process, which allows for creative introduction of each new challenge and, in some cases, the creation of circumstances that change the leadership dynamics. In one instance, a group was presented with a challenge and three women who had naturally assumed the leadership role in previous challenges were made "mute"; they could participate in whatever way they felt comfortable but could not add anything verbally to the solution of the problem. One of the results was that other women came forward as leaders and took the opportunity to test their leadership skills with support and trust from the group. As one participant stated: "The ropes course experience deepened my understanding of some beliefs that I've had about myself, e.g., that I am a leader if I am in a supportive, safe place."

For women who were inclined to take leadership automatically, not having to do so resulted in a sense of relief and new awareness that they did not have to be under the pressure to lead, that others would take on that role and the job would get done. It opened up the possibility of being able to be a learner and to relax in that role. One woman shared her experience this way: "I learned more about my role as 'leader' as 'one who takes charge' in groups and how good it felt not to have to do that–I realized I want to learn how to participate without taking charge."

When women come together in an environment where an activity is perceived as dangerous and problems are in need of a solution, there is a shared sense of resolution through cooperation and support. Two women describe it this way: "I felt like one member of a collective group–at times a leader, other times a follower. There were a lot of strong leaders in the group, and I felt we worked well together, cooperatively." "I led and I followed. I challenged myself to trust and listen to the women I was with and to use my voice to express my fears and concerns." "I've talked with others about the teamwork that occurred when the team was working so well that no one knew whose idea was whose."

Women who have gone through the ropes course experience report other changes in their feelings and awarenesses of themselves: "I gained a bright burst of confidence from the whole experience. I call on certain moments when I doubt my abilities at any given time. I find myself noticing leaders and my own role within groups more." "I learned about the power of constant and non-invasive support. I was high up on a tree, and five women below were almost chanting confidence to me." "I noticed myself passively not participating in the group in the beginning and how that turned around when we processed an exercise. I learned to recognize how I did that and that I could move through that pattern of response."

Although the ropes course has been used for many "special populations" it can be used as a powerful tool for learning and increasing self-awareness and esteem for many women in our society. Sexism and oppression of women create internal and external fears and mistrust. Leadership development is stifled in some women, while others feel the pressure of having to lead. The all-women's ropes course experience presents opportunities for women to explore these fears, build trust in themselves and others, and try out their leadership skills within a safe and supportive environment. Women gain a new sense of possibility through the experience of seeing other women do what society says we should not be doing.

My experience offering *Journey Weavers* programs is a beginning point for exploring the use of the ropes course as a tool for enabling women to overcome the impacts of oppression and sexism. However, additional programs need to be developed addressing the needs of women from a broader range of backgrounds, races, ethnicities and physical abilities. In addition, it is expected that more in-depth research will be developed on the effectiveness of the ropes course as an agent of change.

REFERENCES

Gass, M. (1993). *Adventure Therapy*. Iowa: Kendell/Hunt.
Mitten, D. (1992 February). Empowering Girls and Women in the Outdoors. *Journal of Physical Education, Recreation and Dance*, 56-60.
Schoel, J., Proudy, D. & Radcliffe, P. (1988). *Islands of Healing*. Hamilton, MA: Project Adventure, Inc..
Webster, S. (1989). *Ropes Course Safety Manual*. Iowa: Kendall/Hunt.

Building Self-Efficacy
Through Women-Centered
Ropes Course Experiences

Linda Hart
Linda Silka

SUMMARY. This paper describes our experiences as facilitators in adventure-based ropes course training. It summarizes experiences with different groups that raise rich and complex issues about the use of adventure-based learning for personal growth and professional development. These groups include women executives, women living in public housing who have formed a women's resource group, adolescent women in treatment, adolescents from culturally diverse backgrounds, graduate students, and women who have been sexually abused. These groups reflect the diversity of female participants who have engaged in ropes course training. Although participants are diverse, deep commonalities exist in the kinds of issues they are addressing in ropes course programs. Positive changes in women's abilities to take risks, practice assertive leadership, solve problems

Linda Hart manages the technical assistance and training arm of the Center for Family, Work and Community, University of Massachusetts at Lowell. She holds an MA in Program Evaluation from Lesley College and continues to consult both nonprofit and corporate clients in organizational development, drawing on her 15 years' experience in adventure-based training. Linda Silka holds a PhD in Social Psychology from the University of Kansas. She is coordinator of the Graduate Program in Community and Social Psychology, University of Massachusetts at Lowell. At the Center for Family, Work and Community, Linda consults in program evaluation and other technical assistance and training activities.

[Haworth co-indexing entry note]: "Building Self-Efficacy Through Women-Centered Ropes Course Experiences." Hart, Linda, and Linda Silka. Co-published simultaneously in *Women & Therapy* (The Haworth Press, Inc.) Vol. 15, No. 3/4, 1994, pp. 111-127; and: *Wilderness Therapy for Women: The Power of Adventure* (ed: Ellen Cole, Eve Erdman, and Esther D. Rothblum) The Haworth Press, Inc., 1994, pp. 111-127. Multiple copies of this article/chapter may be purchased from The Haworth Document Delivery Center [1-800-3-HAWORTH; 9:00 a.m. - 5:00 p.m. (EST)].

111

effectively, and feel more competent in general, can result from participation in a ropes course experience. In this article, the reader will see how one fixed ropes course element can be used to create a variety of metaphors for diverse groups of participants.

Adventure-based training is increasingly being embraced as an effective strategy for enhancing personal growth, particularly in the areas of increasing one's sense of self-competence and risk-taking (Snow, 1992). Among the more promising forms of adventure-based experiential learning is ropes course training in which participants engage in facilitated group problem-solving tasks that take place on low and high ropes courses (Rohnke, 1989). Metaphorical experiences are created by the facilitator to engage groups and individuals in examining their ways of dealing with risks and challenges, thereby encouraging personal growth of the participants (Bacon, 1983; Gass, 1991; Gass, Goldman, & Priest 1992; Johnson & Johnson, 1991; Snow, 1992). In this article we will share our metaphorical treatment of the ropes course to increase self-efficacy in women.

Despite the general promise of ropes course facilitation for women, dilemmas are emerging as this adventure-based training is adapted from a largely middle class male model. Physical challenges have often been regarded as distinctively male (Aburdene & Naisbitt, 1992; Fuhrmann, 1986). In established ropes course programs, many facilitators continue to be males who receive little training in supporting the growth of women and these facilitators may use the ropes course experience to perpetuate gender-based stereotypes in physical settings. Unmodified, adventure-based training can become an exercise in proving one's physical prowess rather than an opportunity for growth.

How then can adventure-based training best be used to enhance women's lives and build on their competencies? Can physical challenges become an effective way to promote personal growth in women? Can the ropes course experience be tailored to meet the developmental needs of women? Will women be more prone to take appropriate risks after participating in ropes course training? Will women have greater confidence in their competence as problem solvers? Based on various training experiences with women from a broad array of backgrounds, we have developed a model of ropes course training that emphasizes self-efficacy (see model in Figure 1).

Our model emphasizes using the ropes course as a "learning laboratory." Change is promoted through carefully crafted initiatives that promote new, more self-efficacious behaviors. Central to this model is the importance of: (a) applying feminist metaphors (Gilligan, Lyons, & Hammer, 1990; Hooks, 1984; Jordan, Kaplan, Miller, Stiver, & Surrey, 1991), as opposed to the war and sports metaphors (Lakoff & Johnson, 1980) typically used in ropes training (and society as a whole); (b) using ropes course experiences to empower women-centered skills including communication and community-building skills (Jordan, Kaplan, Miller, Stiver, & Surrey, 1991); (c) presenting physical challenges for empowering women; (d) engaging participants in a new arena so that they cannot simply depend on old coping mechanisms but instead are brought out of the "comfort zones" so that issues can be addressed; (e) tailoring the facilitation process to participants' personal goals and recognizing the cultural challenges that women face (Aburdene & Naisbitt, 1992; Melia, 1986); and (f) using a systems perspective in which the facilitator acts as a catalyst that "disturbs" the system and in so doing provides opportunities for growth.

This model can be used to facilitate a process by which women can learn to take risks without losing other strengths in the process. The goals of adventure-based experiences for women are to help them enjoy a high level of self-respect, take appropriate emotional risks, turn crises into opportunities for growth, resolve interpersonal conflicts in a manner that preserves personal integrity, clearly understand their personal and professional potential, ask for what they need, and recognize life's accomplishments. The challenge is for women to come through this metamorphosis as more competent risk-takers with higher levels of self-respect, while preserving positive qualities such as communication skills and community-building skills. In ropes course training, these particular goals are approached from an analogical distance (Bacon, 1983). When women are comfortable with their new behaviors, those behaviors can be applied to "real-life" situations. As an individual woman progresses through these goals, she becomes a more self-efficacious individual in that she produces desired personal and professional outcomes.

FIGURE 1. Building self-efficacy through women-centered ropes course experiences.

BUILDING SELF-EFFICACY THROUGH
WOMEN-CENTERED
ROPES COURSE EXPERIENCES

ROPES COURSE
AS A "LEARNING
LABORATORY"

CRISIS

CHANGE

NEW BEHAVIORS

The woman engaging in adventure-based therapy:

• enjoys a high level of self-respect.
• takes appropriate emotional risks.
• turns crisis into opportunities for growth.
• resolves interpersonal and intrapersonal conflicts in manner that
  preserves personal integrity.
• clearly understands her personal and professional potential.
• asks for help when such action is in her best interest.
• recognizes what she has accomplished in her life.

A MORE
SELF-EFFICACIOUS
INDIVIDUAL

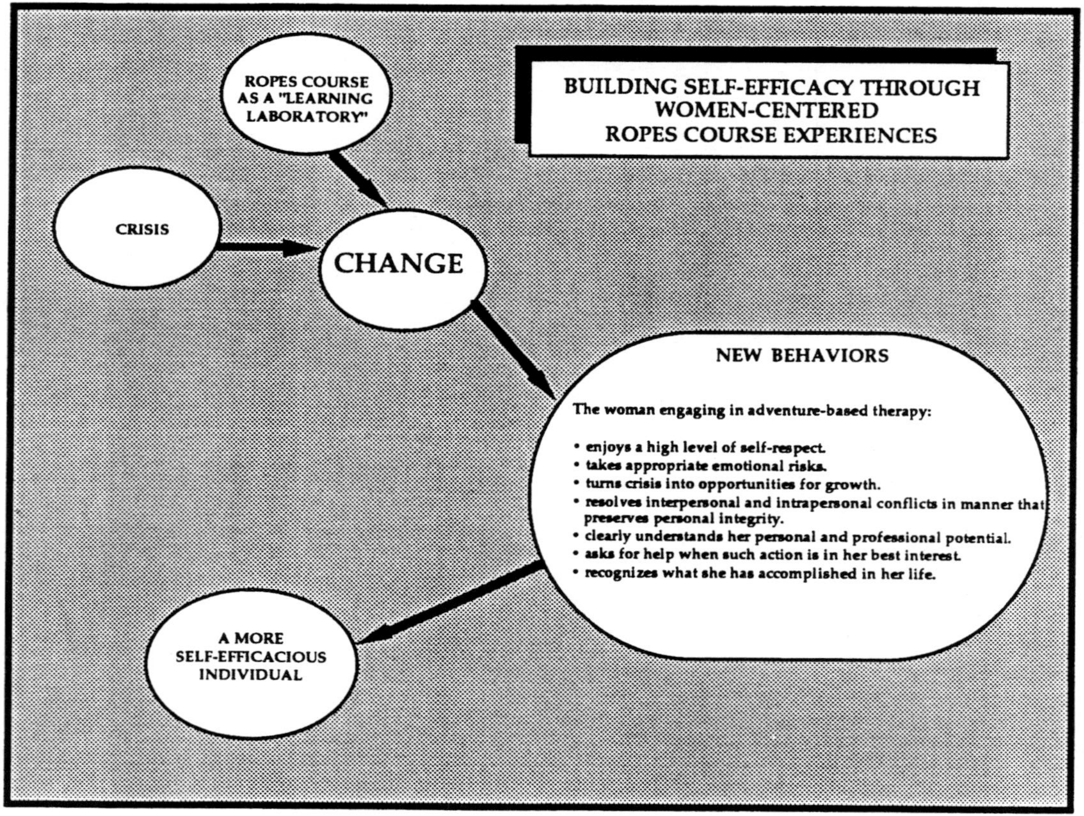

The basic components of the model in action are illustrated in the following discussion as it explores actual scenarios that develop on the ropes course. The prepared physical course sets the stage for the metaphorical experience. A typical "low ropes" element is the "Mohawk Walk"[1] (Rohnke, 1989) in which wires are tightly strung one foot above the ground between four or more large trees to form a sequential path. When the group arrives at the course, the facilitator might begin the metaphorical experience by communicating a framework to the group–perhaps a group of age-diverse women from various occupational and educational backgrounds–in which the ropes course element represents an upcoming or recurring common challenge in each woman's life. The group has several decisions to make at this point. They must decide what challenges they share, how many "setbacks" or steps off the wire the task will require, and what time pressures they will impose upon themselves. Frequently, the trees become milestones while the stretches of wire represent specific difficulties within the larger metachallenge. Thus, the task is a game, but a game that is tailored to replicate important and often problematic features of each woman's life. While scrambling around trees and overcoming various obstacles, women work together to meet the challenges presented by the "game." In the process, poor communication and lack of teamwork can come to the surface.

Afterwards, team members use the raw materials from the metaphorical experience to reflect on the strategies they used to solve the initiative and to consider how those strategies carry over to their day-to-day lives. For example, women have approached the "Mohawk Walk" by believing they will need much more time and many more touchdowns than they actually use. On the other hand, they may devote so much time to planning in an effort to create a "risk-free" environment that the task remains unfinished. The facilitator's role is then to draw out the meaning of these experiences and inspire the participants to initiate changes in their own personal action plans.

This initiative can also be used to explore gender issues. In our own work, a group of predominantly male fifth graders was participating on the ropes course as a form of leadership training (as they entered the top grade offered by their grade school). The males were enthusiastic as the group began their experience on the high ropes course whereas the girls were quite reluctant to participate. At this point, the group was presented with the low ropes course element, the "Mohawk Walk," and a framework was designed to emphasize the importance of women as leaders. We introduced the initiative as follows:

> Imagine that all of you are traveling by wagon train through the midwestern prairie in the middle of the 1800s. Just as you are about to cross the Rocky Mountains all of your oxen die (of a communicable disease). Determined to reach an outpost (on the other side of the Rockies) you proceed on foot through a mountain pass. You then encounter a group of native Americans who explain that crossing the land directly ahead of you would upset their ancestors as it is an ancient burial ground. They believe that the spirit world would be disrupted by the steps of strangers. There is good news, however. The native Americans are willing to build a system of tree-to-tree cables across the burial ground for you to traverse. The native Americans now consent to the crossing as long as the white men and women's feet touch the burial ground no more than five times and that the crossing take no more than 40 minutes. The Native Americans include one additional stipulation. It is the belief of this tribe that women are especially close to the earth and thus more favored by the spirit world. Thus, they insist that two women lead the group through the burial ground.

The boys and the girls in the class reacted strongly to the framing story. Two of the previously reluctant girls were now very eager to assume this challenge. The boys who had consistently fought for group leadership, on the other hand, were outraged at being excluded from leadership. They claimed that the group would never succeed with girls as leaders. In fact, two boys so purposefully attempted to sabotage the activity that they were asked to timeout for a portion of the exercise. After the timeout they were able to successfully re-enter the exercise. The style of leadership displayed by the girls was very different from that shown by the boys. The male leadership style in this group had consisted of one boy putting his solution forward and telling the rest of the group what needed to be done. Another boy might then challenge the leadership with a new idea. In contrast, the girls asked the group as a whole for their ideas and developed together a plan which was a hybrid of several ideas. One of them decided to be at the front of the line while the other female leader remained at the end of the line. The task was completed very successfully with a great deal of communication and involvement from all group members.

An extended debrief explored the leadership issues that emerged: What style of leadership did the girls use? If you were used to leading, how did it feel to become a "follower" and fellow group member? If you were usually in a follower role, how did it feel to become a leader? Two of the boys who had consistently assumed strong leadership roles remained angry at only girls being allowed to be leaders and continued to view the situation as unfair. Other boys and many of the girls spoke in support of the girls' leadership; these youth stated that they felt more central to the decision-making process than they had in previous initiatives. The girls who led the group were clearly affected by the opportunity to display and practice their leadership skills. The impact extended beyond the students; their teacher saw a potential in at least those two girls that she had previously not seen.

In using this framework the facilitator took a risk. What if the girls had failed? Would the group automatically assume that female leadership couldn't work? Suppose none of the girls was willing to take the lead role? Although the risks were considerable, the facilitator felt that in this group (like so many others) the view of males as leaders was so entrenched (Aburdene & Naisbitt, 1992; Melia, 1986) that it was worth the risk to "disturb" the system. It seemed better to expose the gender issues than keep them hidden. Even though negative reactions might emerge, the skilled facilitator would address them during the debrief which is another of the complex benefits of the action-reflection approach (Friere, 1973) we use when delivering ropes course programs.

The youth example indicates how the "Mohawk Walk" element can be used to explore leadership issues. The same element can facilitate exploration of cooperation and mastery. The latter can be seen in a training with incoming graduate students in a program in Community and Social Psychology. Central to this program is community building. All but 2 of the 15 graduate students were female and many were mid-career professionals returning to school after many years. Many described graduate school as seeming quite daunting. The "Mohawk Walk" was used with the students as a metaphor for the upcoming year with the trees representing milestones and the cable representing challenges. As with graduate school, the task at first seemed overwhelming, with individuals questioning the possibility of reaching their goals. As they worked together to create support, all were able to get through "the year." In completing the ropes course program, participants found they could advise and observe one another but in many ways still had to find a method that worked best for them as individuals. Here the academic environment metaphor was direct: During the debrief, students in the graduate program discussed the benefits of strong community support, but also became aware of the need for each student to find her own way through the challenges of graduate school.

Ropes course training is not simply about group functioning; it is also about how individuals confront challenges and deal with risk and change. The work on the high course elements emphasizes risk taking and developing confidence in one's abilities while using the community for support. Once again, the facilitator helps participants develop a framework for exploring the high ropes elements in ways that apply to the individual's work and family life.

High ropes course elements can be used successfully with survivors of sexual abuse, for example. Sexual abuse often leaves survivors unable to trust others and having a heightened need for control. This lack of trust in relationships, together with a need for control, can create problems for abuse survivors in their daily interactions (Bass & Davis, 1988). The high ropes course event called the "Pamper Pole" (Rohnke, 1989) provides an opportunity for survivors to confront both issues. The "Pamper Pole" is a telephone pole that rises 25 feet in the air. Widely spaced metal footholds provide a means for climbing to the top of the pole. Once the climber has made the difficult climb to the top, a trapeze is strategically placed ten feet away to entice the participant to jump. This physical challenge encourages participants to look at how they handle issues of trust and control. In one case, an abuse survivor spent over an hour on this event climbing part way up the pole, falling off, attempting the climb again, and again falling off. Each time she reached a higher position on the pole, and she was finally able to reach the top of the pole and leap off. Her progression during this hour was videotaped for use in therapy sessions. Watching the videotape, she was able to see the lack of trust she had in herself, in the belayer (the person controlling the climber's safety rope), and in the system. As the event progressed, she was able to observe the growth in her level of trust. She described the leap as signifying a willingness to give up some control, knowing she would safely emerge from the experience. The several falls off the pole signified for her that one can continue "to climb" after experiencing a setback.

The "Dangle Duo" (Rohnke, 1989) is yet another high ropes event with rich metaphorical applications. The physical apparatus is a series of elevated logs placed approximately 5 to 6 feet apart and rising 45 feet into the air. Two participants climb the event together. Success is virtually impossible if either of the two women attempts this event alone. Participants will succeed, however, if they work together and communicate effectively by reaching out for one another at the right moment, and taking risks for one another. The "Dangle Duo" can supply useful metaphors for a therapist and client, couples, friends, mothers and daughters, and other twosomes desiring relational work.

Finally, the high ropes course event, the "Multivine" (Rohnke, 1989), provides a particularly strong metaphor for women with respect to risk-taking. The "Multivine" consists of a high cable strung between two trees 30 to 100 feet apart. Above the cable is a series of "vines" or ropes which the participant can use for support as she proceeds across the cable. Of course, the "vines" are not quite long enough to provide a sense of security before the next vine is reached. In order to progress from "vine" to "vine," the participant must let go of the rope behind her and reach for the rope in front of her. The analogies to life outside the ropes course emerge: the necessity of sometimes letting go of the past in order to reach for the future, the sense of being overwhelmed by the enormity of the tasks ahead, and yet the possibility of summoning up the confidence to proceed and be assertive while reaching for accomplishment.

Although the ropes course experience is intended to enhance women's sense of achievement, cultural conditioning sometimes undermines acknowledgement of the women's competencies shown in the experience and may call for additional intervention on the part of the facilitator. A frequent issue in debriefing women on the high ropes course experiences is the need of participants to somehow look at how they failed rather than how they succeeded. One woman successfully climbed 50 feet up a tree and proceeded across a high wire to reach her goal tree, only to claim, once she was back on the ground, not really to have "done it." When the facilitator questioned her about this, she said that she couldn't claim full credit because she had not looked down. To encourage the participant to take credit for this success (and by analogy other successes in her life), the facilitator asked her to explore her route visually and explore ways to fully credit herself for her accomplishments. The next step was to discuss with the participant other areas of accomplishment in her life for which she had previously been unable to take credit. As the example suggests, the ropes course experience provides the analogical distance to allow participants to begin to look at recurrent patterns in their lives.

Again, it is the metaphorical character of the experience that provides opportunities for growth. Once on the high element, each participant places herself in the hands of others in order to feel safe; one's response to situations in which trust is required becomes apparent. This high ropes experience involves personal risk taking, but at the same time it involves learning about one's interactions with others. Participants are engaged in a new arena so that they cannot simply depend on old coping mechanisms, but instead are brought out of their "comfort zones" so that issues can be addressed. An important aspect of the experience is that while the physical dangers feel very real, they are not. Although each participant is high off the ground, she is roped to a belayer so that the fears she experiences are based on perceived rather than real risks. The analogical distance allows people to consider how they approach risks, examine the degree to which they can trust, and reflect on ways in which they might change (Bacon, 1983).

Application of these ideas to different groups shows how the training is carried out, while at the same time raising rich and complex issues about the use of adventure-based learning for personal growth and professional development. In the remainder of the paper we highlight other dilemmas and concerns that must be addressed if ropes course training is to have its full impact for women of various backgrounds confronting different issues.

The skilled facilitator deliberately uses the ropes course as a tool that is adapted to the client's needs. The same physical setting can be used to create very different metaphors for different groups. To illustrate this point, consider different approaches taken in work with court-adjudicated female adolescents in a secure facility, and work with women executives. For both groups, ropes course experiences have served as a facilitative process, and in both cases the analogical distance has been helpful, as has been "disturbing" the system in order to help people look at their behaviors in a different way. The juxtaposition of the two cases illustrates the versatility of the ropes course.

The experiential training initially helped the facilitators to diagnose a severe lack of problem-solving skills in the court adjudicated adolescents. Once identified, the training could be used to help the teens build skills in problem-solving and conflict management. For example, on the first training date the teens were led through an exercise asking them to create a behavioral contract with paints and markers on a sheet. Once the contract was complete, they were charged with the task of placing the contract high on the wall of their gymnasium. This task was extremely challenging for the teens. They were unable to sequence the tasks (e.g., some of the teens were "hanging out" on one another's shoulders close to the wall while others were far from finishing the task of applying tape to the contract). In subsequent sessions, the teens were faced with numbers of new problem-solving initiatives. Over the course of time they developed the awareness that their problem-solving success depended on their ability to plan, focus, and follow through. In this case, the low ropes course experience was used to develop fundamental problem-solving skills.

In contrast to the teens, the female executives were a high functioning group possessing sophisticated problem-solving skills. Their concerns focused on using all of their team members as a resource and having the confidence to apply their problem-solving skills to unfamiliar contexts. Many were heads of their own companies or teams and tended to be strong leaders who were comfortable in asserting control in groups. The challenge for these individuals was in trying out new behaviors. After leading a ropes course exercise emphasizing a shared leadership style, the facilitator used the debriefing process to help participants examine the links between group process and outcomes. The analogical distance of the "learning laboratory" gave the participants the safety to diagnose behaviors and make plans for change where appropriate. For example, one very strong leader realized that she frequently prevented the ideas of quieter colleagues from emerging for group consideration. She used the next exercise to participate in a manner that allowed her own ideas as well as those of her colleagues to be heard.

Although female professionals like those described above often have strong problem-solving skills, they may not always have the confidence to strike out in new directions and take risks in using those skills in unfamiliar contexts (Jordan, Kaplan, Miller, Stiver, & Surrey, 1991; Melia, 1986). The female president of a public relations firm that we worked with raised exactly these concerns with regard to her employees. She hoped to turn more responsibility over to her largely female employees, while at the same time she wanted the group to engage in the kind of risk-taking that would ensure the firm's continued success. As the team leader, she also knew it was important for the team to understand the ways in which their work fates were interdependent. Improving and maintaining communication within the group was thus an important priority. This is like many team development situations involving women, in which risks are an important part of work life, yet where risk-taking may be difficult for women to engage in comfortably. So, how does one increase risk taking without losing important communication and community building skills? Often in competitive situations of this sort we hear people resorting to war metaphors such as "we are at war," or "the competition is killing us." How, then, does one avoid war metaphors yet obtain high performance and risk taking? Ropes course initiatives, when carefully tailored, provide ideal opportunities for exploring risk-taking while maintaining good communication and avoiding war metaphors. In the aforementioned consultation, the facilitator used the low ropes initiatives described earlier to focus on building a strong team. Once the group had established their effectiveness as a team, they then shifted into combining team activities with a focus on personal growth–or as the team put it–how to "live by the ropes." Personal growth metaphors were developed on the high ropes course with participants focusing on a real risk each wanted to take in her daily life. This intact work team who had experienced a series of ropes course trainings with themes related to risk-taking, gathering one's resources, welcoming new members, and reaching for more in tough times, observed shifts not only in their professional experiences but also in their personal lives. One team member who had been unhappily living with her spouse's "old world parents" described the risk-taking on the "Pamper Pole" as enabling her to risk family conflict so that she and her spouse could take the long-wanted step of moving to their own home. Another team member was able to bring about change in one of the most debilitating parts of her life. Years ago she had given up driving, but through the conscious focus on appropriate risk-taking, she successfully attempted driving again after the ropes course training and thus found a bridge to the new behaviors that she wanted to adopt.

The situations that we have discussed thus far have dealt with cultural specifics related to gender. Many additional cultural issues having to do with race and ethnicity have emerged in our work with women. Although ropes course training is intended to be culturally neutral, its roots in white suburban experiences show up in a variety of ways and can often be impediments. We are frequently reminded of the potential limitations of ropes course training that must be overcome if the training is to resonate with various cultural backgrounds. For example, an African-American consultant who has been working with us exploring the possible uses of ropes course training with inner city youth, discussed how alien the woods environment might be to urban youth, perhaps creating too much analogical distance for the ropes course experience to be growth enhancing. Moreover, she raised concerns about the deeply racist "jungle" stereotypes some people hold toward African-Americans. On the course that day the adolescents themselves were concerned with how those not from African-American heritage would view them as they climbed high in the trees. How, then, does the facilitator ensure that the ropes course activities work for all participants?

The best approach to ensuring culturally responsive ropes course programs is, of course, to have culturally diverse program designs delivered by facilitators from a variety of cultural backgrounds. Unfortunately, most facilitators continue to reflect a narrow spectrum of American culture. Consideration should be given to careful inclusion of trainers from many cultural groups. It is equally important that all facilitators, regardless of their cultural background, look at ways of creating positive experiences for all participants (Reddy & Jamison, 1988).

When presented effectively, the ropes course can be a dramatic and dynamic tool for personal and professional growth. We continue to explore ways of developing inclusive ropes course experiences. In one recent example, one of our groups included recent immigrants from Asian communities who were clearly uncomfortable at being expected to be assertive in a large group. In order to encourage participants to bring their ideas forward, we redesigned the experience to emphasize planning periods and debriefs in pods of three. We learned that individuals who find it culturally unacceptable to speak out in large groups make many contributions in more intimate settings. The larger message for the facilitator is to constantly consider the group's concerns and potential areas for growth. Moreover, we challenge facilitators to take the ropes course experience beyond the culturally "sensitive" arena into the direct use of the course as a forum for addressing issues such as racism, prejudice, and intercultural conflict. Too little is currently being done to explore the potential of the ropes course to impact deeply held cultural beliefs.

FINAL CONSIDERATIONS

Throughout this paper we have discussed ways in which the ropes course is beginning to be used to facilitate personal and professional growth in women. We have suggested that the course can be adapted to widely diverse groups dealing with different issues. We have indicated that the analogical distance and the metaphorical presentation may well be key to the experience. Given the richness of this experience, how does one begin to look at impact? Only recently have facilitators begun to look beyond the initial responses they observe at the ropes course and consider possible impacts for participants and their teams. The few extant evaluations have focused almost entirely on social development in adolescents (Snow, 1992). An interesting paradox becomes apparent when one begins to consider why ropes course training would have an impact: The success of the ropes course seems to depend on analogical distance, yet other work indicates that the closer an experience is to one's day-to-day life, the greater the likelihood of transfer. The paradoxical effectiveness of distancing may depend on effective debriefing that links the training back to personal experience (Eitington, 1984; Gass, 1991; Gass, Goldman, & Priest, 1992; Snow, 1992). Subtleties in the debriefing process will thus be an important focus for study.

Concerns with impact will also need to be tied to questions of how the impact to participants and their teams can be prolonged (Eitington, 1984; Gass, 1991; Gass, Goldman, & Priest, 1992; Snow, 1992). Special consideration of women's experiences will be important here, too. As indicated earlier, we have found that participants may attempt to minimize their experience, which could reduce impact. The response of significant others can exacerbate this minimizing because sometimes significant others simply don't believe participants completed a high ropes course experience, or are unable to comprehend fully what participants have accomplished. We have explored various strategies for prolonging impact. Among our methods has been to use photographs of participants at dramatic points in the ropes course training. For example, while working with emotionally disturbed adolescents, we would enlarge photographs of particularly healthy moments into poster-sized pictures and hang them throughout the school. Videotapes have also proved effective as reminders of the experience. Yet for greatest impact, visualization strategies may need to be combined with a host of other carryover techniques. The debrief is likely to be the most important carryover technique, especially when expanded into the development of a written personal or team action plan. Ideally these action plans express visions, goals, techniques, and strategies individuals will use to attain those goals (Dahl & Sykes, 1988). A final way to renew and build on the training is to hold a series of spaced train-ings—perhaps about every four to eight months (Reddy & Jamison, 1988). Each experience in sequenced training must then be care-fully crafted and focused on a particular theme appropriate to the group's needs at that point. Ultimately, these variations in the training and follow-up will be important to conceptualize theoreti-cally if future evaluations are to be effective in capturing the differ-ences in the impact of various ropes course trainings on women's personal and professional growth. The model we have proposed and illustrated here may provide a starting point for initiating next steps in characterizing when ropes courses will enhance women's lives.

NOTE

1. About 15 years ago Karl Rohnke was running a workshop for current and prospective ropes course trainers at Triton High School in Byfield, Massachusetts (K.R. Rohnke, personal communication, August 18, 1993). At that time workshop participants would work on inventing new initiatives as part of the ropes course construction aspect of the workshop. What is currently "The Mohawk Walk" was invented by participants in the Triton workshop. When deciding on a name for the new event, two of the creators were Kahanwake Indians from the Mohawk Tribe. The two suggested that the initiative be named "The Mohawk Walk" after their tribe. Given the Mohawk Indians' unique ability for working high construction, the name was doubly appropriate.

REFERENCES

Aburdene, P., & Naisbitt, J. (1992). *Megatrends for women.* New York: Villard Books.

Bacon, S. (1983). *The conscious use of metaphor in Outward Bound.* Denver: Colorado Outward Bound School.

Bass, E., & Davis, L. (1988). *The courage to heal.* New York: Harper & Row.

Dahl, D., & Sykes, R. (1988). *Charting your goals.* New York: Harper & Row.

Eitington, J.E. (1984). *The winning trainer* (2nd ed.). Houston: Gulf Publishing Company.

Friere, P. (1973). *Pedagogy of the oppressed.* New York: Seabury Press.

Fuhrmann, B.S. (1986). *Adolescence, adolescents.* Boston: Little, Brown & Company.

Gass, M.A. (1991). Enhancing metaphoric transfer in adventure therapy pro-grams. *Journal of Experiential Education, 14*(2), 6-13.

Gass, M.A., Goldman, K., & Priest, S. (1992). Constructing effective corporate adventure training programs. *Journal of Experiential Education, 15*(1), 35-42.

Gilligan, C., Lyons, N.P., & Hammer, T.J. (1990). *Making connections.* Cambridge: Harvard University Press.

Hooks, B. (1984) . *Feminist theory: From margin to center.* Boston: South End Press.

Johnson, D.W., & Johnson, F.P. (1991). *Joining together* (4th ed.). Englewood Cliffs, NJ: Prentice Hall.

Jordan, J.V., Kaplan, A.G., Miller, J.B., Stiver, I.P., & Surrey, J.L. (1991). *Women's growth in connection.* New York: The Guilford Press.

Lakoff, G., & Johnson, M. (1980). *Metaphors we live by.* Chicago: The University of Chicago Press.

Melia, J. (1986). *Breaking into the boardroom.* New York: St. Martin's Press.

Reddy, W.B., & Jamison, K. (1988). *Team building: Blueprints for productivity and satisfaction.* San Diego: NTL Institute for Applied Behavioral Science and University Associates, Inc.

Rohnke, K. (1989). *Cowtails and cobras II.* Hamilton, MA: Project Adventure.

Snow, H. (1992). *The power of team building using ropes techniques.* San Diego: Pfeiffer & Company.

What Is the Therapeutic Value of Camping for Emotionally Disturbed Girls?

Lynn Levitt

SUMMARY. Therapeutic camping in a wilderness or similar natural environment has led to personal, social, emotional, and cognitive benefits for emotionally disturbed girls. While emotionally disturbed boys derive similar benefits, there appears to be some evidence for differential effects of therapeutic camping based on gender. Criticisms of past research include the lack of control groups, random assignment of subjects, valid and reliable measures, statistical analyses, and long-term follow-up studies. Suggestions for the future include: (1) the development and analysis of more therapeutic camping programs for girls in same-gender and mixed-gender groups, (2) increased use of true experimental or quasi-experimental designs, (3) more research into the generalizability of therapeutic camping benefits to other populations and non-wilderness settings, (4) systematic research into what aspects of camping are therapeutic, and (5) the development of community-based programs and services incorporating those aspects of the camping programs found to be therapeutic.

Therapeutic camping for emotionally disturbed children and adolescents has existed for over 50 years. The goals of such programs are to foster normal behavior patterns, emotions, and attitudes through camping in wilderness or similar natural environments.[1]

Lynn Levitt is Professor of Psychology in the Behavioral Sciences Department at New York Institute of Technology. She received her PhD degree from Colorado State University, and her research interests include environmental and social issues.

[Haworth co-indexing entry note]: "What Is the Therapeutic Value of Camping for Emotionally Disturbed Girls?" Levitt, Lynn. Co-published simultaneously in *Women & Therapy* (The Haworth Press, Inc.) Vol. 15, No. 3/4, 1994, pp. 129-137; and: *Wilderness Therapy for Women: The Power of Adventure* (ed: Ellen Cole, Eve Erdman, and Esther D. Rothblum) The Haworth Press, Inc., 1994, pp. 129-137. Multiple copies of this article/chapter may be purchased from The Haworth Document Delivery Center [1-800-3-HAWORTH; 9:00 a.m. - 5:00 p.m. (EST)].

However, many of these programs involved emotionally disturbed boys in same-gender groups. Do emotionally disturbed girls derive these same benefits from therapeutic camping programs? The purpose of this paper is to examine the effects of therapeutic camping for emotionally disturbed girls and provide suggestions for future research.

When examining the effect of therapeutic camping on emotionally disturbed girls, one has to look primarily at studies that involve girls in mixed-gender groups because of the paucity of studies involving same-gender groups (Eells, 1947; Goodrich, 1947; Ryan & Johnson, 1972). Thus, it will be presumed that the benefits of therapeutic camping for emotionally disturbed girls in mixed-gender groups apply to both sexes unless some differentiation based on gender has been made by the researchers.

Therapeutic camping programs differ widely in terms of the type of outdoor setting, duration of the program, activities, patients, staff, staff/patient ratio, etc. Usually mountainous, forested regions of the United States with developed facilities such as cabins and recreation buildings are used (e.g., Ryan & Johnson, 1972) although some programs include backpacking into rugged wilderness areas (Berman & Anton, 1988; Davis-Berman & Berman, 1989; Kole & Busse, 1969). Generally, small groups of less than 10 to 30 patients are taken camping (e.g., Durkin, 1988; Polenz & Rubitz, 1977; Ryan & Johnson, 1972; Stoudenmire, Temple, Pavlov, & Batman, 1988) for short-term periods ranging from day camps to a few weeks in length (e.g., Burdsal & Force, 1983; Rawson & Barnett, 1993; Rawson & McIntosh, 1991). Girls with a variety of diagnoses are referred to the camping programs primarily through child welfare systems, community mental health centers, schools, and psychiatric or correctional institutions. The staffs consist of a combination of professionals and non-professionals, some of whom are volunteers. Staff/patient ratios generally range from 1:1 to 1:5 (e.g., Hughes, 1979; Rawson & Bennett, 1993; Ryan & Johnson, 1972).

RESEARCH RESULTS

While a review of the literature indicates that therapeutic camping can have no effects or even negative effects on certain behaviors of emotionally disturbed children and adolescents (Polenz & Rubitz, 1977; Ritter & Mock 1980; Ryan & Johnson, 1972), most studies have indicated that camping in a wilderness or similar natural environment is therapeutic for emotionally disturbed girls. The personal, social, emotional, and cognitive benefits include the following:

1. Enhanced self-concept, confidence, and self-esteem (Berman & Anton, 1988; Davis-Berman & Berman, 1989; Durkin, 1988; Porter, 1975; Rawson & McIntosh, 1991);
2. Improved social and school attitudes and behaviors (Eells, 1947; Hughes, 1979; Hughes & Dudley, 1973; Kaplan & Reneau, 1965);
3. Decreased pathological symptoms (Berman & Anton, 1988; Davis-Berman & Berman, 1989; Durkin, 1988; Jensen, McCreary-Juhasz, Brown, & Hepinstall, 1968; Rawson & Barnett, 1993; Ritter & Mock, 1980);
4. Enhanced patient-staff relations (Berman & Anton, 1988; Kaplan & Reneau, 1965); and
5. Improved quality and quantity of social interactions (Goodrich, 1947; Herr, 1977; Polenz & Rubitz, 1977; Rosen, 1959).

Although almost all of the benefits listed above are based on data from mixed-gender groups, very few of these investigators did separate analyses for males and females to determine if there were any gender differences in response to therapeutic camping. While no gender differences in either anxiety or self-esteem have been reported (Rawson & Barnett, 1993; Rawson & McIntosh, 1991), other researchers have found gender differences. Gawronska, Mikulska-Meder, and Stancgak (1984) reported that females in rehabilitation camps were more sociable, better able to deal with difficulty, tidier, and less withdrawn than males. Burdsal and Force (1983) reported that the boy campers became significantly less dependent on the counselors for dealing with their basic needs following the third camping trip, but the girls did not show any significant changes on this or other measures taken. However, Burdsal and Force caution that these results were based on a relatively smaller sample of girls. Using same-gender groups, Ryan and Johnson (1972) reported an increase in depression, hostility, and anxiety among girls upon their return to the hospital. Boys, on the other hand, showed decreased depression, hostility, and anxiety mid-way during the trip, but somewhat increased depression and hostility upon their return to the hospital. They attributed these gender differences during the trip to the boys having had more successful camping experiences in the past.

Thus, it appears that there are gender differences in response to therapeutic camping, but these differences are, in part, based on the time of testing and the dependent variables measured. The reasons for these gender differences are as yet unclear.

CRITIQUE OF THERAPEUTIC CAMPING STUDIES

While camping appears to be therapeutic for emotionally disturbed girls, the results are questionable from a scientific viewpoint. Many of the earlier studies used some variation of Campbell and Stanley's (1970) one-shot case study where disturbed children are taken camping and changes in their behaviors are assessed, or the pretest-posttest design where emotionally disturbed children are tested before and after the therapeutic camping experience to assess any behavioral changes. Because these two designs lack control groups and fail to randomly assign subjects to treatment conditions, the internal and external validity of these designs is weak (Campbell & Stanley, 1970, p. 8). Without control groups or random assignment of subjects, we do not know if the treatment, i.e., therapeutic camping, or some other explanation (e.g., spontaneous remission, the novelty of the environment, environmental change, the Hawthorne effect, or other therapies used in conjunction with camping therapy) caused the beneficial effects. Moreover, many of these earlier studies were anecdotal or observational in nature, lacked valid and reliable measures, lacked statistical analyses, or were based on small sample size.

Regarding external validity, we still do not know to what populations, settings, treatment variables, and measurement variables the effects can be generalized. While there are relatively few follow-up studies, the results of some indicate that certain therapeutic camping benefits do generalize to non-wilderness settings (e.g., school) and do not dissipate with time (Hobbs, 1966; Porter, 1975; Ritter & Mock, 1980; Rosen, 1974).

While many of the earlier studies suffered from the above criticisms, more recent research has shown improvements in experimental design and methodology (Davis-Berman & Berman, 1989; Durkin, 1988; Hughes, 1979; Rawson & Burnett, 1993; Rawson & McIntosh, 1991; Ritter & Mock, 1980). The results of these studies support earlier research that show camping to be therapeutic for emotionally disturbed girls.

WHAT IS THERAPEUTIC ABOUT CAMPING?

It is still uncertain whether the beneficial effects of therapeutic camping programs can be attributed to something inherent or unique about wilderness or similar natural environments, something about the camping program itself, or some interaction between the two (Bernstein, 1972; Klusman, 1950). For those who love the wilderness and wish to argue for its preservation, one would hope to show that it is something inherent or unique about wilderness (e.g., the flora and fauna, novelty, isolation) that is causing these beneficial effects. Perhaps, the therapeutic changes occur because wilderness evokes coping behaviors rather than defensive behaviors (Bernstein, 1972); it is a different, natural, or healthful environment (Hughes & Dudley, 1973; Thomas, 1981); it provides restorative experiences (Mang, 1984); or it affords the opportunity to interact with and/or observe animals and plants which in itself has been found to be therapeutic (Cable & Udd, 1988).

On the other hand, therapeutic gains may be due to some aspect of the camping program. Results of research have already indicated that the type of camping program, the staff type activities, participation of family members in the program, and length of the program are all related to the effectiveness of the camping program (e.g., Berman & Anton, 1988; Durkin, 1988; Kaplan, 1979; Kobayashi & Murata, 1977; Marx, 1988; Perlman, 1947; Rosen, 1959). Moreover, certain therapeutic aspects of the camping program (e.g., group activities) may prove more effective in wilderness rather than non-wilderness settings (Kobayashi & Murata, 1977).

WHERE ARE WE HEADED IN THE FUTURE?

Several suggestions for future research are warranted. First, more therapeutic camping programs for emotionally disturbed girls in both same- and mixed-gender groups need to be developed. Comparisons of the effectiveness of these programs with those for emotionally disturbed boys will help to determine if there are differential effects of therapeutic camping based on gender.

Second, the use of true experimental designs, if possible, or quasi-experimental designs, is recommended. If a control group is not available, an appropriate comparison group or a variety of single-subject designs can be used. Ethical problems of the control group not receiving the treatment might possibly be resolved by either giving the control group the treatment after the study has ended or as another phase of the study. In addition, data should be collected from multiple sources such as patients, parents, or staff as various groups may perceive the camping experience differently (e.g., Polenz & Rubitz, 1977).

Third, we need to examine if the effects of therapeutic camping for young, white, emotionally-disturbed girls generalizes to other populations. While camping has led to therapeutic benefits for older, mentally-ill female patients (e.g., Banaka & Young, 1985), literally nothing is known about other demographic variables (e.g., color, race).

Fourth, since the ultimate value of therapeutic camping programs lies in determining if the therapeutic gains derived in the wilderness transfer to non-wilderness settings in the community, it is imperative that researchers conduct long-term, follow-up studies.

Finally, systematic research is required which explores aspects of camping that are therapeutic. Support services in the community can then integrate these aspects into their programs. For example, if it is discovered that there is something inherent about wilderness that is therapeutic, such as the flora or fauna, then community support services might arrange to take the emotionally disturbed girls to city parks, zoos, or botanical gardens. Indeed, Kaplan (1979) has suggested that outdoor programs be one component of community-based programs to help the child or adolescent make the transition to the community. The importance of these follow-up programs and services for maintaining the therapeutic gains in the community has also been stressed by others (Durkin, 1988; Marx, 1988).

It is hoped that future researchers will incorporate some of these suggestions and that these findings will be disseminated to professionals and other concerned personnel and agencies interested in the effects of therapeutic camping for emotionally disturbed girls.

NOTE

1. Wilderness in this context refers to those federal lands protected by the Wilderness Act of 1964 and other areas not protected by this Act but that retain the essential ingredients of wilderness (i.e., roadless tracts of land where the human is a "visitor who does not remain" and where the impact of human endeavors is kept to an absolute minimum).

REFERENCES

Banaka, W. H., & Young, D. (1985). Community coping skills enhanced by an adventure camp for adult chronic psychiatric patients. *Hospital and Community Psychiatry, 36*(6), 746-748.

Berman, D. S., & Anton, M. T. (1988). A wilderness therapy program as an alternative to adolescent psychiatric hospitalization. *Residential Treatment for Children & Youth, 5,* 41-53.

Bernstein, A. (1972). Wilderness as a therapeutic behavior setting. *Therapeutic Recreation Journal, 6,* 160-161, 185.

Burdsal, C., & Force, R. C. (1983). An examination of counselor ratings of behavior problem youth in an early stage, community-based intervention program. *Journal of Clinical Psychology, 39*(3), 353-360.

Cable, T. T., & Udd, E. (1988). Therapeutic benefits of a wildlife observation program. *Therapeutic Recreation Journal, 4,* 65-70.

Campbell, T. T., & Stanley, J. C. (1970). *Experimental and quasi-experimental designs for research.* Illinois: Rand McNally and Company.

Davis-Berman, J., & Berman, D. S. (1989). The wilderness therapy program: An empirical study of its effects with adolescents in an outpatient setting. *Journal of Contemporary Psychotherapy, 19*(4), 271-281.

Durkin, R. (1988). A competency-oriented summer camp for troubled teenagers and their families. *Residential Treatment for Children & Youth, 6*(1), 63-85.

Eells, E. (1947). From the Sunset Camp Service League: Camp as a therapeutic community. *Nervous Child, 6,* 225-231.

Gawronska, B., Mikulska-Meder, J., & Stanczak, T. (1984). Turnusy rehabilitacyjne (doswiadczenis wlasne). (Rehabilitative camps: An experiment). *Psy-

chiatria Polska, 18(5), 445-450. (From *Psychological Abstracts*, 1986, *73*, Abstract No. 20540).

Goodrich, L. (1947). How much decentralized camping can do for the child. *Nervous Child, 6*, 202-206.

Herr, D. E. (1977). Institutionalized adolescents' perceptions of a summer camp program. *Adolescence, 12*(47), 421-431.

Hobbs, N. (1966). Helping disturbed children: Psychological and ecological strategies. *American Psychologist, 21*, 1105-1115.

Hughes, A., & Dudley, H. K., Jr. (1973). An old idea for a new problem: Camping as a treatment for the emotionally disturbed in our state hospitals. *Adolescence, 8*, 43-50.

Hughes, H. M. (1979). Behavior change in children at a therapeutic summer camp as a function of feedback and individual versus group contingencies. *Journal of Abnormal Child Psychology, 7*(2), 211-219.

Jensen, S. E., McCreary-Juhasz, A., Brown, J. S., & Hepinstall, E. M. (1968). Disturbed children in a camp milieu. *Canadian Psychiatric Association Journal, 13*, 371-373.

Kaplan, H. D., & Reneau, R. F. (1965). Young patients enjoy therapeutic camping. *Hospital and Community Psychiatry, 16*, 235-237.

Kaplan, L. (1979). Outward Bound: A treatment modality unexplored by the social work profession. *Child Welfare, 58*(1), 37-47.

Klusman, W. H. (1950). The value of wilderness to youth. *Camping Magazine*, pp. 11-12.

Kobayashi, R., & Murata, T. (1977). [A consideration of the effectiveness of therapeutic camping for autistic children]. *Japanese Journal of Child Psychiatry, 18*(4), 221-234. (From *Psychological Abstracts*, 1980, *64*, Abstract No. 12857).

Kole, D. M., & Busse, H. (1969). Trail camping for delinquents. *Hospital and Community Psychiatry, 20*, 150-153.

Mang, M. (1984). The restorative effects of wilderness backpacking (From *Dissertation Abstracts International*, 1985, *45*, 3057-3058-B).

Marx, J. D. (1988). An outdoor adventure counseling program for adolescents. *Social Work, 33*, 517-520.

Perlman, J. (1947). Camps for maladjusted children. *Nervous Child, 6*, 155-160.

Polenz, D., & Rubitz, F. (1977). Staff perceptions of the effect of therapeutic camping upon psychiatric patients' affect. *Therapeutic Recreation Journal, 11*, 70-73.

Porter, W. (1975). The development and evaluation of a therapeutic wilderness program for problem youth. Unpublished thesis, University of Denver, 1975.

Rawson, H. E., & Barnett, T. (1993). Changes in children's manifest-anxiety in a therapeutic short-term camping experience: An exploratory study. *Therapeutic Recreation Journal, 27*, 22-32.

Rawson, H. E., & McIntosh, D. (1991). The effects of therapeutic camping on the self-esteem of children with severe behavior problems. *Therapeutic Recreation Journal, 25*, 41-49.

Ritter, D. R., & Mock, T. J. (1980). Carryover effects of a summer therapeutic daycamp program on children's classroom behavior: A one-year follow-up. *Journal of School Psychology, 18*(4), 333-337.

Rosen, E. J. (1974). Tikvah: A special program of integrated summer camping and its effects upon emotionally disturbed adolescents and their normal peers. (From *Dissertation Abstracts*, 1974, *35*, 288-289-A).

Rosen, H. (1959). Camping for the emotionally disturbed. *Children, 6*(3), 86-91.

Ryan, J., & Johnson, D. (1972). Therapeutic camping: A comparative study. *Therapeutic Recreation Journal, 6*, 178-180.

Stoudenmire, J., Temple, A., Pavlov, M., & Batman, D. (1988). Modeling of holistic living behaviors in therapeutic summer camps. *Journal of Social Behavior and Personality, 3*(1), 141-146.

Thomas, J. C. (1981). Treed? Bushed? Stoned? Implications of cognitive psychology for wilderness therapy. Presented at the Second Annual Convention of the Wilderness Psychology Group, Missoula, Montana.

Equine Psychotherapy:
Worth More than Just a Horse Laugh

Judith J. Tyler

SUMMARY. Equine psychotherapy, first begun in Europe, is a fledgling therapeutic resource for a very broad range of diagnoses. It is a powerfully effective tool in assisting clients who are fearful, anxious, depressed, angry, dissociative, or who have a variety of other emotional problems. Introducing therapeutic work with the horse to a client who is accustomed to conventional "office therapy" is, in itself, a change. Work with horses breaks through the client's defensive barriers and requires the client to develop fresh insights and new perspectives from old relationship and behavioral patterns. Work with the horse requires cooperative affective and behavioral consistency in clients who have learned a habit of thinking one way, feeling otherwise, and behaving in a manner that may be totally unrelated to either. We, as therapists, may not discern this important dissonance in the office, but the horse seems to sense the incongruity and will display confusion until the client is internally consistent.

Having been an avid horsewoman for most of my life, including packing, jumping, outfitting, hunting and camping by horseback, I

Judith J. Tyler was formerly a Special Education Counselor with the Mesa Public Schools, Arizona, and she has been a clinical therapist in public mental health and in private practice for four years in Springerville, AZ. She is a Certified Professional Counselor in Arizona and is nationally certified as well, holding a Master of Counseling degree from Arizona State University. Currently, she is a Doctor of Psychology candidate, enrolled at the Massachusetts School of Professional Psychology. She has been a life-long horsewoman.

[Haworth co-indexing entry note]: "Equine Psychotherapy: Worth More than Just a Horse Laugh." Tyler, Judith J. Co-published simultaneously in *Women & Therapy* (The Haworth Press, Inc.) Vol. 15, No. 3/4, 1994, pp. 139-146; and: *Wilderness Therapy for Women: The Power of Adventure* (ed: Ellen Cole, Eve Erdman, and Esther D. Rothblum) The Haworth Press, Inc., 1994, pp. 139-146. Multiple copies of this article/chapter may be purchased from The Haworth Document Delivery Center [1-800-3-HAWORTH; 9:00 a.m. - 5:00 p.m. (EST)].

have enjoyed finding ways to blend my enthusiasm for conventional forms of therapy with my first avocational love and form of personal therapy, horseback riding. I live in one of Arizona's most rural areas, and I am fortunate to have hundreds of square miles of vast, rugged, very primitive mountains just outside of town, accessible only by foot or by horse.

Many of us are familiar with the beneficial effects of *physical* therapy on horseback. The North American Riding for the Handicapped Association Inc. (NARHA), based in Denver, Colorado, has expanded from ten therapeutic riding centers in 1969 to over 450 centers currently in operation throughout the U.S. (You Can Make A Difference, 1993). NARHA lists benefits to "individuals with just about any disability," with the emphasis on physical and speech therapy:

Muscular dystrophy	Cerebral palsy
Visual impairments	Down's syndrome
Mental retardation	Autism
Learning disabilities	Paralysis
Hearing impairments	Spina bifida
Emotional disabilities	Brain impaired
Multiple sclerosis	Amputations

At New Mexico State University in Las Cruces, I recently had the opportunity to observe Therapeutic Horsemanship of El Paso, under the direction of Joy Ferguson and Luanne Reiter, conduct classes for handicapped children. The program consists of professional, qualified and certified (by NARHA) instructors, dedicated volunteers, determined and enthusiastic riders and, of course, gentle and willing horses. A holistic approach, with attention to the clients' emotional as well as physical development, is clearly evident. Those working with the clients emphasize confidence, improvement of self-esteem, and a sense of control and empowerment as they also work on the clients' physical disability (*THEP Steps*, 1992). Occasionally, a client is enrolled who is not physically impaired but who manifests an emotional impairment. In Las Cruces, for example, one eight-year-old boy, who manifested a conversion disorder affecting his speech due to severe trauma, began to talk to his horse during the third therapeutic riding session (L. Reiter, personal communication, April 17, 1993).

My emphasis, however, is essentially on the use of horses and varied horseback riding experiences in the treatment of *emotional* problems in clients. This type of therapy is useful with a broad variety of diagnoses, and it is appropriate for any age and either gender. It is appropriate cross-culturally and, of course, for persons who are physically and mentally impaired as well as for those who are not. Equine therapy should be considered a very useful supplement to skilled conventional psychotherapy. Winston Churchill stated succinctly and intuitively a concept which I am simply putting into practice: "The outside of a horse is good for the inside of a man [or woman]."

There are several types of clients for whom horseback therapy seems to be especially suited. Because this type of therapy is expensive and time-consuming, clients should be screened carefully and, generally speaking, horse therapy should be limited to those clients who are inaccessible by more conventional therapeutic modes, or who need a "boost" therapeutically. A few therapists, however, such as Barbara Rector at Sierra Tucson (a residential treatment center in Arizona), work full-time in Equine Psychotherapy, either individually or to provide a resource as part of a larger, more general therapeutic model (B. Rector, personal communication, May 22, 1993). Whatever the counselor's emphasis, it goes without saying for ethical reasons that the client and therapist should both have an understanding of the reasons for introducing horses into therapy, with clear therapeutic goals in mind. If a client is likely to confuse use of horses in therapy with a social outing, that client should not be included in a horseback program. This potential problem became clear to me when a colleague referred a man, who already enjoyed riding, to me for help with chronic depression. She mentioned to him that I sometimes used horses as part of therapy, and it was clear when he arrived at my office that he already had a "set" that I was to be his friend. As a result, his therapy did not include the use of horses, and his inaccurate expectations also interfered with the effectiveness of conventional therapy, because the client was "set up," albeit inadvertently, for some feelings of rejection or abandonment when his expectations were not realized. The therapist who uses horses as part of therapy, or the colleague who refers clients, should know the client well and should lay careful therapeutic groundwork before horseback therapy is considered.

One client for whom horses seem effective is the adolescent with Oppositional Defiant Disorder, particularly if the client is "counselor wise." Most of the defensive behavior that this type of client customarily uses disappears when attention is focused on a horse. Teenage girls, especially, seem to have a natural affinity for horses, and boys of this type are able to demonstrate their "machismo." On one occasion, I supervised a ride for a group of emotionally handicapped high school students, many of whom were behaviorally disordered and who had severe acting-out problems. We paired these students up with horses who had similar personalities. The students felt challenged; many who had abysmal self-esteem or who felt that they had little control over their lives suddenly felt empowered and proud of their literally higher social position. Although they were reluctant to admit it, many students clearly demonstrated affection toward and trust in their horses, vulnerable feelings which they did not feel safe in expressing toward people close to them. For days afterward, students who rarely spoke with peers talked enthusiastically about their personal experience with horseback riding. Many of these students' only escape from highly stressful home situations was through alcohol, drugs, sex or other addictions; the horseback riding experience was one of the few "natural highs"–a wholesome form of relaxation and recreation–that many of them had ever experienced. Similarly, inner-city youth who have a very narrow range of positive experience may find therapeutic horseback riding to be a challenge when it is planned to be a successful and rewarding experience for them. Through other types of therapy, of course, an initial positive experience on horseback may be utilized as a springboard toward other experiences which foster feelings of self-confidence and an improved ability to relate and to communicate with others.

Clients who are experiencing difficulties related to control in their lives are also especially responsive to horse therapy. Clients who over-control seem to diffuse this need while managing the horse, and are less likely to attempt to control the therapy session. "Here and now" parallels may also be drawn by the therapist between the client's overcontrol of the horse and overcontrol of personal relationships. Issues surrounding control, or the loss of it, are paramount, of course, for those clients with a history of childhood trauma. For one such client, a young woman with a history of severe depression and childhood abuse, a "maiden voyage" on horseback initiated a much deeper level of therapy. I had been seeing this client for several months, and, despite a great deal of shame and fear, she was beginning to detail horrific physical and sexual abuse in her childhood. One day I suggested we go for a horseback ride. This was a tremendous step for a young woman who had many phobias, including horses, who had never ridden, and who even had refused to touch the horses until recently. I hoped the experience would accelerate the trust she was beginning to show in me as her therapist, and would give her some sense of empowerment and self-confidence, as well as helping her to relax. We rode along the base of a beautiful Ponderosa-pine covered mountain, across brooks and through glades filled with fallen logs and ferns. It was a beautiful spring morning, and wildflowers were just beginning to show their colors in the meadow grass. When we stopped to rest, dismounting and sitting on a sunny log, she proceeded to introduce me to a whole new diagnosis. "I have something strange happening to me," she started hesitantly. "I've been to several libraries the past few weeks reading every psychology book I can find. I thought I might be schizophrenic, but I've decided that I'm not. I know I'm different, but I don't know what to call it. You know how some children have imaginary playmates? Well, I'm not a child, but I have two other parts of me that are sort of like imaginary playmates . . ."

Thus I was introduced to my first case of Multiple Personality Disorder. I believe the combination of increased trust and diminished anxiety which this young woman increasingly felt during our horseback ride enabled her to gather the courage to share her "secret" with me, her therapist.

Since I frequently work with survivors of severe trauma, many clients present, to some degree, with dissociative symptoms. This type of client is especially adept (albeit unconsciously) at "spacing off" traditional therapy, primarily verbal in nature, in a traditional office setting. Additionally, the therapist may not know during verbal dialogue which words or phrases may be triggering dissociative episodes in the traumatized client. In contrast, this type of client is actually forced, through bombardment of a variety of stimuli, to stay "present" while riding. Obviously, they must manage the horse and guide it through varied terrain and around obstacles. The client's senses are stimulated by changing sights, sounds, smells, temperature, and the physical feel of the horse under her or him. The client must stay in control of both him or herself and the horse, and must remain consciously aware of the continuous changes in environmental surroundings. Similarly, NARHA encourages all of their clients, including children with Attention Deficit Disorder, to groom, stroke and talk to their horses, both for tactile stimulation, to help bond the client with the horse, and to help the child learn to focus.

Depressed or severely stressed clients may begin therapy with one or two horseback rides. The lulling rhythm of the horse combined with the sights, scents and sounds of natural surroundings in Arizona's White Mountains elevates the spirit, alleviates tension, and may be used as an adjunct or an introduction to more conventional forms of therapy and visual imagery in the office.

Similarly, a horseback ride tends to "break the ice" and eliminate the therapeutic double-bind for the sort of angry client who simultaneously is asking for help, but who comes into therapy with a belligerent, displaced anger which overflows onto the therapist. Therapy on horseback seems to dissipate anger and to avoid tension or a power struggle which might ensue in an office setting.

One such client seemed unable to relax in my office. She had many serious conflicts to deal with at home; her anger and stress in regard to those conflicts were evident, and in some ways obstructive, to therapeutic process in the clinic. A horseback ride promoted an immediate and lasting change in her presentation. Her rapid, shrill speech slowed almost immediately to match the rhythm of the horse's walk. There were even comfortable silences as she took a few deep breaths and began to enjoy the mountain scenery passing by as we rode at a leisurely pace up a trail. Her constant nervous laughter lessened and became more appropriate. In such an utterly foreign environment (for her) as horseback riding, she seemed able to break the cycle of old relationship and perceptual habits. She appeared able to distance herself from the family conflict and tension in order to better "sort it out" and to objectively view her and others' roles. On the trip home, this client commented on how much she was enjoying the mountain scenery, adding, "I haven't slowed down and taken the time to relax and get away from my problems for years! The colors are more vibrant–everything is more beautiful than I had remembered it."

Group therapy on horseback also evolves naturally and very easily for the therapist using horses as "co-facilitators." Elements of teamwork, cooperation, communication, successful challenge, healthy competition and improved socialization are all easily introduced and coordinated, using the horse as a medium. Whatever the type of client or the purpose in assigning that client to equine therapy, there are some specific guidelines to ensure the client's safety and a successful therapeutic experience:

1. Treatment plan: What are the specific goals to be accomplished through the use of horses in this client's therapy? What proportion of the client's total therapeutic experience should be allotted to equine therapy?
2. Seasoned "players": The horses selected for such a program should be gentle and mature, with specific experience in therapeutic riding. Therapists should be comfortable with variety and versatility in therapeutic approaches. If not experienced horsepersons, they should work on an equal-partnership basis with someone who is.
3. Volunteers: Since equine therapy is so labor-intensive, volunteers need to be recruited and trained. NARHA holds clinics (with the current emphasis on physically handicapped riders) throughout the U.S. for instructors and for volunteers, and those who go through their program are certified (NARHA, 1993).
4. Location and equipment: For an effective program, a fenced arena with some specialized equipment for mounting and dismounting should be available. The arena should be lighted, as well, for evening riding. An adjacent trail system, available for more independent clients, would add another therapeutic dimension. A variety of saddle types and other tack in good

condition should be on hand to meet diverse physical, therapeutic and skill-level needs of clients.

A well-planned program with trained personnel can be a creative therapeutic adjunct to office therapy. It offers many clients a powerful new dimension to their therapeutic experience. It goes without saying, too, that a change in routine is beneficial for the therapist and, in turn, for the client. I find that interspersal of "equine therapy" into my daily office routine is a wonderful deterrent to "burn-out" and it keeps alive the joy and enthusiasm I feel for the work I love.

REFERENCES

THEP Steps (1992, December), *4* (1).
You can make a difference (1993). [NARHA informational pamphlet]

RECOMMENDED READING

Engel, B. (1992). *Therapeutic Riding Programs: Instruction and Rehabilitation.* Durango, Colorado. Barbara Engel Therapy Services.
Engel, B. (1992). *The Horse, The Handicapped and the Riding Team.* Durango, Colorado. Barbara Engel Therapy Services.
Engel, B. (1992). *Bibliography for Therapeutic Riding.* Durango, Colorado. Barbara Engel Therapy Services.
Heiperty, W. (1981). *Therapeutic Riding,* Ottawa, Ontario, Canada. Canadian Equestrian Foundation.
Joswick, F. (1986). *Aspects and Answers.* Augusta, Michigan. The Cheff Center for the Handicapped.
Lamphear, M. (1992, May). Horseback Riding–Therapeutic for Clients and Therapists. Physical Therapy Forum.

Two Bears, Dancing:
A Mid-Life Vision Quest

Darion Gracen

SUMMARY. The life-altering personal experience of the author on her first three-day vision quest is interwoven in this article with the experiences of other women questers and the knowledge the author has gained as a leader of wilderness experiences and as a therapist with women questers. Five phases of any quest, or wilderness experience, are described using personal and anecdotal descriptions of each phase to offer both a subjective and objective understanding of the questing process. The five phases are *preparation, severance, threshold, reincorporation,* and *implementation.* The threshold phase, the time spent alone and fasting in the wilderness, is described in

Darion Gracen, MA, MSW, is a graduate of Mount Holyoke College and Smith College School for Social Work. She is a psychotherapist in private practice in Boulder, CO and conducts workshops, retreats, and spirit quests nationally. She is writing a book, *Tracks of the Bear*, that draws on her work with visions, life purpose, and relationship with self, other, nature, and Spirit. Her work combines Native North and South American and Buddhist traditions as well as humanistic and transpersonal psychology.

[Haworth co-indexing entry note]: "Two Bears, Dancing: A Mid-Life Vision Quest." Gracen, Darion. Co-published simultaneously in *Women & Therapy* (The Haworth Press, Inc.) Vol. 15, No. 3/4, 1994, pp. 147-159; and: *Wilderness Therapy for Women: The Power of Adventure* (ed: Ellen Cole, Eve Erdman, and Esther D. Rothblum) The Haworth Press, Inc., 1994, pp. 147-159. Multiple copies of this article/chapter may be purchased from The Haworth Document Delivery Center [1-800-3-HAWORTH; 9:00 a.m. - 5:00 p.m. (EST)].

greater depth than the other phases. This is often the most memorable part of the questing experience. The final section of the paper offers thoughts on the lasting benefits of this type of wilderness experience. Included in this section are thoughts on why the awakenings from such experiences are life-altering for some and seemingly more transitory for others.

Years have passed since I completed my first vision quest at age 38, yet as I begin to write this I stand again, in my memory, face to the warm Montana wind on a steep slope of the Rocky Mountains. The life transforming experiences of my three day quest, including a 4 a.m. encounter with two black bears, continue to affect many aspects of my life. The "implementation" phase of this vision quest experience is ongoing.

My own personal vision questing experiences are now inextricably interwoven with the knowledge and wisdom I've gained in working as a facilitator of quests and as a therapist with women who have completed one or more quests. The stories included here were gathered from women aged 18 to 72. The questing women came to this experience for hundreds of different reasons, ranging from wanting a wilderness experience away from the city, to desiring a reconnection with Spirit, to wanting to uncover a new direction in their lives. Some initially came to leave something behind, whether it was a fear or a lack of clarity, and some simply had a hunger for spiritual reconnection. The results of the quests ranged from fun or mild confusion to transformation of self concept, life purpose, and all relationships whether with another person, Spirit, or their own wild nature.

I've had the privilege to stay in touch with many questers over several years. I've also done some ongoing therapy work with women who are experienced vision questers. Although the long-term impact of a vision quest varies greatly, nearly everyone continues to delineate their life as having a time before quests and a time afterwards.

THE FIVE PHASES

Steven Foster and Meredith Little are the founders of the School of Lost Borders located in the Eastern Sierras. In their book *The*

Book of the Vision Quest (1980), they describe their long years of work in guiding individuals through wilderness rites of passage including the vision quest. In their chapter entitled "The Rite," they credit Arnold Van Gennep in his book *Rites of Passage* (1972) with identifying the three phases of a "passage" that underlie all initiatory ceremonies. They are the *severance, threshold,* and *incorporation* phases. These are described as similar to opening a door, entering a new room, and returning to the world through a door on the other side of the room.

To these three standard phases, I have added two more. An additional one at the start of the process is the *preparation* phase. One I have added at the end, to create a place to consider longer term effects, is the *implementation* phase. They are not actually discretely different from the severance or incorporation phases, but really are additions to the beginning and the ending of the questing process, emphasizing the importance of the opening and closing of any wilderness experience.

Preparation phase. I was 38 years old when I was caught off guard while reading a magazine in my New England bathroom one spring morning. I saw an advertisement for Brooke Medicine Eagle's (1991) first vision quest camp in Montana and immediately knew I was going and that there would be no coming back to life as I had known it. The fear that welled up in me about the changes ahead was nothing compared to the excitement. This was a time of psychic preparation for me as the months passed before it was time to pack.

As I made my physical preparations for the trip, and the time away from home and work, my excitement and fear both grew. Once in Montana I would come to discover the impressive difference between fear generated from an unseen future and one from a seen present. At this point I couldn't tell the difference. Both kinds of fear can offer incredible growth opportunities and I believe that a person's willingness and ability to work *with* fear is one major factor in determining the value of an individual's questing experience.

Although I had not been diagnosed at the time, I also had Chronic Fatigue Syndrome as I dreamed of upcoming Montana nights. During the previous few years my energy level had dwindled and yet I had managed to live around this increasing limitation. As I faced this first quest in Montana, I began to physically exercise in a way that I had not tried for years. I was astonished and horrified at my inability to regain my strength quickly. I would be facing this quest truly handicapped on a physical level. I have since completely recovered from chronic fatigue with the help of homeopathy, acupuncture and enormous life changes. I needed to grow a life that was big enough for me. This first quest was instrumental in giving me the clarity about what needed to shift for me both internally and externally.

Severance phase. This is the time from the actual departure from your "old" life to the beginning of the solo quest time. This includes deciding what to take along with you, literally and metaphorically. For most everyone a quest involves travel to some distant place even if it's simply a place in your county where you've not spent much time.

Jennifer from Manhattan arrived in Montana and immediately had to confront many fears–the deep quiet, a river to cross with no bridge in place, eerie northern lights, a full moon keeping her awake, spiders in her tent. I have seen women from the country, accustomed to isolation and self reliance, experiencing fear of being part of a loving community of women. Nancy, a successful businesswoman, had to face her unexpected fear of literally having too much fun. There's a major adjustment for everyone just in arriving and settling into the community of questers. It's different for everyone–often in surprising ways. Part of the quest experience, however, is learning that we are not in this alone. There is enormous power in shared intention. We truly learn a new way to live together as we gather for this experience.

The second phase of severance is leaving the busy-ness of ordinary life. All are required to turn from doing to being; from an outward focus to an inward one. Silence, meditation, physical exercise, sweatlodge, and small group sharing, are forums for the inner world to become the focus. Amy learned that simply walking around humming was a way for her to get from there to here. Penny experimented with a whole day of silence and when she started talking again all she wanted to talk about were her dreams, intuitions, and observations of nature. During the severance phase, the emphasis in the community becomes one of respect for the weather signs, the dream omens, and the tender explorations into one's own psyche.

Another part of the severance period is cleansing the body and preparing for the fasting during the quest. Leila had a difficult time believing that a human could go for a few days with no food and decided to eat as much as she could to "stock up" before the quest started. By the time she was sitting alone on the mountain, she was bloated and miserable. Maryanne wanted nothing much to do with food and started fasting early and then, unknown to the questing staff, refused to drink water while on her quest. Her eyes dried out considerably so that her vision was affected for about a year afterwards. Gluttony, denial, and simply not listening to or respecting our own bodies all soon equate with not only immediate consequences in the wild, but are also clear metaphors for how we treat the earth and one another.

The last part of the severance period, just before the solo time begins, usually involves selecting a questing site and learning about a common symbolic language for keeping track and later discussing what happens during the actual quest. The Native American medicine wheel serves both these purposes very well. Although the medicine wheel becomes an increasingly intricate system as you study it, it's also enormously useful at the outset for both inner and outer orientation, and their interconnection (Medicine Eagle, 1991; Sams, 1990). This great circle represents the cycles of life and the seasons, and can help all of us to keep track of where we are in our lives. Questers are confronted with having to tell the truth about what's trying to happen in their lives as they orient themselves on the wheel. Are things falling away in their lives? Is it time to let go? Is it really time to manifest their dreams? Soon, it becomes clear which sector of this wheel each woman is inhabiting as she faces her solo questing time.

When a fundamental understanding of the wheel is gained then something called a medicine walk can be made. This is a long hike in a great circle around the center camp. The questers are learning to watch for signs, to notice how they feel internally in different places along the walk. They are also seeking their solo questing sites. At what points do they feel tired or energized? What do the birds and four-legged animals have to say to them or show them? When does a spider drop from the tree into their path? In which direction is the snake crawling?

By the time I went out on my medicine walk, I was fairly sure that I belonged in the west for my solo quest. Many things were trying to fall away in my life and it felt like a relief to be able to acknowledge that, and not have to try to hold things together. I began my walk by heading south, then thinking that I would make a big loop and head west. I was immediately in trouble in the south. I got caught in barbed wire, fell in a stream, ripped my pants on a log, dropped my water container–all this from a person who is not normally clumsy. Finally I slogged my way out of the south and headed west, resigned to get on with the task of facing the west. I was already learning to quit stalling about where I knew I needed to go in my life!

As I surrendered to my knowing, I headed west and everything changed immediately. The wind shifted, a field filled with purple lupine opened up in front of me, two crows (symbols of the west for the Plains Indians) cawing wildly flew close overhead. It took me a long time to get to what felt like the west. I was experientially learning that the work of the west is not done quickly. It takes time to see and cut away what you no longer need. At last I was drawn to a log in the shade of a huge old ponderosa pine. I sat down and my period arrived. Letting go was apparently already happening! This was the spot. I sat there for a few minutes, shut my eyes and began having the most welcoming sensation come over me. Deep peace and a sense of coming home are the best way I can describe it. I tied my bandanna to the tree to mark my spot and headed down the mountain to camp, down to the last full meal we were having before the quest began.

We gathered for a sweat lodge (Brown, 1953) early the next morning, equipped with the bare essentials of sleeping bag, tarp, layers of clothes, and plenty of water. After completing many hours of ceremony we received our blessings from the leader, and each other, and headed out in silence to our sites.

Threshold phase. This phase begins with the marking of the sacred circle, in which the solo time is completed. Sitting in a circle, eight feet in diameter, for several days, is a quick way to alter your perceptions. Soon, everything around you becomes not so different from what is going on inside. The oneness of all of life becomes evident very soon. Allison pondered afterwards about where this sense of oneness goes when you're in the middle of the city? How could five of us wake up at the same moment to see three turquoise

light. In between swaying steps with the bear, I rebundled my few things. I also reached out and gently picked up the stone that marked the west side of my circle that lay near the feet of the bear. As I headed down the slope I mistakenly assumed that the barbed wire fences would keep the bear from following me down the mountainside. The long grass soaked my jeans as I walked quickly away from the bear, and climbed through the first barbed wire fence. I looked back as I continued down the slope, and saw the bear following exactly in my footsteps, padding along in the zig-zag path I had left in the trampled grass. She climbed through the fence and continued ten feet behind me through more fences, around trees, over a rocky precipice, right up to the edge of camp. I realized at that moment that I was going into mild shock and needed to lie down. I made it across one last field to my tent, considered going to find a staff person, and finally decided that I could be in shock just as well in my tent as I could walking to find someone else. So I lay quietly in my tent, and never heard from the bears again—at least not in person.

The morning grew hotter, and soon the heat in my tent woke me. I wandered out into the tent field and ran into a staff person. Although we had been asked to be in silence, this woman noticed that I looked profoundly different and asked how I was. I told her about the bears and she started screaming—telling me she would have wet her pants, run down the hill, gone yelling for help. She could not believe that I had just stayed there; that I had joined this dance with the bear. Oh, my God! I quickly began to realize that coming back to this other life, even within the protection of camp, was going to be a task. I also realized that in ordinary reality perhaps I had done something extraordinary. It had not felt like that to me at the time but simply what was natural and there to be done.

Reincorporation. This phase had begun by the time I talked to that staff person. After our quest leader officially blessed our safe return, we began to bring our bodies back to ordinary life. Some women had grown stiff and too tired during their quest. They needed time alone in their tents to rest. Others suffered from hypoglycemia. A mild vegetable broth was eaten just after the quest to break the fast. Fruit and lots of fluids were also offered. Still others were so elated that sleeping or even quiet was almost too much for them. Not everyone was able to manage the silence at the end of the threshold phase and quiet buzzing conversations could be heard as you traveled through camp. Big discoveries were made and needed to be talked about right away by some.

A large gathering to reunite the questing group followed the period of silence. Here, each woman is given a chance to briefly tell her quest story. Carla told of her equipment blowing away and learning about how well she can survive with nearly nothing on the physical plane. She surprised herself with the fact that, at age 62, she was not afraid of anything! Madeline was glowing at her visit from three coyotes, and her sense of humor seemed to have been recovered from childhood. Each woman, in turn, stood with twenty others there as her witnesses, and was given a chance to begin to tell her story and rejoin the circle of questers after their days apart from one another and from ordinary reality. There are usually funny animal stories told and tales of who was visited by what. Often the most profound changes happen for people who simply were spoken to by a star, or visited by a dream that showed them how they trip themselves each time they get clear on a new direction.

One woman I remember counseling after her quest was certain that nothing had happened for her. She had slept, eaten some contraband food, walked around outside of her circle, and generally felt that she had cheated and so really deserved no revelations. As we talked several times during the first day of reincorporation, it began to be clear that much actually had happened for her. Her dreams had been vivid. Her eyes sparkled each time she told the story of "breaking the rules." In her everyday life, this was a rather passive woman. I finally asked her one last time about any "visitors" she had during the quest. She responded that she had thought about that all day and finally realized that the ONLY visitors she had were ants. She actually had to move her sacred circle because the ants gathered in a huge milling heap right in the center of her circle. Ants, in the medicine cards created by Jamie Sams and David Carson (1988), represent patience, either too much or not enough. This woman, for once, had broken her long standing patience and made some fun for herself, bending rules, sneaking food, moving around, even exploring far outside the area in which she was supposed to be sitting. Her personal noose of patience had been broken.

Penny was convinced that her entire quest was really about the herd of small mule deer that had come to visit her at dawn each morning of her quest. She saw their beauty, speed, and alertness as qualities that she lacked in her overweight body. She had begun to feel like a "beached whale" sitting there in a field as these sleek creatures circled around her, snorting, stamping and blinking with deep curiosity. I talked with her about other ways she could learn from these deer. Could she become them and learn from that perspective, rather than seeing only what she lacked by comparison?

She spent the morning pondering this question and came back to me excited with her answer. She responded that she knew that they were surprised by her presence, were welcoming her, and that actually their reaction to newness, change, and her own loving presence were really what she wanted to adopt from the exchange with the deer. She already knew a lot about feeling bad about herself and her body. By the time she headed for home, she was already practicing "leading" with her curiosity and loving kindness, rather than shrinking her energy from contact with others out of fear of their reaction to her physical size. The last time I saw her she was sitting in the middle of a large group of women, leading them in a song she had made up on her quest.

For me, in my meeting with the bears, I only knew that the bears and I had become one in some elemental way and that I could no longer live my life hiding my power and resources in a cave of questioning and shyness. The bears and I were unusual together on that hillside, we stood out to one another, and yet we danced and learned deeply from one another. Since then I have learned to carry my power into situations where it clearly did stand out, to stand my ground and share with those who were willing to dance with me, even through our differences. Previously, I would have spent more time hiding in my own self-created bear cave and only venturing forth when the coast was clear. The first days after my quest, though, my learning was much more experiential than intellectual. I knew that deep change had happened from the many visions and visitors during that first quest, and I also knew that there was no going back. People gave me all kinds of bear presents and reminders before I headed for home and I carried them carefully, wanting and needing their reminders at first. Very soon, though, my own life would become the reminder.

Incorporation. During the *incorporation* phase we can start to see which women will allow the changes and awarenesses from their quests to become lasting parts of their daily lives. This is a fairly difficult thing to measure. One thing I know for sure is that a quest is not something easily forgotten and I believe that they echo into our futures in ways that are sometimes subtle yet very powerful. Our elemental selves are fed in a deep and lasting way on a quest in nature, and that nurturance feeds the roots of much growth in our lives even if it does not always sustain flashy new projects or blatantly new ways of being.

I think that some key personal qualities, certain pre-quest intentions, and a woman's phase of life all make a difference in the long-term benefits gained from a quest. A collection of personal qualities that I've come to call "knowing how to live like a river" are very valuable in integrating new awarenesses and in facing change. People with these qualities know how to meet the challenge of a sudden waterfall plunge in their lives as well as how to metaphorically spin in circles when caught in an eddy of life. They come to a quest knowing how to sit still *and* how to stay awake. Their curiosity is alive and their fear is interesting to them rather than debilitating. These are the people who are also good at not getting caught in the "mud" of their own personality level selves. They come with an understanding of how they "work" inside so that their awareness is freed up enough to attend to the unseen and metaphorical worlds in a clear way.

The leader, or midwife, of any quest has as much to do with the pre-quest expectations as does a woman's personal experience of facing the unknown and her previous successes or experienced failures in facing a challenge. Comfort with the unknown and a willingness to surrender control are certainly factors in determining the potency of a quest. A woman's pre-quest belief in her ability to make change happen has much to do with her ability to carry out the revelations from a quest. For many, the ongoing support and connection among the participants seem a very important part of overcoming the inertia and old habits that tend to stifle change and blur intentions after the quest. The group's bonding process before the quest is a crucial element in making this support possible and useful later on.

Implementation. Finally, there is the question of life phase. I believe that certain life phases are much more conducive to assimilating a quest in a long lasting way. I do not assume that "long lasting" is necessarily better or desirable for everyone, but I do know that many measure success in this way. Women at early mid-life, and at menopause, seem particularly adept at using this kind of psychological and psychic opening. These are the women who have watched the wrinkles set in on their faces, have experienced some deep losses and powerful joys, and know that they no longer have forever to create the kind of experience for which they hunger. Also, quite young women, in their late teens or twenties, tend to integrate the questing insights so quickly into their psyches that the change is nearly overnight and seemingly everlasting.

For some the pressure of a dissatisfying life can go two ways. It can either create a longing in a woman that results in successful reaching for a change, or it can create a lowered horizon that makes something like spiritual connection seem like another task to tax her resources. This leads me back to where I started in this section. The underlying personality characteristics of knowing how to be "like a river" seem to be the most significant in terms of supporting lasting change.

The bears and I have lived together inside my psyche ever since my first quest. When I forget how to live like a river, or don't dare to make my wisdom or power available to the world, I am quickly reminded either from inside or out. I send this article out as one of those reminders for you–and for me. Keep on!

REFERENCES

Brown, J. E. (Ed.) (1953). *The sacred pipe.* Norman, OK: University of Oklahoma Press.

Carson, D., & Sams, J. (1988). *Medicine cards.* Santa Fe, NM: Bear & Company.

Foster, S., & Little, M. (1980). *The book of the Vision Quest.* New York: Prentice Hall.

Medicine Eagle, B. (1991). *Buffalo woman comes singing.* New York: Ballantine Books.

Sams, J. (1990). *The sacred path cards.* San Francisco, CA: HarperCollins.

Van Gennep, A. (1972). *The rites of passage.* Chicago: Chicago University Press.

Therapeutic Considerations
of Wilderness Experiences
for Incest and Rape Survivors

Shirley Joseph Asher
Gayle Quick Huffaker
Marte McNally

SUMMARY. The purpose of this article is to examine the relevancy of traditional wilderness programs, such as Outward Bound, to women who have been violated by experiences of childhood incest and/or adult sexual assault. Applications to African-American women, women with physical challenges, and women who are economically disenfranchised will be emphasized. The overview is from a feminist perspective, one that advocates empowerment over struggle and resisting revictimization on any level.

The Rape Assistance and Awareness Program (RAAP) is a nonprofit agency in Denver, Colorado, dedicated to providing low-cost group psychotherapy for women who have been recently sexually assaulted as well as for women with histories of incest. About five years ago, a three-day Colorado Outward Bound School (COBS)

Shirley Joseph Asher, PhD, is a psychologist in private practice in Denver, CO, and Clinical Supervisor at the Rape Assistance and Awareness Program. Gayle Quick Huffaker, MA, LPC, is a psychotherapist in private practice in Denver, CO, and Group Facilitator, Rape Assistance and Awareness Program. Marte McNally, MA, is Director of Victim Services, Rape Assistance and Awareness Program, and facilitates groups for both incest and rape survivors.

[Haworth co-indexing entry note]: "Therapeutic Considerations of Wilderness Experiences for Incest and Rape Survivors." Asher, Shirley Joseph, Gayle Quick Huffaker, and Marte McNally. Co-published simultaneously in *Women & Therapy* (The Haworth Press, Inc.) Vol. 15, No. 3/4, 1994, pp. 161-174; and: *Wilderness Therapy for Women: The Power of Adventure* (ed: Ellen Cole, Eve Erdman, and Esther D. Rothblum) The Haworth Press, Inc., 1994, pp. 161-174. Multiple copies of this article/chapter may be purchased from The Haworth Document Delivery Center [1-800-3-HAWORTH; 9:00 a.m. - 5:00 p.m. (EST)].

161

experience was incorporated into RAAP's treatment program. While the COBS weekend generally has been viewed positively by most of the clients and group facilitators, aspects of this element of the program have become increasingly problematic. Its applicability to women with physical disabilities and women with conflicting social and economic priorities is questioned. When RAAP received a special grant to provide sexual assault services specifically targeting women of color, groups for Latinas and African-American women were established and facilitated by therapists of color. These women of color, both clients and therapists, consistently challenge the relevance and practicality for them of the COBS experience.

In this article, we contend that wilderness experiences, in their traditional application, do not support the feminist, woman-centered approach to life which is advocated and nurtured at RAAP, nor does it specifically honor cultural diversity or ethnic multiplicity. Recommendations for wilderness experiences attracting a broader range of the feminine experience are made.

During the past ten years, wilderness experiences and adventure-based programs, such as those sponsored by Outward Bound schools, have become an increasingly accepted adjunct to the treatment of incest and recent sexual assault survivors (Courtois, 1988; Goodwin & Talwar, 1989; Herman, 1992). The physical challenges posed in the wilderness courses often evoke feelings of fear and powerlessness that are associated with the original victimization. By voluntarily exposing themselves to these dangers, abuse survivors learn "to master them and regain some of their personal efficacy and self-respect" (Courtois, 1988, p. 210). Other issues central to abuse survivors, such as the ability to develop trusting relationships and utilize problem-solving skills, can also be addressed in wilderness therapy.

The Rape Assistance and Awareness Program (RAAP) is an agency that provides low-cost group therapy for women who have recently been sexually assaulted as well as for women with a history of incest. In 1987, RAAP incorporated a three-day Colorado Outward Bound School (COBS) experience into the treatment program. Over 100 RAAP clients have participated in the COBS Survivors of Violence Recovery Program since the inception of the program. Rape survivors participate in a 16-week structured course of treatment with the COBS experience occurring at about the tenth week. The retrospective incest therapy groups are 45 weeks in length with the wilderness experience occurring between the 25th and 30th weeks.

The COBS experience is a three-day therapeutic wilderness program consisting of sequentially designed activities that may include trust exercises, group initiatives, a ropes course, rock climbing and rappelling, orienteering, snowshoeing, cross country skiing, or an extended time alone in the wilderness. Much time is spent debriefing and processing. The group processing sessions are essential in that they help facilitate the transfer of learning from the wilderness to the everyday lives of the women (Webb, 1993). Through accomplishing tasks that once appeared impossible, and carefully moving just beyond one's "comfort zone," women can begin to feel an increased sense of competence, of mastery, and of increased self-esteem (Oliver, 1988; Pfirman, 1988). They may begin to understand that asking for help can be a strength, and that they can, with support, continue to move toward a goal, even when extremely fearful. Many survivors' lives are circumvented by fear, isolation, shame, numbness, and the constant and exhausting need to be in control. Feeling competent, trusting oneself and others, asking for what one needs, making choices, setting boundaries, confronting conflict, and moving through fear are giant steps towards healing.

While once viewed as a central and essential part of the treatment program, the COBS component is now an option that is offered to the clients. Currently, one-half to two-thirds of the women choose to participate in a COBS course. Virtually all of the clients and facilitators who have participated in a COBS course feel that it has been a very positive experience, but aspects of the program have become increasingly problematic. Decreased emphasis on the COBS portion of the treatment program has been in response to the needs and concerns voiced by some women of color, physically challenged women, and those with few economic resources. In this article, we will delineate the problematic aspects of wilderness therapy for these three groups of women from a feminist perspective. We will offer some modifications of typical outdoor programs and alternatives that have served similar purposes and achieved similar goals.

FEMINIST PERSPECTIVE

Important considerations in viewing wilderness therapy from a feminist perspective are the issues of relevancy and accessibility. Is wilderness therapy helpful for everyone? Does everyone benefit equally from wilderness experiences? Is the therapeutic value of wilderness experience based on assumptions that may not be universal with regard to race, gender, and class?

Historically, Outward Bound has been viewed as a "white male" organization (Hoffman, 1992; Knapp, 1985; Miranda, 1985; Mitten, 1985). Outward Bound was "imported" to the United States in 1961 from England and Scotland. Based on German-born educator Kurt Hahn's model, Outward Bound was initially designed to help better prepare WW II British merchant seamen, and later to benefit upper class youth. It was innovative in that it strongly emphasized both mental preparation and experiential learning (Berman & Anton, 1988; Miner & Boldt, 1981).

A metaphor employed to understand the appeal of adventure experiences has been that of the heroic initiation quest prevalent in classical and contemporary literature. The participant leaves home, his senses heightened and receptivity enhanced. He survives some travail in the woods, reflects on the experience and returns home with new insights about his life, his "character having been strengthened" (Warren, 1985, p. 13). We wonder if this metaphor is applicable to all participants. The growth of "women in the wilderness" programs as an alternative to programs like Outward Bound speaks to the fact that women may view the wilderness differently than men do (Giammatteo, 1993). Women, and particularly women of color, may not subscribe to the heroic myth metaphor at all. They may seek solidarity rather than confrontation with nature and community building rather than competition (Mitten, 1985).

AFRICAN-AMERICAN WOMEN

In 1990, groups for African-American women and Latinas were established when RAAP received a special grant to provide sexual assault intervention services specifically targeting women of color.

These groups are facilitated by women of color. RAAP has more experience with African-American clients than with other women of color; consequently, this article emphasizes their experience. It should be noted, however, that women of various ethnic and racial backgrounds participate in the program and each woman is recognized and honored as bringing a unique worldview.

African-American women, through their groups at RAAP, were able to explore, embrace, enhance, and clarify their connectedness to African values and to one another. The Afrocentric values that they integrated into their lives became a critical factor in their healing. The perspective described below was the product of a unique circumstance and therefore cannot be generalized to all African-American women. These African-American participants chose to deal with their sexual violations in a group of only African-American women facilitated by an African-American woman.

African-American women proceed through life with a need for relevancy, a pragmatic view of what is important, and how it can be applied. The challenge of a wilderness experience for African-American women is for it to be practical with useful application for their everyday use. It cannot be an isolated experience.

Traditional African-American families appreciate communal values, extended families, and closely-knit support systems. All living organisms are perceived in African tradition as being endowed with the same force, spirit, and universal energy. This is referred to as "being in the universe" (Nobles, 1978, p. 685). Humans are valued as being one with nature. The African culture is one of "rhythm" that comprises both emotional and physical movement. This is a process for understanding and organizing reality. Nature does not represent a struggle or a force to be conquered, but rather a unified, harmonious force with which all people are connected. African-American women are linked to nature and may choose, when provided with the option, to connect spiritually with a tree rather than to climb it. They may embrace a wilderness experience as an avenue to communicate with their ancestors rather than to ascend a mountain.

The African values of spontaneity and community may run counter to Western values of control and individualism. In the egalitarian atmosphere appreciated by African-Americans, there may be no clear division of responsibility or singularly recognized voice of authority. The wilderness experience, in order to be relevant to African-American women, may not involve any reference to time, being late, or ending an activity. The freedom of spontaneous versus planned activities allows each woman to maintain her life's rhythm. Furthermore, the absence of an authoritarian leader allows for a sense of inter-connectedness in which all people are authorities of their own experiences.

Women are often encouraged to undertake wilderness experiences in order to confront their female victimizations and move beyond them. Sexual victimization is seen as an expression of contempt in a sexist society. The concept of sexual victimization as primary oppression may escape or even alienate African-American women who are in the position of "double jeopardy," being targets of both racial and sexual oppression (Smith & Stewart, 1983). According to Hooks (1984), "White women may be victimized by sexism, but racism enables them to act as exploiters and oppressors of black people" (p. 15). Giddings (1984) reinforces this idea by quoting La Rue, "Blacks are oppressed. . . . White women are suppressed. . . . and there is a difference" (p. 308). Women of color may not embrace a wilderness experience with Anglo women as an automatic statement of their feminist solidarity. "Women of Color view feminism as yet another system in which they have to define and justify their reality which makes it [feminism] just as oppressive as the traditional sexist patriarchal system" (Boyd-Franklin, 1983, p. 162). In this capacity, participants, therapists, and wilderness course instructors who are unable to accept the differences in worldview and experience that women of color represent, become oppressors. Whatever difference is ignored or denied will become the focus of the woman of color. In crisis or confrontation, many women of color will call upon their cultural/ethnic traditions for personal power (Boyd-Franklin, 1983). These defenses may include isolation, nondisclosure, confrontation, and denial. When denied acknowledgement of who they really are, women of color are compelled to process rage and anger either internally or with others (Lorde, 1984).

African-American women suffer a loss of self-esteem when isolated from other same-race support systems and role models

(Myers, 1980). African-American women, more than any other race or sex group, indulge in touching behavior with other African-American females to express feelings and to demonstrate affection. They need one another for safe emotional expression (Smith, 1983). In order to enhance the opportunity for an empowering experience, women of color ought to experience a wilderness event with other women of color in all capacities of participation. It should be noted that while women of color need not be exclusively with other women of color, they should not have to handle the experience in isolation.

One of the authors, who is an African-American woman, participated in a COBS weekend as a group member in preparation for taking her own groups to COBS. As a participant, she experienced feeling invisible and invalidated. Her ethnicity was challenged by both instructors and participants who repeatedly remarked that she did not actually "look or sound like a Black woman." She was the only individual dropped on the trust fall by her fellow participants–all white. Furthermore, the specific racial implications of this incident were not processed in the debriefing sessions. In that all those present, including the COBS instructors and the facilitator, were apparently uneducated and uncomfortable regarding cultural differences, she remained an outsider. She compensated by being physically competitive, confrontive regarding every cultural or ethnic slight, and emotionally distant. Never did she feel connected to nature in ways that were meaningful. Although African-American women tend to view struggle as potentially unifying, this experience of struggle was divisive and unempowering.

THE ISSUE OF PHYSICAL ACCESSIBILITY

The fact that many women who have been traumatized at some point in their lives have a variety of physical health problems has been well documented (Follingstad, Brennan, Hause, Polek, & Rutledge, 1991; Goodman, Koss, & Russo, 1993; Leidig, 1992). It is in keeping with the literature, that a significant number of the clients at RAAP (between 20% and 50% of the members of any given group) have health problems that preclude them from engaging in strenuous physical activity. The women have suffered from asthma, post-polio syndrome, chronic fatigue syndrome, rheumatoid arthritis, severe hypertension, and reflex sympathetic dystrophy (RSD). As a result of their physical conditions, the women are unable to participate in the wilderness course. When the programs at RAAP were first developed, we considered excluding women who could not participate in COBS. Realizing this would be discriminatory, we decided that some flexibility needed to be introduced into the plan.

Some interesting dynamics have developed in groups when the women are confronted with the dilemma that not all will be able to participate in the COBS experience. Inevitably, the group will consider the possibility that if not all can go, none will go. Consideration of not participating in the course leads to feelings of anger and resentment in the able-bodied incest survivors. Once again, as in their family of origin, they must sacrifice their needs and desires for someone else. To assert their wish to attend COBS often results in internal conflicts and feelings of guilt. The able-bodied women feel selfish and may contain their enthusiasm both before and after the wilderness experience.

The conflicts between the able-bodied and physically challenged women also recapitulate family of origin issues for those whose physical limitations date from childhood. They were vulnerable to abuse and ridicule as children and learned that silence and compliance were important for survival (Courtois, 1988). They could not express anger and disappointment at constantly being left behind for fear of causing further disruption in the family. They were dependent on the family for care and could not jeopardize their only sense of security. Expressing the anger, fears, and frustrations of being left behind in the group is a major challenge for these women. The risks feel similar to the risks in childhood—incurring the anger of others, fearing rejection, and jeopardizing their tenuous position in the group/family.

The women whose limiting medical conditions are more recent may feel that their bodies have betrayed them. These feelings may be reminiscent of their abuse experiences. Although some of the women have learned to silence their needs in order to obtain the cooperation of their caretakers, their rage and frustration over physical limitations tend to be closer to the surface than those whose limiting conditions date from childhood. One client, whose group went on a one-day COBS outing, was encouraged by a COBS instructor to be "the voice of the group" when she could not participate in a particular exercise. Despite this attempt to include her, she became totally enraged at the suggestion. She stated she was tired of being the voice of others, that she was there to be her own voice, and expressed enormous frustration at not being able to contribute equally in all aspects of her life.

Among the women who are able to participate in COBS, there is great variability in their physical conditions. Some are physically fit and are not particularly challenged by the rigors of the course. Instead, they may be challenged on a solo outing or on a trust walk where they must confront feelings of vulnerability and mistrust. They may experience enormous anxiety just in being away from familiar routines, the comforts of home, and their support systems. What can be accomplished on a wilderness trip in terms of healing from sexual assault cannot be measured in direct proportion to the degree of physical difficulty of the course.

THE ISSUE OF ECONOMIC ACCESSIBILITY

Economic accessibility is as much of an issue for the women clients at RAAP as is physical accessibility. COBS has been extremely generous in granting tuition scholarships but that does not cover all costs of the weekend such as child care and loss of wages, since the women need to miss a day of work. Childcare and employment problems have prevented several women from participating in COBS.

One barrier to participation in COBS related to finances is socioeconomic class. Outdoor programs which can include technical climbing, white water rafting, and cross-country skiing, all of which require specialized equipment, are generally considered to be middle class experiences. A woman with little outdoor experience may have difficulty imagining how she could benefit from it. The very thought of it may feel alien and overwhelming. A weekend spent living outdoors may be viewed as deprivation rather than as a nurturing and growth experience. For these women, such a trip may also be viewed as frivolous and trivial (Warren, 1985). Some women have expressed surprise, confusion, and indignation at the amount of money spent so that they may experience nature. Thus, some clients resist involvement in the wilderness component of the program based on fears of the unknown as well as concerns about whether the experience will be practical or relevant.

RECOMMENDATIONS FOR REDUCING BARRIERS

As the staff at RAAP has become increasingly aware of the physical, socioeconomic, cultural, and philosophical barriers that prevent clients from benefiting from COBS courses, the commitment to confronting these issues and seeking solutions has also grown. Alternative settings are actively being explored. Some Colorado wilderness organizations, such as the Breckenridge Outdoor Education Center, accommodate people with a variety of physical problems. A therapeutic horseback program that accepts people with differing physical abilities has recently been located. Giammatteo (1993) describes wilderness experiences adapted to inner-city settings.

At this time, economic accessibility remains an insurmountable obstacle to women's participation in a three-day wilderness program that takes them away from their children and jobs. Assisting single mothers in locating low cost childcare or developing a cadre of volunteers to care for the children is one solution. As a result of their abuse, the women are very reluctant to leave their children with people they do not know very well. Providing on-site childcare is a solution that the mothers might find more palatable.

Taking time from work to attend COBS has been impossible for several women, particularly those who are newly employed or in low paying jobs. Several have been threatened with termination when they requested the time off. For some women, it was too threatening to tell employers why they needed the time off, while others who explained their request still were denied. Until sexual abuse is more widely acknowledged and the healing process gains acceptance, this barrier will remain.

Maintaining group cohesiveness when some women are unable to participate in COBS has been problematic, but some strategies have been developed to minimize the impact on the group. Women who cannot participate in COBS are urged to set personal goals for that weekend just as those who are going on COBS do. They are encouraged to spend some time alone and to challenge themselves, take risks, and reflect. Their activities can range from taking a day alone, to writing a letter to a family member, or getting a massage. Some groups choose to spend a day together combining nurturing activities, such as meal preparation, with other projects, such as making collages, representing their victimization. All of the activities are structured so that all of the women can participate equally.

Traditional wilderness excursions need to be more flexible in order to attract more women of color. We do not suggest that activities requiring physical conditioning or a willingness to explore one's physical nature be eliminated; however, we recommend that alternative approaches to growth be available to all participants. These options need to be culturally diverse and facilitated by persons not only trained in wilderness survival but also in cultural multiplicity. Culturally-based options offer some diversity to a traditional Eurocentric masculine view of nature and competition.

As previously mentioned, African-American women often appreciate a more spontaneous approach to life. Consistent with the African value placed on creative expression, options such as singing, painting and mask-making, dancing and drumming, and ancestral storytelling in the oral tradition may be offered as activities counter or supplemental to the ropes course, mountain climbing, skiing, etc. As a result of deep ethnic and spiritual affinity to nature, women of color may be more inclined to meditate using the open space to facilitate inner monologues, to honor the earth by planting, to participate in activities geared toward worshiping the sun, and to use nature as a guide to communicate with ancestors.

The author who earlier described her wilderness excursion, had a second COBS experience about one year later. She participated as the therapist for a group of African-American women who had been in therapy with her for about eight months. She worked closely with the COBS staff to develop a culturally honoring experience for the women. Most importantly, the staff instructors were racially diverse. Unfortunately, due to physical challenges confronting a couple of the women, COBS was unable to assume liability for them for a wilderness weekend, but was willing to devote staff for a one day excursion in a park outside of Denver. Stresses were apparent at times and, at one point, the white instructor openly discussed feeling anxious at handling time and activities so spontaneously and approaching nature more spiritually than competitively. She discussed her reactions to spending an entire day and evening with a group of African-American women exploring their heritage and its connection to nature. Due to her ability and willingness to be flexible and move beyond her perceptions of what "should be," she was completely embraced by the women and she, in turn, was able to embrace them. This example serves to emphasize how a culturally diverse experience may prove beneficial and growth-enhancing for all persons involved, not just persons of color.

When using typical outdoor programs with women who are survivors of violence, a reassessment of these programs' philosophies is indicated. For these women, using a feminist model that employs principles such as pluralism, egalitarianism, and building on strengths, may create a more inclusive, safer, and empowering environment for healing the wounds of sexual abuse and assault. Specifically, an egalitarian perspective in wilderness therapy promotes shared decision-making. Rather than being led from activity to activity, seldom being informed of what is coming next, women would be told about their options and allowed to decide which activities would facilitate their growth. Less emphasis would be placed on facilitators and instructors to "be in charge." Participants would be trusted with their own process, while facilitators provide support.

In previous COBS courses, individuals have been given the choice whether to participate in any activity or to choose an alternate form of the activity. In theory, the instructors and therapists are to insure that neither coercion, nor peer pressure, pushes a participant to engage in an activity in which she feels unsafe. In reality, even with encouragement, many women, especially women who have survived victimizations, are unable to assert themselves enough to set these limits. Women who choose to say no to certain activities rarely experience this as an accomplishment, but generally feel it as failure.

Since COBS is limited in its accessibility for an increasing number of RAAP clients, the search for other adjuncts to psychotherapy that will foster the women's self-esteem, ability to trust, sense of empowerment, and safety in the world will continue.

Women who have kept secrets and pain buried for so long need to be able to fully and spontaneously express themselves at any given moment. Diversity must be explicitly celebrated. Opportunities to express diversity in terms of ethnicity, color, age, physical abilities and sexual orientation must be specifically provided. Rather than viewing nature as a force to conquer, nature would be seen as a gentle teacher. Each woman brings unique gifts. These gifts include those typically viewed as useful to outdoor survival such as physical strength or "leadership abilities," but they may also include less obvious but equally important outdoor skills. It is time that we recognize that ". . . a sunset watcher is as important as a firebuilder" (Mitten, 1985, p. 22).

REFERENCES

Berman, D. S., & Anton, M. T. (1988). A wilderness therapy program as an alternative to adolescent psychiatric hospitalization. *Residential treatment for children & youth, 5*(3), 41-55.

Boyd-Franklin, N. (1983). Black family life styles: A lesson in survival. In A. Swerdlow & H. Lessinger (Eds.). *Class, race and sex: The dynamics of control.* Boston: G. K. Hall & Co.

Courtois, C. (1988). *Healing the incest wound: Adult survivors in therapy.* New York: W. W. Norton & Co.

Follingstad, D. R., Brennan, A. F., Hause, E. S., Polek, D. S., & Rutledge, L. L. (1991). Factors moderating physical and psychological symptoms of battered women. *Journal of Family Violence, 6*, 81-95.

Giammatteo, H. (1993, March/April). Into the woods. *Ms.*, pp. 44-45.

Giddings, P. (1984). *When and where I enter.* New York: Bantam Books.

Goodman, L. A., Koss, M. P., & Russo, N. F. (1993). Violence against women: Physical and mental health effects. Part I: Research findings. *Applied and Preventive Psychology, 2*, 79-89.

Goodwin, J. M., & Talwar, N. (1989). Group therapy for victims of incest. *Psychiatric Clinics of North America, 12*, 279-293.

Herman, J. L. (1992). *Trauma and recovery.* United States: Basic Books.

Hoffman, H. (1992, Fall). Was Kurt Hahn's model flawed from the very beginning? *Beyond: Alumni magazine of the Colorado and Pacific Crest Outward Bound Schools*, pp. 3-4.

Hooks, B. (1984). *Feminist theory from margin to center.* Boston: South End Press.

Knapp, C. E. (1985). Escaping the gender trap: The ultimate challenge for experimental educators. *Journal of Experiential Education, 8*(2) 16-19.

Leidig, M. W. (1992). The continuum of violence against women: Psychological and physical consequences. *Journal of American College Health, 40*, 149-155.

Lorde, A. (1984). *Sister outsider.* New York: Crossing Press.

Miner, J. L., & Boldt, J. (1981). *Outward Bound USA.* New York: William Morrow & Co.

Miranda, W. (1985). "Heading for the hills" and the search for gender solidarity. *Journal of Experiential Education, 8*(2), 6-9.

Mitten, D. (1985). A philosophical basis for a women's outdoor adventure program. *Journal of Experiential Education, 8*(2), 20-24.

Myers, L. W. (1980). *Black women: Do they cope better?* Englewood Cliffs: Prentice-Hall, Inc.

Nobles, W. W. (1978). Toward an empirical and theoretical framework for defining Black families. *Journal of Marriage and the Family, 40,* 679-688.

Oliver, J. (1988). *An evaluation of the Colorado Outward Bound School's Victim of Violence Recovery Program.* Unpublished master's thesis, University of Denver, Denver, CO.

Pfirman, E. S. (1988). *The effects of a wilderness challenge course on victims of rape in locus of control, self-concept, and fear.* Unpublished manuscript, University of Northern Colorado, Greeley, CO.

Smith, A. (1983). Nonverbal communication among black female dyads: An assessment of intimacy, gender, and race. *Journal of Social Issues, 39*(3), 55-67.

Smith, A., & Stewart, A. J. (1983). Approaches to studying racism and sexism in Black women's lives. *Journal of Social Issues, 34*(3), 1-15.

Warren, K. (1985). Women's outdoor adventures: Myth and reality. *Journal of Experiential Education, 8*(2), 10-14.

Webb, B. J. (1993). The use of a three-day therapeutic wilderness adjunct by the Colorado Outward Bound School with survivors of violence. In M.A. Gass (Ed.), *Therapeutic applications of adventure programming* (pp. 95-102). Dubuque, IA: Kendall/Hunt.

Breaking Through Barriers: Wilderness Therapy for Sexual Assault Survivors

Deborah Levine

SUMMARY. This article presents wilderness therapy for sexual assault survivors. A form of treatment that combines counseling with rigorous outdoor activities, it creates situations that relate metaphorically to the original assault. Women engage in activities designed to promote team building, trust, self-esteem, confidence, intimacy and personal growth. They are then faced with physically challenging situations that evoke the feelings of helplessness that were experienced during the assault, only this time they are provided with the chance to conquer them, by climbing to the mountaintop, hiking the hill, or simply knowing and asserting their physical limits.

This article substantiates wilderness therapeutic programming by looking at its appropriateness for sexual assault survivors. Descriptions of wilderness experiences will be provided along with a discussion of variables which contribute to treatment efficacy. In familiarizing the readers with wilderness programming, the author hopes to build more widespread acceptance and subsequent use of this model for survivors.

Deborah Levine, MA, is Health Educator at Columbia University in New York, providing sexual assault programming for students and faculty. She is presently coordinating a joint project with Victim Services and New York City Outward Bound, and has previously worked at Ithaca Rape Crisis, Planned Parenthood, and the Santa Fe Mountain Center, a therapeutic wilderness center in New Mexico. She has consulted with various non-profit and educational groups about the effects of violence on youth.

[Haworth co-indexing entry note]: "Breaking Through Barriers: Wilderness Therapy for Sexual Assault Survivors." Levine, Deborah. Co-published simultaneously in *Women & Therapy* (The Haworth Press, Inc.) Vol. 15, No. 3/4, 1994, pp. 175-184; and: *Wilderness Therapy for Women: The Power of Adventure* (ed: Ellen Cole, Eve Erdman, and Esther D. Rothblum) The Haworth Press, Inc., 1994, pp. 175-184. Multiple copies of this article/chapter may be purchased from The Haworth Document Delivery Center [1-800-3-HAWORTH; 9:00 a.m. - 5:00 p.m. (EST)].

175

INTRODUCTION

Existing modes of treatment for adult rape and incest survivors include self-help, group therapy, twelve-step programs, and individual psychotherapy. However, an innovative, non-traditional treatment approach being used by a handful of agencies in the U.S. is wilderness therapy. This form of treatment combines counseling with rigorous outdoor activities to create a situation that relates metaphorically to the original abuse and emphasizes developing new coping strategies. It involves a one to three-day group experience in the outdoors that engages women in activities designed to promote trust, team-building, self-esteem, confidence, intimacy, and overall personal growth. Women are encouraged to face their fears in a supportive environment that is separate from their daily lives, yet carries constant references to their abusive situation. They are faced with physically demanding activities that evoke the feelings of helplessness that were experienced during the abuse, and then are provided with the chance to surmount them by climbing to the mountaintop, hiking the hill, or simply knowing and asserting their physical limits.

Wilderness therapy is a combination of experiential education and traditional therapeutic group processing. The experience differs dramatically from "taking a walk in the woods" or camping out for the weekend. Distinguishing factors include the processing of the activities, which facilitates transfer of the learnings to daily life; the role of the group leader in helping the participants to understand their experience; and the integral part that trust plays throughout the programming. In addition, structured risk and induced fear in a safe environment are tools to build confidence and strength.

Before describing specific activities involved in wilderness therapy as applied to rape and incest survivors, it is important to cover some of the short and long term effects of sexual assault. Whiston (1981) compares the reactions of a victim after a sexual assault to a grief model, and illuminates the losses suffered by the survivor. She enumerates loss of self-identity, loss of security, loss of power and control, and loss of sexual identification as common reactions to the trauma of rape. Other authors have described the psychological implications of the assault as also including depression, fears of one's environment and circumstances, guilt, self-blame, shame and a loss of self-esteem (Burgess, 1988; Burgess and Holmstrom, 1976; Sgroi, 1982; Walker, 1988). If the abuse has not been dealt with in a supportive manner soon after its occurrence, it will continue to have negative, sometimes debilitating effects for many years afterward.

Wilderness programs for sexual assault survivors are usually one to three-day programs. They consist of a creative combination of physical activities, beginning with the simplest icebreakers and moving to more complicated tasks. The three activities that have been most effective with sexual assault survivors are the climbing wall, the ropes course, and the three-day rock-climbing trip.

THE CLIMBING WALL

I worked on the climbing wall with an adult sexual assault survivors' group that had been meeting for eight weeks prior to their wilderness experience, and with a group of adolescent girls living in a juvenile detention center, all of whom had been sexually abused. Both of the groups had participants of mixed ethnicities—Anglo, Latina, and Native American.

The climbing wall is a simulation of an actual rock climbing site. It is used when there isn't time enough or there aren't appropriate resources to do a "real" rock climbing expedition. It is a 40-foot wall with two different climbs on each side, of varying degrees of difficulty. There are pegs as well as clay and wooden grips for the climber's hands and feet. A belay rope system provides back-up safety if the climber falls. The women learn how to put on their harnesses and helmets, and they receive basic information about safety and how to climb, but overall, the technical information conveyed is fairly simple. Before climbing the wall, the belayer (a staff person on the ground who handles rope safety for the climber) asks the client what her goals are and together they assess the reality of those goals within the parameters of the person's emotional and physical capabilities. As the woman reaches her goals on the wall, again an assessment is made: Can you go further? Do you want to stop here? How does it feel to reach your goal?

Working with a group of adults was much easier on many levels than working with the adolescents. There wasn't the confusion of the usual adolescent issues with the survivors' issues. The group members were ready and willing to experience whatever we had planned and were committed to their personal growth and healing. This particular group was articulate and members had no trouble applying what they gained from the wilderness experience to their daily lives.

Some of the most poignant comments about the climbing wall from women in this group were as follows:

> I could see [from the climbing wall] how I just walk through all the problems in my life without a plan, and eventually I get stuck and entangled with no place to go. I panic then because I can't see the next step. I did the same thing on the wall: scrambled up, got stuck, and then realized that the only way to do it was one step at a time–to look ahead and see what's next and plan.

> The climbing wall helped me with my fears and my problems in my life. I was totally surprised that these exercises actually had relevance to my problems.

> My strength in climbing the wall completely surprised me. I learned that I can do more than what I think.

> I don't have to be so afraid all the time that people think bad things about me.

> My strongest memory is the feeling I had when I was halfway up the wall and felt stuck. It was so powerful to overcome that and make it to the top.

> The most difficult thing for me today was climbing the middle part of the wall and overcoming the idea that I can't do it.

In working with the adolescent survivors on the climbing wall, I encountered one particularly moving experience which I would like to use as an illustration of the activity's effectiveness. One Native American girl had a revelation at the point where the particular wall we were working on angles out about 45 degrees. This is approximately three-fourths of the way up the wall. She had scrambled up to that point, and then got stuck there for an unusually long time.

Periodically, she would try to climb, then give up and sit back in the harness. When asked, she clearly didn't want to come down. She must have made between six and eight attempts to climb to the top. Finally, she put one foot in front of the other and reached the top. She stayed there for awhile, then rappelled down. At the bottom, she was in tears and had difficulty talking. She began to tell me what had happened to her. At the point on the wall where she got stuck, all the "bad" things in her life–her sexual abuse, as well as all the "bad" things she did herself as a result of the abuse–flashed before her. Every time she tried to climb, she couldn't, until the images were finished. She just sat in the harness with the memories–"stuff I don't usually think about during the day." This was quite an intense moment for her, especially when she made the conscious decision, after the images were over, to have it be her past, not her present or her future. Her present involved overcoming her past and making it to the top of the wall.

THE ROPES COURSE

The ropes course is designed by experiential educators to help people overcome their fears in a safe, structured manner. One model is a 40-foot tall apparatus that contains four to eight different activities within it, each involving rope tied between two poles. In some activities, balance is required, in some it is an issue of problem solving, and in some it's solely where to place your arms and legs at each given moment. The activities increase in difficulty as you move along the course. Each participant is tied in to a harness as well as a safety rope system to ensure minimal risk. It is not a physically demanding course; in actuality, the hardest physical challenge is climbing up the ladder to begin the course. The course is geared more to overcoming emotional and mental blocks than physical ones.

Making choices and defining boundaries are areas of weakness for sexual assault survivors. The ropes course gives women a chance to decide what their limits are, and, if possible, to push beyond them. When I worked with a group of severely sexually abused teenagers from a family assistance center, there were two girls who didn't want to complete the course. One didn't attempt the course at all, and one climbed the ladder to the first platform and then decided to go back down. Both girls felt sure that they were making the right decisions for themselves at that moment. They were supported by both the staff and their peers for making their own decisions and affirming their boundaries, and also for continuing to stay with the group and give support and encouragement to the other girls who did complete the ropes course activities.

Another moving experience occurred with a Latina adolescent from this group as she completed the ropes course. She had managed to finish all the activities, but then was afraid to rappel from the platform. She was at the top for a long time, crying and trying to overcome her fears, but essentially paralyzed. A wilderness instructor suggested that she let go of one thing in her life that she doesn't like as she pushes off the platform and rappels to the ground. It worked, and she went down apparently fearlessly. During the group processing session afterwards, we asked her what she let go of. She answered, "The abuse my father did to me."

A THREE-DAY TRIP

On a three-day trip to a national park, we worked with a group of ten girls of various ethnicities, aged thirteen to seventeen, all living together in a group home, and all dealing with issues stemming from child sexual abuse and neglect. The length of stay in the group home ranged from three months to one and a half years. The advantage of their situation was that we, as wilderness therapists, had enough background information about the girls to formulate individual goals for the trip. The girls in this group had major presenting issues of abandonment, disrespect for authority, low self-esteem, sexual promiscuity, and substance abuse. In addition to individual goals, the group goals were to develop cohesion and trust, to develop respect for individual differences, and to assume responsibility for one's own actions, including understanding their consequences.

The three-day course began with a full day of initiative and trust-building activities. The second day we went rock climbing in the mountains, and the third involved a solo reflective period. On the second day, the rappelling was quite a dramatic experience for most of the girls, and clearly the highlight of the trip. All their issues came up poignantly–that they self-impose limitations on their abilities to succeed, that others are available to provide safety and support, that it is possible to overcome fears. Many abuse survivors have an inordinate amount of fears and phobias. Once a person is sexually abused, so much has happened that is outside the realm of normal experience that the survivor begins to feel that anything at all can happen at any time. This generates irrational, yet real, fears of just about anything. One common fear is a fear of heights which we were asking these girls to face and overcome on the mountain.

Every one of the girls tried the rappel, and all but one successfully completed the journey down the mountain. Climbing up seemed easy for the girls after coming down the mountain backwards (rappelling). They scrambled up with new found confidence and were constantly challenging themselves with more difficult climbs. Even the one girl who was too afraid to rappel down the mountain managed to climb the easiest route up the rock face. There was a marked change in the girls after the climbing–an easing of tension and a noticeable increase in self-esteem and confidence.

THE GOALS OF WILDERNESS THERAPY

Every survivor who participates in wilderness therapy has some sort of experience, be it positive or negative. In addition, some individuals have major life-changing experiences during the span of a wilderness course. The key to this programming is continuity in the treatment plans. It is not helpful to provide a major transformative event for someone and then send her back to her life without adequate processing. It is also important to give survivors the tools to transfer the growth to other more common experiences. Ideally, the therapist or counselor who has been working with the group on sexual assault issues prior to the wilderness therapy joins the group in its wilderness activities and then provides follow-up in their regular group sessions.

Wilderness therapy is an innovative concept in the mental health field. Although the roots of adventure programming are deep and there are hundreds of outdoor experiential schools and programs in the country, the use of the wilderness as a therapeutic tool remains revolutionary to traditional schools of psychotherapeutic practice. And, within the experiential education field, using wilderness tools for survivors of rape and child sexual abuse is considered creative and underutilized. When one considers the widely documented extent of child sexual abuse, the timeliness of introducing this form of treatment becomes clear.

Wilderness adventure programming combines counseling with rigorous outdoor activities and an appreciation for the environment. The result can be a restoration of power that is concrete and instantaneous, a goal that could take six months of traditional therapy to achieve. The immediacy of the environment allows women to deal with issues as they surface, and allows the facilitators to structure the activities to the needs of the particular group and the individuals involved.

During each program there is noticeable growth in some of the participants in the areas of self-esteem and confidence, overcoming fears, giving and receiving support, trust, power and control issues, and problem-solving. More rarely, there are participants who have extraordinary, life-changing experiences while participating in a wilderness adventure. And perhaps regularly, after each program there is some resolution or change for the survivors that the wilderness therapists may never see.

PROGRAMMATIC EVALUATION

Common controversies surrounding wilderness therapy for sexual abuse survivors include the value of imposing stress on survivors, the perceived rigor of the programming experience, and how the program considers the traditional therapy in which survivors might also be engaged. The intentional use of stress is central to the change process of wilderness therapy. Stress is often created by the participants' perception of risk. In the case of sexual assault survivors, however, it is important to confront the potential pitfalls of self-challenging physical experiences. Urging individuals to push themselves beyond their perceived limits may give survivors the sense that in some ways they failed during their assault for not trying hard enough to deter it. Also, it brings into question the usefulness of confronting a perpetrator during an attack, especially if a weapon is involved. Many see wilderness programming as always promoting direct confrontation, as it does in confronting participants' fears on the mountain or in the ropes course.

In a study done in 1988 by Carter, Prentky, and Burgess, it was found that different victims' response strategies were effective depending upon the psychology of the perpetrator. Many cognitive self-defense suggestions may be forgotten in the moment of panic when a victim is confronted by a potential rapist. Nevertheless, knowledge can bring an added sense of confidence to an unpredictable and volatile situation, and may be the only weapon a victim has in a dangerous situation. It thus becomes clear that in different situations, different response strategies are appropriate and the key is the victim being able to attain the presence of mind and confidence to find a method of danger reduction. Wilderness programming focuses on building self-esteem and confidence, as well as reducing fears, so that even though the wilderness activities may not be specifically transferred to a future sexual assault or abusive situation, there can be non-specific transfer in terms of principles and attitudes.

Programming for sexual assault survivors takes place at a much slower and gentler pace than most traditional outdoor adventure programs. First, there is so much room for individuals' issues to surface because of the parallels to the abuse situation, that the groups must move slowly so as not to miss opportunities for processing and growth. Second, this experience for female survivors is not about the "macho" feeling of having to make it to the top, or having to complete all the tasks to be successful. Working with survivors is an effort to help the participants make their own choices and define their own limits and boundaries. It is important to remember that these are people who have already had their boundaries tested and abused and have been pushed beyond human limitations. For survivors, this is not a test of endurance, stamina or physical abilities; it is an emotional test of belief in oneself and one's capabilities, as well as one's ability to say no and mean it.

Wilderness therapy should not in any way supersede or replace traditional therapy. This type of programming complements other forms of treatment in which a survivor might be engaged. Wilderness therapy deals with the more "typical" survivors' issues, such as body image and self-imposed limitations, in a poignant and immediate manner. It is important to note that a woman who may have a transformational experience on a wilderness course may not be able to return to her daily life and transfer the learning. The therapy or support system the survivor has in place before the program begins would then come into play afterwards. The most successful programs occur when the participants, therapists, counselors, family, and friends are informed about the nature of the wilderness experience. A good support system can help to effectively transfer the learnings back to the daily environment and activate change.

One day in the field with a group of survivors of various ethnicities and backgrounds tells the whole story. In one survivor's words:

> This experience exceeded my expectations. It was wonderful to see all of us open up and become closer and more trusting. WE ALL CAN MAKE IT!!!

REFERENCES

Burgess, A.W. (1988). *Rape and sexual assault II*. New York: Garland Publishers, Inc.

Burgess, A.W. & Holmstrom, L.L. (1976). Coping behavior of the rape victim. *American Journal of Psychiatry, 113*(4), 413-418.

Carter, D.L., Prentky, R.A., & Burgess, A.W. Victim response strategies in sexual assault. In Burgess, A.W. (Ed.) (1988). *Rape and sexual assault II*. New York: Garland Publishers, Inc.

Sgroi, S.M. (Ed.) (1982). *Handbook of clinical intervention in child sexual abuse*. Lexington, MA: Lexington Books.

Walker, L.E.A. (Ed.) (1988). *Handbook on sexual abuse of children*. New York: Springer Pub. Co.

Whiston, S.K. (1981). Counseling sexual assault victims: A loss model. *Personnel and Guidance Journal, 59*(6), 363-366.

Women's Adventure Group:
Experiential Therapy in an HMO Setting

Margaret J. Kessell

SUMMARY. Over a six-year period, the author has led 14 groups of women in a program consisting of three sessions of yoga, a dance therapy session, an initiatives course in the woods, and a four-day rock climbing experience. Women with diagnoses of major depression, post-traumatic stress disorder, dysthymia, anxiety, and adjustment disorder participated in a bi-weekly group meeting eight times, in activities to reconnect them with their bodies, their feelings, their spiritual selves, and with each other.

The design of the group is based on the theory that women with these diagnoses have learned in our culture to make decisions based on fear, to be unassertive, to feel little control over their lives, to be disconnected from and abusive to their bodies, to be ashamed of their feelings, and to isolate themselves from community, especially the community of other women. Long-term follow-up of group members indicated that this was an ignition experience, sparking changes in life-style and attitudes of many of the women, leading to higher self-esteem, healthier coping strategies, a sense of some control over their lives, and more connectedness with other women.

Margaret J. Kessell is a Licensed Independent Clinical Social Worker, working part-time for Group Health, Inc., a large HMO in Minneapolis, MN. She earned her MSW at the University of Minnesota in 1981. Prior to using experiential group therapy with women, she worked for Outward Bound and coordinated an adventure-based program for disabled adolescents. She currently has a part-time private practice and a small corporation called Personal Challenges, Inc., which runs women's groups uniting the body and spirit in the outdoors.

[Haworth co-indexing entry note]: "Women's Adventure Group: Experiential Therapy in an HMO Setting." Kessell, Margaret J. Co-published simultaneously in *Women & Therapy* (The Haworth Press, Inc.) Vol. 15, No. 3/4, 1994, pp. 185-203; and: *Wilderness Therapy for Women: The Power of Adventure* (ed: Ellen Cole, Eve Erdman, and Esther D. Rothblum) The Haworth Press, Inc., 1994, pp. 185-203. Multiple copies of this article/chapter may be purchased from The Haworth Document Delivery Center [1-800-3-HAWORTH; 9:00 a.m. - 5:00 p.m. (EST)].

"There's nothing to hang onto–my leg is shaking–I want to come down!" Fear is evident in her trembling voice as Glenda clings to the rock face 25 feet above ground. Tied in through her harness to a rope securely held by her belayer, she is in little physical danger, but perceived danger paralyzes her mind and causes her body to stiffen. "Breathe, lower your heels, and breathe again. Look for a foothold, something small, look around you, test it out. I've got you. Trust your feet." Her belayer shouts up encouragement.

Inch by inch, Glenda moves up the rock, pausing to breathe, to search for tiny nubbins that will hold her and move her to the next vantage point from which she has a different perspective of the climb. Finally reaching the top amid shouts of joy from the women watching below–"All right! You *did* it! Beautiful!"–Glenda dissolves in tears in the arms of the woman waiting at the top–tears of relief, disbelief, amazement at herself, pride, and thankfulness. She will share these feelings tonight as the group talks over the events of the day: each woman with her experience of accomplishment, of recognized limitations, of new definitions of success, of being supported in fear and going through the fear, or of saying no and not being shamed by the group.

DEVELOPMENT OF THE GROUP

This is therapy in an HMO setting? For the past seven years this kind of group has been offered at Group Health, Inc., in Minneapolis, Minnesota. The author has led two groups a year, ranging from four or five women in the early groups to nine women in later groups. The idea began as a program for single mothers of teenagers–women who were overwhelmed by that role and isolated from support systems. The idea grew, and other therapists began to refer clients, so that the women have ranged from age 25-62: never-married, separated, divorced, lesbian, happily or unhappily coupled, widowed, mothers and non-mothers, grandmothers, all in a mix. Their diagnoses ranged from adjustment disorder through major depression, dysthymia, anxiety, panic attacks, post-traumatic stress disorder (many survivors of incest or other sexual abuse), and alcohol and other drug dependencies in remission. Feelings of low self-esteem were common. Many women felt stuck with no options in an unrewarding and underpaid job, or in a marriage or relationship that was abusive. The sense of paralysis–"I'm stuck–I can't go up and I can't go down–I see no options,"–no wonder they recognize that feeling on the rocks.

In earlier work with Outward Bound running a program for adolescents with physical disabilities and chronic illness (Kessell, Resnick, & Blum, 1985), the author became well acquainted with the blocks that hold people back: not only real physical limitations, but also perceived limitations, fear of failure, societal attitudes that include the need of others to protect them, and lack of opportunity to test one's limits. The result of such blocks is low self-esteem, little self-confidence, lack of trust in self and others, and alienation from one's body. A person learns not to risk. Struck by the similarity between physically disabled teenagers and many of the women seen in therapy, the author sought to develop a program that would reconnect a woman to her body and to other women, that would give opportunity for physical and emotional risk-taking in a safe environment along with the chance to reflect on the experience. Thus was born the Women's Adventure Group, affectionately shortened to WAG. A name that did not reflect pathology was intentional, as this was to be a group that focused on women's strengths.

STRUCTURE OF THE GROUP

Each group met eight times over a three month period. There were four distinct activities, culminating in a four-day rock climb. The other activities were yoga (three sessions), dance therapy (one session), and an initiatives course at Wilder Forest, a retreat center near the Twin Cities.

A. Yoga sessions were interspersed with the other sessions. The women committed to practicing yoga on a daily basis for the duration of the course. Yoga teaches relaxation, correct breathing, and flexibility; reconnects a woman to her body, and helps her to become aware of where she stores tension and emotions. Knowing how to relax and breathe, and becoming more flexible, were valuable assets on the rock climb.

B. Dance therapy, similarly, helped the women to identify emotions held in the body, such as fear, anger, and sadness, and to express these emotions in nonverbal ways. Body movement tends to bypass the normal defenses people erect to deny or repress their feelings, which then find expression in anxiety, panic, or depression. The women were encouraged to discuss with their therapist, or with one of the leaders, any issues that surfaced during this session.

C. The initiatives course was a bonding experience. The women were presented with a series of obstacles and problems that can be solved only by group cooperation. Issues discussed were: being willing to risk sharing ideas with the group; leadership; trust; willingness to try something new; and advantages of being tall or short, thin or heavy. Activities included: a blind trust walk in pairs; getting everyone through a huge spiderweb without touching the web; and scaling a 12-foot wall through cooperative thinking and effort. At this session, the women had fun, let down their guard in their common effort to solve the puzzles, and began building trust in one another and in themselves; this trust served them well on the rock climb. Scaling the wall became a metaphor for doing the seemingly impossible with the support of other women. Women who had learned to be ashamed of their size (apparently everyone over a size 8) were amazed that other women could easily lift them. Tall women found that their height had advantages and was respected. All body sizes and shapes had their advantages and disadvantages. By working together each woman brought a gift to the group.

D. The rock climb is described in detail in the next section. A month after the rock climb, the women met again at a potluck dinner to share photos of the trip, tell tales of their homecomings, and report what had happened in the interim. They also decided on how they wished to continue relating now that the group had formally ended. This was a crucial piece if they were to retain and build upon the gains they had made.

THE ROCK CLIMB

The rock climb took place 250 miles from Minneapolis, at Devil's Lake, Wisconsin. The women carpooled, which gave them a chance to get better acquainted and to share their jitters. The group stayed at a nearby retreat center where they cooked meals together, which provided an opportunity to deal with eating habits and teach nutrition experientially. Those who had good eating habits shared their ideas and recipes. Food is a central issue for many women: food as comfort, nurturance, fulfillment, compulsion, punishment or reward, escape from boredom. With menus planned, meals cooked together, and lunches packed for eating at the climbing site, participants became aware of how they use food in their lives, and lively discussion ensued. A surprising number of the women have changed their eating habits following this experience.

Safety procedures were key to the rock climb, as a feeling of safety and control was paramount if the women were to trust themselves and the equipment enough to risk on the rocks. The first afternoon was spent in "ground school" where the women learned and practiced knot tying, care of equipment, safety procedures, and belaying. The word *belay* comes from a nautical term meaning "to make fast or secure." The belayer is securely anchored and takes in the climbing rope through a belaying device as the climber ascends. It takes practice to feel comfortable doing this. Each belayer had a back-up belayer. Many of the women were awed by the sense of responsibility they felt while belaying. A sense of intimacy developed between climber and belayer as the climber moved through difficult spots. Some climbers moved slowly and steadily, some with bold moves and great pauses, or some quickly without thinking. The belayer got a sense of how the climber lives her life. Did the climber allow herself to trust her belayer? Did the belayer trust herself? The belayer was there to protect the climber should she fall, but the climber had to do her own climbing. Mothers who had a hard time letting their children take their own risks found this metaphor particularly useful. The idea of being a belayer or being belayed in other life situations brought new insights into why a person might feel stuck. If a woman believed that her belayer was not well anchored or did not know what she was doing, it was difficult to climb with any security. Better to find a support system she could trust, so that she could climb! Transferring this idea to other areas of life, a number of the women reexamined their "belayer" at home or on the job, and realized why they were afraid to move.

After learning the basics, the women practiced on low boulders. "Bouldering" allows climbers to test their balance, foot placement, and handholds close to the ground. Next, they tried short easy climbs, and then they had the opportunity to climb blindfolded, if they wished. Climbing blindfolded teaches reliance on touch and on the feet, and diminishes the fear of heights. It is a way to be very present in the moment, just where you are, using your sense of touch and your body, tapping into the feeling of security these two offer. "The body does not lie, and the cognitive self cannot take one up a rock" (Mason, 1987, p. 91). Self confidence goes up dramatically when a woman climbs blindfolded.

There were a few rules other than those which pertained to safety:

1. Everything is voluntary; you will be given opportunity, support, and encouragement, but *you* decide what you will and will not do.
2. Ask for what you want.
3. Do not help unless the person requests help; do not take away her opportunity to test her limits.
4. Success does not necessarily mean reaching the top. You are in charge of setting your goals. Success might mean being the first one to try a climb, or trying a difficult climb and finding you can make it halfway.

Following these rules helped to create an environment in which it was safe to risk, to change your mind, to try again, to say no, to cry, and to ask for what you want. Becky climbed once the first day and felt that she had accomplished what she came for. She was included in the group as a belayer and cheerleader, the group accepting her decision not to climb again. On the last day, she confessed with tears that she had been waiting the entire time to be rejected for saying no. In her relationship with her mother and with her children and men, saying no was either disbelieved or punished by ridicule or retribution.

Irene took the risk of going first on a challenging climb. She moved skillfully, until she encountered a difficult move which stopped her momentum three quarters of the way up. As she struggled, she began to cry. Assured by her belayer that she was secure, she was encouraged to take her time and breathe. After some minutes of silence and no movement, Irene moved a foot and passed through the crux. To the small group of women who had held their breath and climbed every step with her, she confided what was happening during those silent moments. Her husband of 27 years, emotionally abusive and having a flagrant affair, was talking to her, telling her how worthless she was and how she couldn't do it. With the encouraging words of her belayer in the background, she fought with him and decided, yes she *could* do it, and she did it. Not long after the climb she began divorce proceedings, which, like the marriage, were long and grueling. Irene frequently asked for, and received, support from friends in the climbing group. This is similar to a client described by Mason (1991, p. 61) who struggled through a climb and said

> . . . it had been the first time anyone ever told her she had the right to be afraid. This, she recalled, was the conversation she had wanted for 32 years–that she could still do something even if she was afraid, and people would stick with her if she had trouble. . . . When we make the decision to no longer live safely but to risk, we become more of ourselves.

Sylvia was terrified of heights. She became increasingly nervous as we hiked up to the cliff the first day and could not bring herself to look down from the start of the climb. She didn't know how she would bring herself to climb. Almost paralyzed by fear on her first short climb, she decided to try it again blindfolded. Free to focus on touch and balance, she moved gracefully up the rock and back down. Realizing that it was her mind that had held her back, she became one of the most daring climbers in the group, looking out over the lake from the top of a climb with great joy. Sylvia had been in therapy for two years dealing with issues of abuse as a child and low self-esteem which caused difficulty in her relationships. Overcoming her fear of heights and finding joy in her abilities translated into self-confidence in relationships, and soon thereafter Sylvia terminated her therapy.

Mary, who walked with a limp due to post-polio syndrome, often worried about her weight. She wondered how she would fare on the trip. On the hike up to the climbing site, she discovered that everyone has her own pace. Joann, with emphysema, also walked slowly, taking time out to breathe. Others who appeared able-bodied were also taking their time. Climbs of varying difficulty were set up and there was no pressure to rush. Mary was determined, and the whole group shared in her achievement as she set her challenge to match her own capabilities. As Mason (1987, p. 96) states in describing wilderness family therapy, "Climbing, although it can be physically demanding, does not require the climber to meet the body-beautiful image of muscles and sinew. . . . Each person has to find her own 'edge'." Rather than comparing herself with others, Mary had the experience of challenging her own perceived limitations.

Although the climbing itself was central to the retreat, other activities balanced the experience. Mornings began at 6:00 with yoga for centering, stretching sore muscles, and maintaining balance and flexibility. Short readings in a circle before meals fed the spirit. The readings became a ritual which underlined the metaphors of the climb and gave pause for joint reflection. Evenings were processing time, time for talking about what the women had learned about themselves during the events of the day, processing conflicts that had arisen, discussing issues triggered by the climb, and asking for what they wanted on the next day.

On the afternoon of the third day, the women experienced a two hour "solo," each being led to a spot in the woods or meadow where she could sit with her journal, allowing Nature to surround her, observing externally and internally. John Miles (1987, p. 37), talks about spiritual growth within wilderness education. "These spiritual aspects come to be appreciated through one's own experience and not as a result of argument, debate or theorizing. . . . In wilderness . . . we have a chance to . . . get in touch with self and nature." Anderson and Hopkins (1991) encourage women to trust their own experience of the divine, of the spiritual, and pay heed to it. The solo was a brief span of time to give the women the space and quiet to feel the connections that exist between them and their environment. We asked the women to keep silence until we had gathered together again in a circle. The leaders then went around the circle with warm water, soap and a towel, carefully washing and drying the hands of each woman. In the silence of this act, the varying responses–downcast eyes, eye contact, tears, sobbing, smiles–told tales of shame, of neglect, of years of caring for others with little in return, and of awe in this moment. There was the recognition that "I matter." This gesture of caring touched the core. It was a moment of rich reward for the leaders as these brave women, who had been risking their bodies and their fears for two days, now shared their vulnerability and allowed themselves to heal.

When the silence was broken, the women began to talk about the experience of solo. Some had not had two hours alone for years. They had found metaphors in watching a stick maneuver its way down a running brook, an ant carrying a larger insect, or a timid deer who approached without fear. Some wrote poetry and wished to share it. Marie, always polite and smiling, found voice for her anger because another woman, out of sight but not out of hearing, had disturbed her solo by singing loudly. Even a "bad" experience has its uses.

GROUP COMPOSITION

Because this group is composed of women in an HMO in Minnesota, there are built-in constraints as to who can be included. Group Health does serve people on Medical Assistance, which opens the experience to women with limited income. The group is subsidized by the HMO, i.e., the leaders are on salary, so the cost to the participants is the cost of expenses for the trip. The majority of Group Health members are white and this is reflected in the make-up of the group: of 102 women, one was African American, one Asian, one Hispanic, one Native American and one African American/Native American. Each was the only minority member in her particular group, except for one group. No discomfort was evident; in fact, many of the women were appreciative of other cultures and eager to learn more about them. In the case of the African-American woman, she felt a part of the group during the trip, but commented on long-term follow-up that she dropped out of the group as it continued informally because she felt she "had a hard time relating to white concerns." She would like to see an all African-American group, and thought that nothing would have to change. The author's sense is that it would be better to have at least one African-American leader in that case.

There were many women in the groups who had suffered sexual abuse as children or adolescents. They were mixed in with women with different issues, some less profoundly disturbing. We did not sit around and talk about past histories in this group, but some stories came out because of events on the rock. For some women with adjustment disorders, hearing these stories often gave them a new perspective on their own lives. For others, the stories touched repressed memories of their own, and they were able to get in touch with their own pain.

We did one group that was already organized as an incest survivors group, with WAG being a part of their therapy. This was a difficult group. It may have been because the group already had an identity, and we, the leaders, were perceived as outsiders. There also seemed to be a group belief that if we were not survivors of incest we could not understand their fears. There were already indigenous leaders within the group who had worked hard to learn to say no; they found it difficult to say yes to physical or emotional risk or to trusting others. Others in the group who did want to risk felt somewhat ostracized. One member wrote on long-term follow-up:

> Not everyone perceived things in the same way. It took a long time for two of our group to work through their feelings. I found the adventure group to be very positive and helpful for me, but after some of those post-rock climb sessions I felt guilty for feeling so good about it. Later I was able to see that that was how they felt, but that I could have my own feelings.

Another woman, also an incest victim, but not a member of that group, stated that she was afraid of intimate relationships. She had risked and become involved, and did get married some months after the group. She stated: "I attribute a good deal of my ability to trust myself and my partner to learning experiences in the group."

As the women discovered their own strengths and capabilities, and related parts of their histories, much anti-male sentiment was expressed. Support was given for women to leave abusive situations. There was, in almost every group, at least one woman who came on the trip in order to try to get closer to other women, to learn to trust and like other women, but who felt competitive with other women and felt closer to men. They did grow more trusting of women because of the climbing experience. In addition, because of their different perspective on men, they challenged the women on their blanket condemnation of men. Both sides had their views challenged, sometimes with the outcome that both expanded their views.

A number of women were struggling with issues of sexual orientation. Two women found it difficult to get close to the group because they were not ready to talk about their sexual preference for women, and their secret caused them to feel like outsiders. Both of them subsequently dealt with their sexual orientation in individual therapy. A third woman who talked about her childhood abuse on the trip, but did not share that she was lesbian, decided at the follow-up meeting to come out to the group. She was surprised to find that they were not surprised, and that they admired her courage to live her life as she chose.

It worked best to have mixtures of ages, backgrounds, cultural identity, diagnoses, and experiences in each group. As women growing up in America, we have all been subjected to bias, to violence in some form, and to the belief that we are not as strong, as smart, or as capable as men. Some have felt this more destructively than others, but we all recognize it when it is talked about. We must deal with our body image as we compare ourselves with the ideal projected in the media and by our friends and acquaintances. The rock does not care if a woman is tall or short, heavy or thin. It offers to each woman a combination of toe holds and hand holds, allowing her to put them together according to how they fit her body. It will wait patiently and quietly while she cries, or rails, or curses, until she breathes and looks around to see what it offers. It will hold her, if she will just trust herself. "We quickly discover that when we meet the enemy, it is our self we meet. As we learn to trust the right hemisphere of our brain as well as our bodyselves, we can then move carefully up the rock" (Mason, 1987, p. 102). In the end a woman will have a new sense of her body, how it balances, how it serves her and how it moves. Each woman treasures the photo of herself on the rock, taking it home and putting it up to remind herself of what she can do.

Because we as women have common experiences, it is important to have women leading the group. When I began this group, my co-leader was my son, then in his twenties, who was an Outward Bound instructor, and who came as the "rock-jock," or climbing instructor, while I was the "therapist." This worked because the early groups were single mothers who were having trouble with teenagers, and as he and I had survived those tough years and were working together, we offered hope to them. It was difficult to find women "rock jocks," even among Outward Bound instructors, many of whom felt they were not competent enough. The illusion persists, hanging on even in the midst of relatively assertive women, that women are not as competent, strong, or capable as men. After a few more groups with male co-instructors, it dawned on me that I was telling myself that I wasn't competent enough, when actually I was perfectly capable of being my own "rock jock." After that it became easier to bring on another woman therapist who was willing to learn to climb. The women expressed gratitude at having role models at different stages of climbing ability. I am appreciative of the fact that we are all on the same journey, stymied by the same kinds of obstacles, and in need of each other as role models. In our lives, we take turns climbing and belaying one another.

LONG TERM RESULTS

Of 102 women who participated in WAG, 45 (44%) have returned long-term follow-up questionnaires. The groups began in 1986, and in 1990 I realized I wanted to do a long-term study. Thus, the follow-up on the early groups comes from one to four years after they were completed. Thereafter, questionnaires were sent out one year post-experience. Most recent groups were surveyed at six months post-experience in order to include them in this study. Thus the results represent participants' perceptions of the effects of the experience on their lives after six months to four years. Half of the women did not return the survey; a few had moved and were unreachable. Three who had negative feelings did respond; two of them felt excluded by the group and felt like outsiders. One missed the rock climb because of illness and subsequently felt outside the group because she missed the core experience.

Some of the questions participants were asked were: Why did

you join the group? Did it fulfill the purpose for which you joined? Did it lead you to do other things that helped you with the problems for which you joined the group? What events or changes have taken place in your life since doing the group? There were a series of questions relating to physical activity, eating habits, general health, visits to Group Health for physical and mental health issues. Following is a summary of the results.

Why did you join the group? (Some gave more than one reason.)

> Therapist recommended it (16)
> Challenge physical and emotional fears (16)
> Wanted a support group (14)
> Raise my self esteem (7)
> Find out who I am (4)
> Incest group was doing it (4)
> Unable to relate to women (3)
> Difficulties with men (3)
> Deal with incest (3)
> Excitement (3)
> Get unstuck (3)
> Rock climbing (2)
> Depression (2)
> Tired of talking (1)
> Alcohol treatment follow-up (1)
> Self-realization (1)
> Yoga as help with health (1)

The next series of questions were answered on a *less–same–more* scale. The questions included:

1. Level of physical activity since doing the group?
2. Change in eating habits (less healthy, same, more nutrition conscious)?
3. Change in general health?
4. Change in number of visits to Group Health for illness or accidents?
5. Change in number of visits to Group Health for preventive reasons, such as regular check-ups?
6. Change in number of visits to Mental Health Center?

The responses are presented in Table 1. Of the 45 women who responded, over half continue to be more physically active than they were before doing the group. Half are more nutrition conscious than before doing the group. Good nutrition was not taught didactically, but was rather experienced on the four day trip. We ate vegetables, rice, beans, pasta, salads, fruit, yogurt, hummus, and whole grain breads. (There were also some *M&Ms* in the trail mix and occasionally at the top of a climb!) Primarily the women experienced how they felt physically and emotionally when they spent an hour doing yoga in the morning, ate well, and were physically active. Of the three who said their eating habits were less healthy, one stated she "went off Weight Watchers," and one was under extreme pressure the year following the group and gained 30 pounds. Over half of those who responded said that they felt healthier.

Almost half the respondents report fewer visits to Group Health for accidents or illness. For an HMO, where visits are prepaid, this is a significant reduction. The area which had the least change was that of visits for preventive care, regular check-ups. Another significant change was the number of visits to the Mental Health Center,

TABLE 1. Changes in Life Style and Health Care

These numbers indicate the number of women who, for example, exercised less than, the same as, or more than they did prior to the adventure group.

	Less	Same	More	No Answer
1. Exercise	2	19	24	0
2. Nutrition	3	19	22	0
3. Feel Healthy	2	18	24	1

These numbers indicate the number of women who had fewer visits for health care, the same number of visits, or more frequent visits than prior to WAG.

	Less	Same	More	No Answer
4. Med. Visits	20	21	1	3
5. Prev. Care	5	33	4	3
6. MH Visits	29	6	6	4

where two-thirds of the respondents decreased their visits, a number stating that they ended therapy altogether. Six increased their number of visits because of decisions to change their life or explore a repressed issue, e.g., a decision to leave a marriage or work on it in marital therapy, a decision to change career direction, a decision to explore sexual preference, or a need to work on past abuse issues. Those who did not respond to the last three questions remarked that they had lost their Group Health coverage. Had the questions been worded more broadly, not referring strictly to Group Health, the answers might have revealed whether their visits to other providers increased or decreased.

On two other questions regarding self-esteem and isolation vs. connection, participants were asked to rate themselves as to how they were before the group, right after, and at present, on a 1-10 scale. Results are tabulated below in Tables 2 and 3.

In both of these questions, 86% of the respondents report positive gain in self-esteem and positive growth in connection with support systems.

The participants' comments provide qualitative data about the long-term results of the experience. A primary result was the bonding that took place among the women. The first three groups were small, and the women wanted to continue adventure experi-

TABLE 2. Changes in Self Esteem

Women rated themselves prior to doing the group, right after the group, and at long-term follow-up (6 months-4 years). Numbers on the left indicate examples of the three ratings on a 1-10 scale with 1 being low self esteem and 10 being high self esteem.

	Number of respondents
Worse right after the group but higher now than before the group; e.g., 5-2-7	4
Higher right after the group, now down but still higher than before the group; e.g., 2-10-8	13
Higher right after the group, continue to maintain or go higher; e.g., 2-8-9	26
No reply	2

TABLE 3. Changes from Isolation Toward Connectedness

Women rated themselves prior to the group, right after the group, and at long-term follow-up (6 months-4 years). Numbers on the left are examples of the three ratings on a 1-10 scale, with one being isolated and 10 being connected.

	Number of respondents
No change; e.g., 8-8-8	1
Negative change right after followed by positive change now; e.g., 4-1-6	1
No change right after, then negative change (due to illness); e.g., 8-8-3	1
Positive change right after, some decrease long term but overall gain; e.g., 2-9-7	12
Positive change after group, continues to maintain or go higher; e.g., 3-5-7	26
No reply	2

ences, including climbing. Leaders developed and this group of women continued to invite women from subsequent groups to join them. Not all of the original women joined, but a substantial number did. They went white water rafting, did a high ropes course, canoed in the Boundary Waters Canoe Area, went biking, had monthly dinners, participated in a Native American sweat lodge, and developed a newsletter. The later groups were larger in size, and preferred to continue meeting with their own group. Some have been more active than others, and there have been subgroups within the groups who have become very close friends. One of the women who didn't like women reported having a positive experience with women and had continued to seek out activities with women. This connection was an unexpected benefit for the woman, but is supported in theory by Ewert and Heywood (1991, p. 598):

A major tenet underlying this study is that natural environment settings such as wilderness . . . areas are effective places for systematic and purposive group development. Initially the participants are a collection of strangers assigned to a series of objectives . . . , but the relatively small number of people, closer physical proximity, frequent and intense interaction often lead to development of primary types of relationships (McGrath, 1984; Vender Zanden, 1987). Through primary relationships an individual experiences warmth, familiarity, and closeness. These types of relationships are usually more valued than secondary relationships in which there is little commitment to or involvement with another person.

They go on to explain that participants are in a new environment with little past experience in such an environment. Old patterns of behavior or relating are not called forth because the situation is new, giving the person the opportunity to develop new patterns. In a rock climbing situation, feedback is immediate, emotions are close to the surface, and misunderstandings have to be worked through. To be belayed today by someone with whom you argued yesterday means that you talked through the issue and moved on.

Another long-term result was a reduction in fear and anxiety. Some of the women attributed this to staying with their fear on the rock, having support and getting through it. Some said the experience opened them up to asking for help, letting other people in, enabling them to do things they were previously afraid of doing. One woman said: "I hadn't anticipated losing a lot of fear–I am much less anxious and fearful than before the rock climb. I feel as if I am peeling off layer after layer of protection and evasions and am getting closer to my core." Some said they were more relaxed and centered because they continued to do yoga regularly. Ewert (1988), in a study of how an Outward Bound experience can reduce anxiety, talks about an inverse relationship between anxiety and self-confidence. He discusses three clinical techniques for reducing anxiety: desensitization, flooding, and modeling. In the climbing experience, the women were introduced gradually to more difficult tasks, beginning with ones that assured success (desensitization). They were encouraged to try more difficult climbs as they progressed, including ones they were not sure they could complete. When they were in a fearful situation (flooding), they were reminded of the skills they had developed, given suggestions for coping, and reminded that they were in charge; they could decide to go up or come down. They also experienced modeling from other participants who got in and out of tight situations, and from the leaders who were willing to model a challenging climb. Mason (1987) talks about the positive use of stress, a concept she calls eustress. We built in this heightened anxiety, producing stress (why rock climb) for a reason.

> The triggered stress, if and when successfully coped with, activates the dormant strengths that go unrecognized and untapped in most individuals. . . . We need eustress to develop a greater capacity for becoming more of who we are. While stress points out weaknesses and vulnerabilities, it also converts them into strengths. When able to face some aspect of their hidden or "dark sides," most individuals deepen their self-acceptance and strengthen themselves. (Mason, 1987, pp. 94-95)

Ewert (1988) suggests that the feelings of competence gained in the outdoor setting by coping successfully with a stressful situation can carry over into everyday life, enabling a person to be effective in new challenges. Some quotes from the women to substantiate this: "The lesson of acting or moving through the fear was essential to my making moves toward divorce that have made my husband and me more honest with each other." "Every so often when I feel a bit tired or afraid of tackling a problem, I remember how it felt to take a step up the rock and be at a totally different place–the feeling is very optimistic and liberating." "I keep a picture of myself on the rock on my refrigerator. I am very proud of my accomplishment."

In summary, WAG has been for many of the women who participated, an ignition experience, an intense encounter with themselves and other women, where they faced issues they had previously avoided and made some decisions. They came to know and accept their bodies more fully, they learned to let other people in, releasing some of the shame which is a legacy of this culture. For some, it was an acknowledgment of their spiritual self, enabling them to view their lives from a new perspective and heal old wounds. Many found support to take new risks amongst the group as it continued; others were ready to let new people or old friends get closer to them. A number of women left abusive relationships or marriages;

others allowed themselves to try a new relationship and become intimate. Some went back to school; one dropped out of graduate school, followed her dream and became a massage therapist. A few got into intense therapy for their marriage or family, or because of childhood abuse now acknowledged. And some go on climbing. Last summer I received a postcard from two women from my first group who had just finished climbing Devil's Tower, a monolith in Wyoming which stands 865 feet in height!

REFERENCES

Anderson, R., & Hopkins, P. (1991). *The feminine face of god.* New York: Bantam Books.

Ewert, A. (1988). Reduction of trait anxiety through participation in Outward Bound. *Leisure Sciences, 10*(2), 107-17.

Ewert, A., & Heywood, J. (1991). Group development in the natural environment. *Environment and Behavior, 23*(5), 592-615.

Kessell, M., Resnick, M., & Blum, R. (1985). Adventure Etc.: Health promotion program for chronically ill and disabled youth. *Journal of Adolescent Health Care, 6*(6), pp. 433-438.

Mason, M.J. (1987). Wilderness family therapy: Experiential dimensions. *Contemporary Family Therapy, 9*(1-2), 90-105.

Mason, M.J. (1991). *Making our lives our own.* New York: Harper Collins Publishers.

McGrath, J. (1984). *Groups: Interaction and performance.* Englewood Cliffs, NJ: Prentice-Hall.

Miles, J. (1986-7). Wilderness as a learning place. *Journal of Environmental Education, 18*(2), 33-40.

Vander Zanden, J. (1987). *Social psychology* (4th ed.). New York: Random House.

So . . .
What Does Rock Climbing Have to Do with Career Planning?

Annette Aubrey
M. J. MacLeod

SUMMARY. This paper reports on the design and operation of a four-day wilderness camp for single mothers on welfare. As participants in a job readiness program, these women are encouraged to challenge themselves physically and psychologically. They are given the opportunity to address their feelings of powerlessness and low self-esteem through participation in such activities as rock climbing, rappelling, problem solving, and a low-ropes course. Themes such as risk-taking, stepping out of one's "comfort zone," trust building, and developing support systems are developed and explored. Client self-reports and facilitator observations suggest that feelings of

Annette Aubrey is a former Coordinator of the Contemporary Woman Project and currently conducts a private counseling practice. She is an associate of the Pacific Center for Leadership where she uses the outdoor environment to provide experiential learning opportunities for various women's groups and corporate clients. She recently completed a Master's degree in Social Work from the University of Calgary. M. J. MacLeod, former Coordinator of the Contemporary Woman Project, has extensive experience teaching life skills and counseling individuals who are experiencing educational and employment barriers. Since her first exposure to wilderness programming she has incorporated these experiences into all subsequent projects. She has a Bachelor of Education in Special Education from the University of Calgary and is currently enrolled in a Master's degree program in Counseling Psychology through Gonzaga University.

[Haworth co-indexing entry note]: "So . . . What Does Rock Climbing Have to Do with Career Planning?" Aubrey, Annette, and M. J. MacLeod. Co-published simultaneously in *Women & Therapy* (The Haworth Press, Inc.) Vol. 15, No. 3/4, 1994, pp. 205-216; and: *Wilderness Therapy for Women: The Power of Adventure* (ed: Ellen Cole, Eve Erdman, and Esther D. Rothblum) The Haworth Press, Inc., 1994, pp. 205-216. Multiple copies of this article/chapter may be purchased from The Haworth Document Delivery Center [1-800-3-HAWORTH; 9:00 a.m. - 5:00 p.m. (EST)].

205

power and achievement emerge in the camp setting. These are often translated into a higher sense of personal worth and efficacy as they develop and begin to implement career goals. The paper concludes with recommendations for research.

INTRODUCTION

Women who support their families on welfare often feel trapped in a cycle of poverty and dependency and see few alternatives. Financial independence is frequently seen as an unattainable goal. At the same time, they are pressured by caseworkers to leave this system. Some seek escape by entering into the "pink collar ghetto," thereby ensuring their dependence on the welfare system. Others find alternative sources of support in marriage or common-law unions, appealing to the "Cinderella Solution" (Miller, 1990).

The Contemporary Woman Project, offered through the Calgary Board of Education's Further Education Department, seeks to assist women in discovering that they do have choices and to gain a sense of personal power. The purpose of this paper is to outline how one component of the Project, the wilderness experience, provides participants with information and experiences that challenge their beliefs about what they are capable of achieving. The women use this information to develop a career plan concomitant with personal values, skills, interests, and income requirements for self-sufficiency. Recommendations for research are discussed in the final section of this paper.

LITERATURE REVIEW

Wilderness challenge programs have gradually gained acceptance in the therapy community during the past two decades. Accepted for many years as a treatment modality with adolescent groups, the popularity of wilderness programs has spread to adult populations, including adult survivors of sexual abuse (Bass & Davis, 1992) and couple and family units (Mason, 1987). Outside of the therapy community, many diverse groups are using a wilderness challenge concept in team building and leadership training endeavors.

While such programming has long been thought to have positive impacts on people, existing research has produced inconclusive results as to the exact nature of these benefits (Talbot & Kaplan, 1986). Much of the research that has been undertaken has been limited to populations of adolescents, making generalization of results to more diverse groups difficult. Noticeably less represented has been research on women's groups in the wilderness. However, the combined weight of evidence gathered from such sources as participants' journals (Talbot & Kaplan, 1986); therapists' structured observations (Davis-Berman & Berman, 1989); client self-reporting (Mason, 1987); and standardized measures lends significant support to using wilderness experiences in a therapeutic context.

Increased self-esteem is the most commonly reported positive change resulting from wilderness challenge programs (Davis-Berman & Berman, 1989; Gillett, Thomas, Skok, & McLaughlin, 1991; Iso-Ahola, LaVerde, & Graefe, 1988; Mason, 1987). Some additional findings have indicated increases in self-efficacy (Davis-Berman & Berman, 1989) and internal locus of control (Marsh, Richards, & Barnes, 1986). Scherl (1989) differentiated between locus of control and self-control, suggesting the latter better characterizes an individual-wilderness relationship. He postulated that the ability to master one's self in relation to the external, uncontrollable environment will bring about increased feelings of confidence which may be generalizable to other situations.

In non-research-oriented literature, Miranda (1985) identified the need for women and girls to find a "space" to be together in nature. Warren (1985) noted the distinct needs women bring to outdoor adventures and called for a new metaphor for outdoor experiences, for both men and women, which emphasizes bonding with the natural world rather than conquering it. Mitten (1985) noted that women experience different socialization than men, and, as a result, have different needs in relation to outdoor programs. She suggested that outdoor programs for women should be based on a philosophy that is both empowering and accepting of their needs for safety,

inclusion, freedom to make choices, and avoidance of a success/
failure paradigm.

PROGRAM DESCRIPTION

The Contemporary Woman Project (CWP) is a ten-week personal development and career planning program for single mothers
on welfare. In a supportive group environment, participants are
given opportunities to identify those personal, relational and societal factors which have contributed to their welfare dependency.
Presented within a feminist framework and using a psychoeduca-
tional model, this program provides participants with opportunities
to build interpersonal and work-related skills. The women also
examine their interests, skills, and abilities in order to begin to
develop a career plan. In addition, regularly scheduled process
group sessions encourage participants to make connections, share
feelings, and work toward integrating new information and experiences into their personal lives. A ten-day job-shadowing experience
and a four-day wilderness camp complement and enhance personal
growth and career planning.

Each Contemporary Woman Project group is comprised of
twenty participants, all of whom are single mothers receiving social
allowance (welfare) benefits. They range in age from 20 to 50, and
on average they have attained an educational level of grade 10.
These women have been assessed as "non-job-ready" by their
caseworkers and are referred to the CWP in order to develop personal, occupational, and/or educational goals. Upon entering the
program the majority report feelings of low self-esteem and powerlessness, with low expectations for change in these areas. A high
percentage of our participants report having been abused as children or involved in abusive relationships as adults, and many have
experienced drug and/or alcohol-related problems. The wilderness
experience was incorporated into the CWP in response to a perceived need to offset self-limiting beliefs and destructive experiences with significant, positive experiences. We believe that accomplishing challenging tasks and learning difficult new skills, all in a
nurturing and supportive environment, allows participants to alter
their perceptions of what is possible for them.

THE WILDERNESS EXPERIENCE

The wilderness experience occurs during the third week of the program and is four days in duration. Participants are taken to an isolated lodge which provides dormitory style sleeping quarters and a kitchen. These facilities ease the adjustment for those group members who are committed city dwellers. Our goal for this component of the program is to provide a safe, supportive, and fun environment wherein participants can meet the following objectives:

a. Experience the positive outcomes of taking risks and attempting new behaviors;
b. Challenge self-perceptions regarding skills, abilities, and personal limitations;
c. Experientially learn effective ways to approach new tasks.

Our desire to attend to our participants' needs for safety and comfort, while at the same time offering valuable learning experiences, is reflected in the program design. The orientation, timing and duration of the experience, and program activities are discussed in detail below.

1. Orientation

A thorough orientation is held one week prior to the actual wilderness experience. Participants are given a detailed description of the site, facilities, activities, and facilitator expectations. They are assured that while they will be expected to accompany the group during all activities, they will maintain the right to choose their level of participation at all times.

An important aspect of the orientation is providing participants with opportunities to voice their hopes, fears, and expectations in order to validate or allay any of their concerns. Few feel unaffected at this point. Our participants have varying degrees of comfort and experience in the outdoors. Many experience great excitement and enthusiasm for the trip, looking forward to adventure and a "holiday." Some are fearful and would prefer not to leave the familiarity and security of their homes and families to participate in such a venture. Some are loath to leave their children, often for the first time. (We have been surprised that most of our participants have been able to find caregivers for their children within their personal support network. However, funding is made available for those who require the services of a homemaker during their absence.) Others resent the fact that their participation in this excursion is a required element of the Contemporary Woman Project. Many ask, "So, what does rock climbing have to do with career planning?" Facilitators take this opportunity to introduce the concept of "comfort zone," suggesting that positive feelings can result from participation in new challenges. Group members are invited to consider stepping out of their comfort zone in the days ahead.

2. Timing and Duration

During the first two weeks of the CWP, group activities focus largely on inclusion. Participants have opportunities to form bonds with each other and find their place in the group. In addition, their comfort levels tend to increase as they develop a rapport with and confidence in the group leaders. Situating the wilderness experience in the third week allows group members to develop and increase feelings of safety and provides containment for feelings of anxiety about the upcoming trip. The four day duration of the trip provides an opportunity for participants to remove themselves completely from their usual responsibilities. This allows them to focus on their experiences, integrate new learning, and reflect upon their application to daily living.

3. Program Activities

The activities planned for the wilderness experience include trust-building exercises, a low-ropes obstacle course, problem-solving tasks, rock climbing, and rappelling.

a. Day One

The program commences with a series of trust building exercises. In small, incremental steps, through physical activities, the women are taught how to ensure and monitor the physical safety of themselves and others. Through these exercises, they build trust to the point where they are able to fall backwards from a short ladder into the arms of their fellow group members.

The low ropes obstacle course (a series of obstacles constructed of rope and wood) invites participants to utilize their bodies in ways they may not have experienced since childhood. They are encouraged to stretch themselves both physically and mentally and, above all, have fun. The obstacles require varying degrees of agility and/or physical ability as well as a willingness to take risks. Participants are not presented with a prescribed method to successfully complete an obstacle; rather, they are encouraged to negotiate each obstacle in ways that feel safe to them, while using whatever physical or emotional support they need from their team members.

b. Day Two

Participants are presented with a series of problem solving tasks. For example, given only a plank, a rope and a reaching device, their task is to retrieve a "pot of gold" from a "toxic waste pit." These tasks provide participants with numerous opportunities to examine their approaches to problem solving. The remainder of this day is spent learning the climbing safety system, how to belay, and the language of climbing. Thus, prior to confronting the rock face, they are not only familiar with the equipment and safety measures, but have begun to develop the skills necessary for a successful experience.

c. Day Three

Upon arrival at the rock climbing site, an orientation is held, safety lines are set, and all participants are given an opportunity to familiarize themselves with a variety of techniques for moving on rock, or "bouldering." Tension is high as they face the greatest risk of the trip.

Participants are encouraged to set personal goals for this day, choose their own level of participation, and make their support needs known to each other. In small teams of three or four, a decision is made as to which task they will first undertake–belaying? . . .

rock climbing? . . . or rappelling?–and . . . who will go first? Ninety percent of the women choose to attempt all of the activities. Only rarely will we hear a comment such as: "I don't care if the meaning of life is up there! I'm not going!"

d. Day Four

The final day is spent processing experiences and developing action plans that are based on new insight and information. Participants are asked to reflect on how they can apply their new learning to their lives at home and in educational and workplace settings. Frequently, the women are very emotional as they realize the magnitude of their experiences.

OUTCOMES

The wilderness experience has been very well accepted by participants. Such adjectives as "exhilarating!", "incredible!", and "fantastic!" have been used by women in evaluating their experience. One woman stated "It was the best experience in all of my life," while others have said, "I learned a lot about myself," "It gave me hope," "I learned how strong I am," and "This should be mandatory for every insecure woman."

Client self-reporting and facilitator observations indicate the objectives we outlined above are met. First, the women experience the positive outcomes of taking risks and attempting new behaviors. The unique nature of the program provides opportunities for these women to attempt new behaviors in a supportive environment. Many of our clients are fearful of attempting new behaviors, given their limited success and/or longevity in the workplace, educational settings, and relationships. Making a decision to accompany the group to camp is a huge risk for some while others feel they haven't risked until they climb or rappel. Participants readily see the link between these experiences and dealing with their fears surrounding returning to school, entering the workplace, or extricating themselves from the welfare system. A successful step out of a comfort zone is usually accompanied by feelings of exhilaration and a sense of greater possibilities: "I overcame a fear that I thought I never would, and now it makes the other things I was afraid of seem not so hard."

Second, the experience challenges self-perceptions regarding skills, abilities, and personal limitations. Many of our clients feel trapped in the welfare system and are overwhelmed by expectations to become financially independent. They often feel "stuck" with their educational levels and previous work histories and have inaccurate views of their personal attributes, skills, and abilities. The wilderness experience serves to challenge these perceptions in a number of ways. These women, particularly those who are obese or have distorted body images, are often amazed that they have the physical ability to complete the tasks. Many are surprised they were able to trust others, and, more importantly, trust themselves. Problem solving tasks provide concrete demonstrations of their skills and abilities in such areas as brainstorming, communicating, collaborating, organizing, and leadership. Many are pleased to find themselves assuming various new roles and feel good when they realize they can make valuable contributions to the group. Rock climbing and rappelling provide opportunities to overcome fears that had previously been paralyzing. Participants subsequently report feeling more confident about meeting other challenges: "If I can rappel down that rock face, I can do anything!" These insights and changes in self-perception have allowed the participants to expand their view of what they can attain. Approximately 70% of the women, most of whom had previously dropped out of school because they were not experiencing success, are now attending upgrading classes, college, university, or are involved in apprenticeship or other training programs.

Third, participants experience effective ways to approach new tasks. Faced with the challenge of leaving the welfare system and becoming financially independent, our clients often have little sense of where to begin. During the wilderness experience they learn that thorough preparation, knowledge of expectations, and acquisition of specific skills aid their ability to proceed with a problem. They also find that such elements as trust, encouragement, support, and the ability to share their needs and ideas facilitates effective problem solving. Through their experience and discussion about working as part of a team they learn that there is more than one "right" way to accomplish a task. Presented with tasks of increasing difficulty throughout the four-day camp, they learn to approach these and other problems by first reducing them into a series of manageable steps. They reflect that completion of less difficult tasks, such as the trust falls and low ropes obstacle course, was necessary before they could approach the tasks of rappelling and rock climbing. Recognition of the link between a step-by-step approach and the manageability of a task serves to decrease their apprehension about their "real-life" challenge of financial independence.

In addition to the individual learning described above, the wilderness experience affects the group process substantially. It serves to complete any unfinished business with regards to inclusion and to move the group well into a working phase. Sometimes, the work that is done is a response to conflicts that inevitably arise in such a setting, and other times, involves processing the day's events and the feelings these events have evoked. In general, we have found that the euphoria connected with successful completion of difficult, new tasks has led to strong group bonding. We have frequently seen a "together we can conquer all" mentality form in the camp setting which is then carried on throughout the remainder of the program.

CONCLUSION

This paper has reported on the design and operation of a four-day wilderness experience for single mothers on welfare. It provides opportunities for participants to engage in a variety of tasks that are both physically and psychologically challenging. Client self-reports and facilitator observations indicate these experiences challenge participants' views of their skills, abilities, and limitations in addition to teaching them new ways to solve problems. Risking and stepping out of one's comfort zone are themes that are developed throughout the camp. Participants are assisted to establish links between their learning in this setting and their "real-life" challenge of achieving financial independence.

IMPLICATIONS FOR RESEARCH

Gender-based socialization has encouraged women to participate in activities that are characterized by passivity, dependence, and low levels of risk in both work and leisure pursuits. More information is needed about the impact that participation in high-risk activities, such as rock climbing and rappelling, has on women's self-perceptions and locus of control.

Super (1984) states, "Those who lack self-esteem are less likely to make good matches between self concept and occupational concept. Similarly, it is difficult to see how people who have unclear self concepts can see themselves adequately in any occupational role" (pp. 227-228). Future longitudinal research should examine whether this type of wilderness experience assists these women to develop a clearer self-concept and whether they subsequently make career choices that are consistent with their self-concept.

A further question involves the cost-effectiveness of wilderness experience programs: Is this program design an efficient method of assisting women to enter into work that is both financially and personally rewarding?

REFERENCES

Bass, E., & Davis, L. (1992). *The courage to heal.* New York: HarperCollins Publishers, Inc.

Davis-Berman, J., & Berman, D. (1989). The wilderness therapy program: An empirical study of its effects with adolescents in an outpatient setting. *Journal of Contemporary Psychotherapy, 19*(4), 271-281.

Gillett, D. P., Thomas, G. P., Skok, R. L., & McLaughlin, T. F. (1991). The effects of wilderness camping and hiking on the self-concept and the environmental attitudes and knowledge of twelfth graders. *The Journal of Environmental Education, 22*(3), 33-44.

Iso-Ahola, S. E., LaVerde, D., & Graefe, A. R. (1988). Perceived competence as a mediator of the relationship between high risk sports participation and self-esteem. *Journal of Leisure Research, 21*(1), 32-39.

Marsh, H. W., Richards, G. E., & Barnes, J. (1986). Multidimensional self-concepts: The effect of participation in an Outward Bound program. *Journal of Personality and Social Psychology, 50*(1), 195-204.

Mason, M. J. (1987). Wilderness family therapy: Experiential dimensions. *Contemporary Family Therapy, 9*(1-2), 90-105.

Miller, D. (1990). *Women and social welfare: A feminist analysis.* New York: Praeger Publishers.

Miranda, W. (1985). "Heading for the hills" and the search for gender solidarity. *Journal of Experiential Education, 8*(2), 6-9.

Mitten, D. (1985). A philosophical basis for a women's outdoor adventure program. *Journal of Experiential Education, 8*(2), 20-24.

Scherl, L. M. (1989). Self in wilderness: Understanding the psychological benefits of individual-wilderness interaction through self-control. *Leisure Sciences, 11*, 123-135.

Super, D. E. (1984). Career and life development. In Brown, D., Brooks, L., & Associates (Eds.). *Career Choice and Development* (pp. 192-234). San Francisco: Jossey-Bass Publishers.

Talbot, J. F., & Kaplan, S. (1986). Perspectives on wilderness: Re-examining the value of extended wilderness experiences. *Journal of Environmental Psychology, 6*, 177-188.

Warren, K. (1985). Women's outdoor adventures: Myth and reality. *Journal of Experiential Education, 8*(2), 10-14.

VOICES OF EXPERIENCE: PERSONAL NARRATIVES

When I Reach the Place I'm Goin', I Will Surely Know My Way

Lauren Crux

SUMMARY. This is a story of love and courage. As the author describes some of her most memorable experiences while traveling on the first all women's raft trip down the Grand Canyon in 1978, we learn how her love for the outdoors inspires and informs her sense of courage. She learns that courage can be gentle and "quiet" or boisterous and "noisy." She describes how the exigencies of river life require that women learn to cooperate and work together despite discord and differences, and how working together results in an increased sense of competency, self-esteem, and power.

I have a photograph of our faces: six women, ranging in age from mid-twenties to mid-fifties, our sun-weathered skin taut with con-

Lauren Crux works as a licensed psychotherapist and consultant in Santa Cruz, CA. She has presented nationally and internationally on the topics of lesbians in mid-life, women and courage, and most recently, the creative process.

[Haworth co-indexing entry note]: "When I Reach the Place I'm Goin', I Will Surely Know My Way." Crux, Lauren. Co-published simultaneously in *Women & Therapy* (The Haworth Press, Inc.) Vol. 15, No. 3/4, 1994, pp. 217-227; and: *Wilderness Therapy for Women: The Power of Adventure* (ed: Ellen Cole, Eve Erdman, and Esther D. Rothblum) The Haworth Press, Inc., 1994, pp. 217-227. Multiple copies of this article/chapter may be purchased from The Haworth Document Delivery Center [1-800-3-HAWORTH; 9:00 a.m. - 5:00 p.m. (EST)].

centration and fear. One woman holds a finger to her mouth, her teeth ready to clamp down. It was the first all women's trip down the Grand Canyon, 1978 (Galland, 1980), and this was the last rapid, Lava Falls, notoriously dangerous. The water drops thirty-seven feet, and on the Deseret Scale of 1-10, which rates the difficulty of river rapids, Lava is rated a ten. Barbara, our guide, told us to fill the paddle boat partially full of water to give it more stability. When she shouted "Drop" we would dive to the bottom of the raft and stay there until we plunged over the edge. She repeated the instructions, then added, "Once we go over, in case I get knocked out, you'll know when to sit up and paddle when you feel the wave hit, it will be unmistakable." "No matter what," she repeated, "keep the boat straight . . ."

* * *

I don't know how it happened. It puzzles me that from my earliest memories I wanted to be outdoors. I think it was that first tent my father pitched in the back yard one summer. Or the trips to the woods, learning to shoot a rifle, hunting tin cans. And then there were the occasional weeks at the dude ranch, rowing boats, riding horses, pretending I was "Jim," or Roy Rogers, budding baby dyke that I was. Whatever it was, it didn't happen to my sister. She is mostly city and somehow I came out sort of country and definitely a dyke, much to my mother's dismay and my father's initial contempt. My mother tried dolls and permanents to stem the tide, but she also let me sleep in my cowboy boots. Whatever it was, I preferred fishing to shopping, playing football to playing house.

My first backpacking trip in my early twenties should have cured me of any romanticism left over from childhood dude ranches and backyard tents. I had forsaken athletics for the academic life and was not in any kind of shape to speak of. My boots were new and did not fit properly. My feet blistered within the first few hours of a week-long trip. I had altitude sickness. We had no ground pads and couldn't sleep at night from the discomfort. We were caught in a three-day rain storm, pinned inside a plastic tube tent open on both ends. The food, Lipton freeze-dried soups and dessert puddings, was disgusting. And my knees were inflamed and wretched with pain from the strain of hiking. But you know, I loved it.

Other than in my imagination, I had never been in uncultivated land at all. It did not seem wild as the term is often misused—meaning strange, dangerous, something to be tamed or conquered. It was, instead, intensely inviting, thrilling—landscape so vast, skies so huge, that at last I felt this was home, what home should be. The water in the Sierras was clean; there was no giardia. I could drink safely from any stream, something that is only a memory now. The mountains were uncrowded—we hiked for days seeing only two others. The wildflowers stood up to my knees, abundant. There was an ease to the lake water, the meander, the brown trout resting in their cool dark holes.

I keep being called to the outdoors. It's always been that way. If I spend too much time at home a longing starts up and I have to get out—get myself dirty and sweaty and climb some hills, swim some lakes, sit and stare at clouds, revel in wildflowers. It sets my spirit right.

Knowing this, it should come as no surprise that when I heard an announcement about the first all women's raft trip forming to go down the Grand Canyon, my hand shot up before I could even think—*Yes, sign me up.* It didn't matter that I had never been river rafting. I had been swimming since the age of three, loved water, loved to surf; river-rafting ought to be fun. But beyond fun, I knew I *had* to go. It is almost impossible to explain this kind of know-ing—an instantaneous *I must do this.* The voice of the unconscious, of the gods? Regardless, the authority this knowing voice carries is unmistakable.

"People die on that river every year," friends cautioned, and then asked if I had my will made out. Well, yes I had a will, and I assured them, that if I died doing something I wanted to do, it would be a good death. I was not going on this trip to kill myself. I was going to find out something about living.

There are many things a trip down a river of this magnitude can teach you, depending on what needs to be learned. Carol, intensely self-sufficient, who had never been dependent on anyone, severely sprained her ankle and had to rely on all of us to lift and carry her, to look after her. Laree's husband of thirty years had just walked out on her. She considered suicide but decided to try this trip instead, despite the fact that she was in her fifties and had never done anything in the outdoors. She soon discovered herself as physically courageous and a lover of rivers and canyons. Not all the learnings were precipitated by misfortune. Sue, a professor of geology, known affectionately as Dr. Sue, was fulfilling a life-long dream. She would give us inspired informal lectures about the landscape and the geology of the canyon, and at every opportunity was crawling over the rocks with an infectious sense of wonder, exclaiming, "Look at this"; and "Oh, look at *that!*"

There were many opportunities to learn courage or to be reminded of what we already had. The basic instructions for heading into a rapid were: "Brace, lean forward into the waves, use the paddle in the waves to balance, don't fall back, and whatever you do, don't stop paddling." For the more difficult rapids, Barbara, our guide and coach added, "Paddle as if your life depends on it."

We had to stay focused and rely on coordinated teamwork. If someone went overboard, we were taught to ignore our instincts to reach for her, endangering the entire boat. Instead, we kept paddling; we'd pick her up once we were through the rapid. "If you go out, swim away from the boat, keep your feet headed downstream, and always, always, hold on to your paddle." Whining and whimpering, taking a time-out, hesitating, waiting, grandstanding–simply would not do. There was no time to be depressed. If you were feeling hostile, needy, or irritable, you had best get over it quickly. Facing a series of thundering, heaving rapids can set your priorities clear. *Ya wanna live, sweetheart? Then keep paddling.*

Of course there was some strife on this trip: some of us were too hot, or didn't like the food, or were frightened by the rapids. Some hated being outdoors and dirty. Some missed being with men. Some had never traveled with open and out lesbians. But when we were paddling, the river demanded that we overcome those differences. Fear is a great motivator and when we headed into 20-foot standing waves, five of them in a row, we learned to cooperate and even to get along. Meaning is created and destroyed and created continually. An outdoor trip of this kind brings to the surface quickly a person's questions, her fears, her anchors, her frailties, her strengths. There was no hiding. I grew to care deeply for the women I paddled with–I entrusted my life to them.

Midway through the trip, we took a day off to rest and swim in the pools that gather below Havasu Falls. The water in these pools is unlike the Colorado, which tends to run a dirty brown color and is shockingly cold since it has been dammed. Havasu runs freely and so the color is unsullied, the temperature warm. Azure, aquamarine, turquoise–I felt my eyes soften taking it all in. I swam and dipped, and jumped off of high boulders into deep pools, and then found a quiet place to lie back and take it all in. Few women have the opportunity to choose adventure; I was relishing my good fortune.

A little while into my reverie, two of our river guides, Louise and Suzanne, wandered by and invited me to join them and another trip member, Barbara, to explore a nearby cave behind Beaver Falls. Louise told us that there was an entrance to the cave through an underwater tunnel and the cave itself sat somewhere behind the fall's 50-foot drop. Although she had never been there before, she had good directions and a mask to help her find the opening. Did we want to go? No one else had taken them up on this offer.

I have been swimming since the age of three and have a great sense of ease and comfort in a watery environment. By contrast, I intensely dislike spelunking. I do not like to crawl through little tunnels underground and find no pleasure sitting around in tight small places under the earth. The last time I went caving, I had a full blown panic attack and vowed I would never again go willingly into a small underground cave.

But I would follow Louise anywhere. She was one of the most competent women I had ever met. A tall sinewy woman, knife strapped to her waist, clever, stronger than most, she could guide a boat with seeming ease through the toughest rapids, weave a good story, keep an eye on everyone, and tell you anything you wanted to know about the canyon and the river.

I also liked Suzanne a lot. A little bit bad, her spirit was like the wild mane of red hair she never tied down, and she loved to play. So, when she and Louise invited me to go exploring with them, I momentarily forgot that I hated caving. You see, I had learned to like adventures and this was sure to be one.

Barbara, the fourth in our party, was fun-loving, fast-spoken, and had a raucous sense of humor. Early on in the trip she had spent one evening giving me a foot rub, extolling the virtues of massaging the big toe, the one she called the sex toe. She insisted that if you rubbed it enough, it would awaken sexual desire. She rubbed and rubbed, all the while asking me if I "felt it yet," much to my delight and the hilarity of the other lesbians on the trip. That foot rub was quite an ice-breaker and she and I became friends and buddies.

This was our group then—four spirited adventurers, looking for something special. Louise donned the diving mask and went looking for the tunnel entrance. I began to feel a little afraid, Barbara too, but Suzanne kept reassuring us. After much dipping and diving, Louise found what she had been looking for. The entrance to the tunnel was about three feet underwater behind a small log. Wasting no time she moved the log, then told us what she had been told: the tunnel, the diameter of which was very narrow, just shoulder width actually, was about five or six feet long. There was supposed to be air inside the cave once you made it through the tunnel. She could hold her breath for a minute and if she didn't make it through by then, she would wiggle her feet and we were to grab her and yank her back out to safety. If she made it through, Louise would stick a hand back inside the tunnel and the next person would enter, arms forward and outstretched and be guided and pulled to safety by her.

She made it—at least her feet disappeared. There was no denying it, I was afraid and voted to go last. Suzanne went next, then it was Barbara's turn. She was afraid now, too, and quipped, "But I have three kids," and then, "Oh hell, here goes my love life," which was her way of saying that she hoped she didn't die. I didn't want to die either, but that was the risk ultimately. That five feet of tunnel, underwater, so narrow my shoulders touched the sides, was a challenge. I held my breath and went for it, saying a prayer that harked back to early childhood. I didn't bargain with God, but came close. As soon as I felt Barbara's hands grab mine and pull, I knew it was going to be OK. Another quick prayer and hugs all around, we gathered ourselves in waist deep water inside a small dark cave that did not seem worth the trouble. "This is it?" I asked disappointedly. "No," Louise replied, gesturing, "we follow this part along until we come to the real thing." And off she went, our fearless leader.

Crouched, we stepped carefully along a narrow corridor. After a few minutes I heard Louise say, "This is it." Then silence. One by one each woman clambered up a ledge in front of us and stepped through a small arched opening. I was last. I could hear the hushed silence, feel an intensity that drew me through the opening into the chamber beyond.

I still do not know the technical description of where I was and what I saw. I will give you a lay person's view. The outer room we had just left was altogether uninspiring–some dark rock, a few slimy things. This room in which I now sat was a place of stunning beauty and something much much more. We all felt it. Our silence was awe-inspired, reverential. Willa Cather referred to times like this as a miracle, "one of those quiet moments that clutch the heart, and take more courage than the noisy, excited passages in life" (Cather, 1977, p. 331).

Before us was a circular pool of water, glowing a mystical turquoise color. I could see clearly far down to the bottom. Because we sat in darkness, the pool was an offering not only of color and beauty, but also of life itself, the possibilities. There was just enough ledge space for us to sit huddled around the pool. The waterfall fell just on the outside of the cave wall to my left. The illumination entered through an underwater archway which opened to the larger pool on the outside, and flooded our pool with light. With the mask, I dove down and could see water churning as the waterfall outside spilled and crashed. Inside, all was tranquil and hushed. The earth was showing us her underbelly, and it was stunning.

Time hovered around us, lengthening, lingering, suspended. Eternity, a moment–all the same. Timeless time. Only our bodies shivering brought us to voice. It was bitterly cold and we had on no clothes. One cannot hold on to an epiphany, we would have to leave, to let go and remember.

We decided to dive down and out under the waterfall, rather than return the way we had come. This would be dangerous in a different way. The dive down was about eight or ten feet. We did not know how powerful was the waterfall or the current we would enter. It could catch us in a whirlpool and drag us under again, or the current could drag us over the outer travertine ledge, which was sharp and ragged. Again, Louise's courage led us on. She would wear the mask, dive under and try it. If she was successful, we would follow. She cautioned us to stay to the left, so we would not get caught in the waterfall's sucking current. "OK," we all said. Louise dove down and out.

She had disappeared from sight before the obvious struck any of us: we had no way to know if she had made it, if it were safe or not. Furthermore, she had the only mask. Despite our uneasiness, we had a good laugh at ourselves, then were serious. It was time for courage once again.

Feeling a little braver, this time I went second, but I lingered just a moment. I wanted the last few remaining seconds to say goodbye, to say thank you. My lungs full, down I dove, lingering even then, looking at the bottom of the pool, at all the plants and rocks that lay there. And then the effort—strong strokes, quick kicks to swim past the waterfall to safety. Caught by the current, I shot into the middle of the pool outside, but swam quickly and easily to shore. There I joined Louise on shore and sat on a rock waiting for the others. They each popped out, one after the other, and joined us. It was an adventure short in duration and huge in intensity. We hugged and whooped and cheered ourselves. Told our story over and over to all the other travelers, as many times as they would listen.

The story I didn't tell at that time, because I had no words for it, was that in the cave I had encountered something I had been looking for, without knowing it. I understood in the first gasp upon seeing the translucent waters—my moment of quiet courage—that all life is infused with the spirit of strength and beauty I found there. I knew then that nature is not something separate and apart; I was *a part of* nature, not *in* it. I recognized that sometimes I have to take risks to find that place of wonder where the sacred and the erotic entwine. The ancients called the Grand Canyon, the "birth canal of the universe." They knew, as I came to know, that it was sacred space. I had discovered and swum into that which is precious to me (Susan Griffin, personal communication, 1981).

From the sacred to the mundane; life was simple. From my journal:

> *A few rules: Pee in the river, shit in the can. Watch out for pink rattlers, scorpions, tarantulas, red ants, eddies, and holes. Beware too much sun, too little salt, too little water intake. Don't grab the oars to get up. Swim away from the boat. Tie all*

three ties on your life jacket (the woman who drowned last year forgot to tie hers). Tie your jacket down when you leave the boat and never use it as a pillow. Always wear your shoes.

Look for: a billion years of twisting, turning, churning, burning. See the shelves, shifts, cliffs, dikes, red walls, granite and gray glistening exfoliating rock. See the ripple marks, fossils, ancient ruins, caves, salt mines. Gaze at the waterfalls, blue herons, carp, trout. Play in the red mud, scoop up handfuls, throw it at one another, paint faces, bodies. Listen to the song of the canyon wrens–three notes descending, the distant sound of the rapid, that grows louder, louder. Feel the heat deep into your bones, the cold wet of the rain, the furnace blast of the upstream wind. Shiver as the rushing chill of the river water floods over you.

The Colorado flows on carrying us with it, teaching us new ways to live, to think, to feel. It is all so simple. Few clothes. No clothes. A blanket on soft sand at night. Meteor showers and heat lightning every evening. Up at six, on the river at seven. Everything is slowing down.

As we drew near to the "slot," the smooth channel of water free of rocks and obstacles that would soon suck us over, the sound of the rapids increased frighteningly. From a far off rumble it became a devouring roar. We all were silent, afraid, I could feel my heart pumping hard against my life jacket, my hands were sweaty. I sat on the left front, my pal, Nell, a big glorious dyke of a woman, sat on the right. The tongue pulled us slowly into her grinding mouth.

We lined ourselves up carefully, Barb said "Dig," the command to paddle hard, and we headed straight over the edge. Then Barb yelled, "Drop." Down I went to the bottom of the boat and the next thing I remember is feeling something hit us with the intensity of a head-on car crash. That was our cue to sit up and start paddling. We were heading backwards into a huge wave and Nell was down, sloshing in the bottom of the boat. I screamed at her, "Stay in." I kept paddling. I didn't know who was left in the boat. One person kept yelling "Paddle, paddle," so I knew there were at least three of us. But Barb was clearly not giving directions. The raft turned sideways to the next wave–the most dangerous situation we could be in–then tipped up on edge. "Oh shit," was all I remember saying.

My side of the boat was headed into the wave. I arched back and out over the edge of the boat, as I had learned to do sailing, only this time, there was nothing to hold on to, no line to grab. Counterbalancing, I did my part to keep us from flipping. I screamed at Nell, who struggled at my feet, still unable to regain her seat. "Stay in here." Nell, who even in extreme adversity kept her humor, shouted back in her best Georgian drawl, "Well honey, I'm trying."

The other voice continued to yell, "Paddle, paddle." I yelled to straighten it out, but at this point it was only wishful thinking. The next wave slammed into our side. I leaned out and into the wave, again acting as ballast, a ferocity of will surging through me. I wanted to live, I wanted to stay in that boat more than I've ever wanted anything.

Then suddenly, it was all over. We made it. We didn't flip. Nell regained her seat, we were past the rapid and I looked around. Barb, our guide, was missing, and China, one of the other trip members, was also missing. They both had gone out upon first impact. We looked back and could see them speeding towards us, feet downstream. We picked up China first, hauling her in quickly. She was shaken; it had been her worst fear to go out in this rapid. On Barbara's face as she came hurtling down the rapid towards us, I saw fear and something else. When we hauled her in, the first thing she did was yell at China, who apparently at first impact had grabbed Barb, pulling them both overboard. Barb was furious, an anger sparked by intense fear. Once again, our frailties surfaced and once again, the spirit of the river required that we face our furies and continue to work together. Barb recovered quickly as the need for immediate teamwork was required. The boat had taken on so much additional water, that we were in danger of sinking. No time yet to celebrate, we paddled hard over to an eddy and bailed furiously. Then we had to paddle across the river, no small effort, to pick up a life-jacket one of the snout boats had lost.

Our chores finally over, we made our way to the shore and safety. As we pulled up to the lunch spot where the snout boats waited, we raised our paddles in salute while we were cheered and photographed. Nell snatched up an unopened can of beer that had followed us down the rapids, detritus from some other rafters, and I popped it open, pouring it like champagne over the head of our already drenched coach. We were heroes, euphoric with our accomplishment.

One of my outdoor adventure teachers once told me that the difference between an adventure and a suicide is that the adventurer always leaves herself a margin of escape. Our margin of escape was that we were well trained, we had a guide who was highly skilled, and we had intense desire. Until this moment, I had not realized the power of desire in my life. To want something so strongly that I would give it everything I had was not a familiar experience. I was used to hiding a little, holding back. What a relief to let it rip and discover emotional muscle I never knew I had.

The Irish poet, A.E., once said, "Keep in your soul some images of magnificence . . ." (Henderson, 1985, p. 41). I struggle often with self-doubt, fear, insecurity, yet I continue to have my brave moments. The Grand Canyon trip was an important marker in my life. It was there that I learned that "courage is just as infectious as fear." I notice that every year, I get a little braver. Age and experience and desire all come together and the pot gets stirred. I continue to return to the outdoors to renew and refresh my spirit. I never forget what the Canyon taught me, about quiet courage, about excited and noisy courage. About magnificence.

REFERENCES

Cather, W. (1977). *My Antonia.* Boston: Houghton Mifflin Co.

Galland, C. (1980). *Women in the wilderness.* San Francisco: Harper & Row.

Henderson, Joseph L. (1985). The four eagle feathers. In *A testament to the wilderness: Ten essays on an address by C.A. Meier* (pp. 37-44). Santa Monica: The Lapis Press.

Climbing for My Life

Molly Gierasch

SUMMARY. As a woman in my 50th year, as a psychotherapist, a mother, a lesbian, I look back over my years as a technical rock climber. Returning to rock climbing after a 15 year break, I climb now in a new way and only with other women. Here I describe the experience of climbing, and the fulfillment and joy it can bring. I discuss the challenge of being an older woman beginning a sport that is associated with youth and can be risky. I discuss the importance of passionate play within women's lives and its therapeutic value.

In a few months I will be 50 years old. I'm a woman. I'm a lesbian. I'm a psychotherapist. My 18-year-old daughter is leaving home in one month. My periods completely stopped four months ago, one month after I ended an eight-year relationship. For the last several weeks, I have had many hot flashes (power surges?) day and night and I am experiencing menopausal-related insomnia. This has made it nearly impossible to write this article. I am normally a good sleeper and am sure I will be again, but in the meantime I am having to learn what I need to do to stay grounded enough to complete everyday tasks. Needless to say, it appears that I am going through a major life transition.

I'm a rock climber and, more recently, have become a white

Molly Gierasch is a feminist lesbian psychotherapist in Boulder, CO. She is in private practice with a collective called the Women's Institute of Boulder. She received her PhD from Union Institute in Feminist Studies and Psychology.

[Haworth co-indexing entry note]: "Climbing for My Life." Gierasch, Molly. Co-published simultaneously in *Women & Therapy* (The Haworth Press, Inc.) Vol. 15, No. 3/4, 1994, pp. 229-234; and: *Wilderness Therapy for Women: The Power of Adventure* (ed: Ellen Cole, Eve Erdman, and Esther D. Rothblum) The Haworth Press, Inc., 1994, pp. 229-234. Multiple copies of this article/chapter may be purchased from The Haworth Document Delivery Center [1-800-3-HAWORTH; 9:00 a.m. - 5:00 p.m. (EST)].

water kayaker. In my late twenties, because my husband wanted me to, I began to climb. Terribly fearful of heights, I was dragged up the rocks for a couple of years and only gradually did I find small amounts of joy in getting to the top. Then I had a baby, divorced, came out, got a PhD, and four years ago–having climbed only a half dozen times in the previous fifteen years–I returned to this sport in a new way. I am older now and mentally I am very different. Now I climb only with other women and only for fun.

Why do I climb? I can vividly remember a moment last September in Yosemite when I was looking down at Celia. I had found her name in the directory from the Stonewall Climbers' Newsletter, a national newsletter for gay and lesbian rock climbers. I called her after I had impulsively planned a long weekend trip to the rock climber's paradise, Yosemite Valley. In this moment, I am balanced on a small hold with my left foot. The side of my right foot, with knee bent awkwardly, is on a smooth, slight indentation. Hopefully, the friction between my shoe and the rock will be enough to keep me from slipping. Both my hands are holding onto minuscule crystals by the fingertips. As I look down, the heat rises off the almost white granite and I glimpse El Capitan in the distance. Other granite monoliths encircle the valley. What am I doing here? "Celia," I say, "Why am I doing this?" She says, "You're doing great! Go for it!" I only met Celia the day before and she is half my age, but she understands my slightly hysterical question. When climbing, many moments contain that question and the shriek that accompanies it. Climbing also offers surprising gifts that keep us coming back and moving up these rocks.

I have just clipped my rope through a carabineer attached to a bolt drilled into the rock face. On this climb, there are bolts every 15 feet drilled into the white/grey rock slab. These bolts protect my potential 30-foot fall. The guidebook says not to trust them. They are merely concrete expansion bolts that may have been improperly placed by beginners. They may pull out or snap off easily. I'm not feeling very scared. I should be, but I'm having a good day. Yesterday, Celia wasn't scared and I was. Today, I'm not. This climb is harder than any I have previously led. In my head, there is an ongoing debate. Should I go on? Am I strong enough? Is this truly as stupid as it seems? Who do I think I am, anyhow?

I think I see a grain of crystallized rock for my left foot. These holds! I can't even see them unless I am very close. My foot sort of finds it and then my hands move, then my other foot. Every move here must be very slow and deliberate or I will fall. As the distance grows between me and my last protection, fear flits around the periphery of my mind. I cannot surrender to it or to the "what if?" thoughts. There is only me, my hands, my feet, the rock, the movement of my body. A grey and red beetle crawls past my right hand. Okay. Keep moving. A lizard scoots and darts past, daring me to follow. And I do. This is the most difficult stretch of the climb. The sun on my back, shoulders, and arms is white light. The air here is clear, dry, and hot. I am an ant on a massive pile of slick edged boulders. I continue the slow dance, breathing evenly while my heart races. I clip into four more bolts. After what seems like a very long time, I am at the top. With a sigh, I carefully tie in to an anchor before I yell "Off belay, Celia. I did it!" She whoops in return and gets ready to follow up. While I belay Celia, the debate in my mind dies and is replaced by a deep sense of self-satisfaction. I did it! Yes! Right-on, Molly! You're not too old, after all!

As usual, after a climb, I felt a deep sense of accomplishment. From the rocks I take into my life enthusiasm, strength, and connection. When I climb with another woman, I am putting my life in her hands. I have to trust her completely and vice versa. On that day with Celia, we had gotten to know each other carefully. We questioned each other about safety, about climbing ethics, and we repeatedly checked each other's use of equipment. By the end of several days climbing together, we had begun a friendship and had learned we could depend on each other's judgment. These kinds of experiences carry over into the rest of my life. When I work with clients who climb or engage in wilderness activities, I encourage them to do as much as possible with other women. Then I see strength, connection, and joy blossom in their lives.

That climb in Yosemite was six months ago. Today, after leading up an exquisite route on the Rincon wall in Eldorado Canyon, outside of Boulder, I sit in the sun, belaying my friend Marilyn, and reflecting. I feel united with myself. As a child and adolescent, I was a frustrated adventurer. In the 1950s, there was little support in eastern Massachusetts for girls who wanted to act like "Indian braves." I did not know any women then who pursued wilderness activities or strenuous, risky sports. Even in my 20s, there were very few women on the rocks. Until I began to climb again, I did not meet any middle-aged or older women who engaged in such craziness. Rock climbing? And then, kayaking?

When I began to climb again I was in my mid-forties. My lover had been sick with chronic fatigue syndrome for two years and I had lost a good part of myself in her illness. I was depressed and feeling hopeless. I was experiencing the mood swings that often come in pre-menopausal years. And I was aging. I remember having to give myself pep talks. Yes, Molly, you can go out and do this even if most of the other people doing it are young and most are men.

It took me a while to find a woman with whom to climb. Finally, a friend introduced me to Marilyn, another psychotherapist, who was recently separated from her husband who had been her climbing partner for five years. She was a good climber but did not have any confidence in leading. Her ex-husband had discouraged her and had always led the climbs himself. He did not teach her the technical skills necessary to lead and he undermined her with criticism the few times she tried. Unfortunately, hers is not an uncommon story. She remained dependent on him and anxious about her own abilities. Marilyn and I both needed support and gave it freely. She now knows she can lead and I know I can climb no matter how old I get.

Climbing brought my life back. I climbed better than I had 15 years before. I could think more clearly and I had learned how to work with fear. I was easy on myself, and Marilyn and I were both very careful about safety. We were supportive of each other. I began to grow in confidence and felt lighter emotionally. I felt nourished by the time playing in rocks, trees, and sunshine. Play had been missing from my life for too long.

I'm an adult woman and have been married and raised a child. I am a therapist and I hear people's pain. I have known times when my view of the world became colored by too much hurt. I am a feminist and I know the realities and struggles women have in this world. I remember when I was ten, I told my mother I did not want to be eleven, I did not want to grow up, I did not want to get married, and I did not want to have children. Then I stomped off and went to play at the claypit at the edge of the woods. The

Benjamin boys and I climbed cliffs, shimmied up trees, and played cowboys and Indians with their pet black angus calf. I did not know that grownups, especially grownup women, could go out and play. When I was in college, play seemed to become associated with alcohol. And it did seem that grownups played and got silly only when they drank. That may not be true for everyone, but it seemed that way for me. Then, gradually, life became a serious thing. Just like for my parents.

The men I have known always did sports. Sports, I thought, were a serious endeavor. Mountain climbers, in particular, did major expeditions and appeared in *National Geographic*. Now I think men do sports primarily to have fun. How did I miss that? Somehow that message never came through. I have kept in shape by running since my late twenties and have done yoga for a long time. For me, both running and yoga are work, but I do them in order to be healthy so that I can enjoy my life and do the things I want to do. I like to hike, bicycle, and backpack. But I *love* to climb and kayak. To these, I bring passion. I believe all women need to have passionate play that suits their own particular natures. When I was growing up, such an idea would have been absurd. Luckily, things are changing. On her car, my daughter, an avid snowboarder, has a bumper sticker that says, "Hell bent for leisure." "Yes," I tell her. "Go for it!"

A couple of years ago, I decided to take up white water kayaking. I wrestled with the aging issue again. Kayaking seemed scary. Everyone I mentioned it to discouraged me. "Kayaking?" "Getting your head stuck upside down underwater?" "Maybe if you were younger." "Why not rafting?" they said. "Boring," I said. I decided that if it was too hard I could always stay in very easy rivers. I went for it. After a few months of taking classes and participating in Colorado White Water Association trips, I began to meet a few other women who liked to boat with women. Now, most weekends and on vacations, I go out and play with my women friends. I am nurtured by the water, the rocks, and the women. I am now not the oldest woman climber or kayaker I know. I am having a very good time.

Having a good time carries over. I believe I do better work these days, am able to be more present, and hopeful within myself. I can be more emotionally available for my friends. I enjoy my alone time much more than I used to. I heal more quickly from the traumas of life. I feel balanced.

As I sit on this rock waiting for Marilyn to reach the ledge, I think about how special it is that I am able to do this. Women, at least white women, have more permission and opportunity to have wilderness experiences now than they used to. They still are usually introduced to these activities by men. This is changing as women are bringing each other out as adventurers. I now know a few women of color who climb. They are lesbians and have already broken major rules of their culture. Once we stray from the paths society prescribes for us, it is easier to risk straying even further. But I also think the sense of internal privilege that results from growing up middle or upper class makes it easier to pursue wilderness sports. And, of course, having access, enough money, and leisure time are necessary.

Young women are finding their ways onto the rocks and the rivers. I want to encourage women who are in their 40s, 50s, and more to do the same. You don't have to be a jock. You just have to "wanna have fun."

Until fairly recently, it was generally believed that women could not climb as well as men, could not hold their own on demanding routes up the rock. There are women now disproving that myth daily. Today there are women who climb at all levels of ability including those doing first ascents on impossible peaks.

A thunderhead is moving in; I hear a rumble in the distance. A flower growing from a crack in the red rock begins to sway as the wind picks up. A grey cloud covers the sun and in the shade the colors deepen. Black streaks from dripping water decorate the rosy cliff above. The air is turning chilly. In a few minutes it is going to rain. After Marilyn reaches the ledge, we move to a large, safe space beneath the overhanging rocks where we coil the rope. As the storm moves in, we begin the downclimb and the hike to the car. My face is wet and cool, flowers glisten along the trail, and the air smells clean. My leg muscles are tired in a pleasant, danced out way. The moment is perfect.

After the Next Full Moon

Connor Sauer

SUMMARY. The wilderness, love and respect for nature, women's spirituality, and the challenge of new experiences are the basis for creating all-women river trips through the Grand Canyon. They are an opportunity for women to commune with each other, be physically active all day, discover new skills and strengths, create meaningful ceremonies, develop strong bonds, and be close to nature. There are distinct, wondrous, and life-changing shifts in an individual's psyche that occur when faced with the unknown possibilities inherent in wilderness experiences. The grandeur of the canyon walls and the power of the river serve as keys, opening places in the human heart another human cannot open. Sharing that opening together in the Grand Canyon, as women, each of us bestowed with the honor of unbounded love and support, we marvelled with an unshakable reverence for the tenacity of nature.

One by one the women walked to the front of the rolling bus, turned, and faced the rest of us. I listened to them speaking, laughing, and crying, and through the windows dusty hogans, brittle dried sage bushes, and sharp rising cliffs flickered by. Thoughts of woman's abundant moisture and dry desert expanse settled into my psyche. We would not be the same women after the next full moon.

Connor Sauer studies and teaches in the field of spiritual healing and creative expression. She works with movement and dance, voice, energy patterning, drums, wilderness trips, sweatlodge, ceremony, women's circles and blood mysteries. She travels and teaches throughout the United States and Canada, hosting workshops entitled AS A WOMAN; UNFOLDING THE GIFTS.

[Haworth co-indexing entry note]: "After the Next Full Moon." Sauer, Connor. Co-published simultaneously in *Women & Therapy* (The Haworth Press, Inc.) Vol. 15, No. 3/4, 1994, pp. 235-242; and: *Wilderness Therapy for Women: The Power of Adventure* (ed: Ellen Cole, Eve Erdman, and Esther D. Rothblum) The Haworth Press, Inc., 1994, pp. 235-242. Multiple copies of this article/chapter may be purchased from The Haworth Document Delivery Center [1-800-3-HAWORTH; 9:00 a.m. - 5:00 p.m. (EST)].

This circle of women had been gathering and preparing for this journey, THE REMEMBERED GATE, for close to one and a half years. At a surface glance, we appeared to be a collection of white, middle class, excited tourists about to run the Colorado River through the Grand Canyon. Welling up beneath the thin veil of skin and voice was the deep resource of experience each woman brought with her, and a remembered gate each would step through in our being together.

We were women who were daughters, sisters, and mothers. Married to men, with lesbian partners, single, white, mixed Cherokee, East Indian, Tlinqit and Yaqui heritage, women of wealthy and modest means, from cities and rural land, well known and not known by the world, of many ages and several generations. Some of us were survivors of incest and rape, abortions and miscarriages, one of us had taken a life in self-defense, all of us had lost beloveds to death. We were career women, homemakers, long and short limbed, heavy and thin, of many religious and spiritual practices. Our humor was as present as any grief. We were women. Inside the Canyon we would slice clear down to the bones together, and sing spirit into the marrow of The Great New Myth. We would cry for a precious, intelligent, instinctual, and authentic vision of the world in which we longed to live, as individuals and as a collective.

At Lee's Ferry, the launching point, we sat under a cluster of Tamarisk trees, the sand warm, Apache Cicadas buzzing, our boat-women giving river safety instructions. As gracefully as someone offering a hand for a dance, Karen, one of our guides, lifted Betty from sitting and walked her across our circle. Looking to the vacant spot, we became breathless and still as a rattlesnake slithered her way across the sand behind our group. What an omen. Our guides knew we would respond well to the unusual, our drummers and spirit journeyers knew there would be shedding of the old, a rising of the creative, and deep change. Shortly after, we pushed six oar-powered rafts off the shore, each of us snug in our lifejackets, and began a descent into the womb of the great Mother Earth.

At the beginning, the river and land were wide and open. Rusty colored rock and clay rippled through layers of the stately Vermillion Cliffs. Ocean green water swirled around river rocks, sucking at the surface. In quiet moments we could hear oars dipping, groaning, and drizzling. In gusty moments wind whistled in our ears, blocking out all other sounds. This canyon and river have become lover, awakener, transformer, trickster, and soul-tracker to many people over the years. The earth opens her belly wide here, beckoning initiation into instinct, trust, courage, wholeness, and irreverent humor. We slipped into her yawning openness.

Women who row boats in the bottom of the Canyon are extraordinary. The finesse, courage, humility, and trust required for this ability is astonishing to witness. Rowing a boat here is a long-term vision quest for those whose hearts have been stolen by the sacred wilderness. The Canyon is a cathedral that creation offered long before our own footsteps were dreamed. Sensing a spiritual umbilical cord between all living things on our Earth is inescapable here, unless you are asleep to life. The deep, vital richness of communion in this way rippled in the bodies, rang in the voices, and breathed in the magnetism of our guides. Eyes would constantly move, taking in the details of place, reading water, noting rock formations, animals and birds, position of people and items on the boat. Arms would row for hours, hands checking gear, passing things from the bow to the stern. Laughter and stories were always present. Without even knowing it, they were the essence of Artemis alive in her element. As the main contact with the river company, I had asked Ruthie to organize and lead our guides. Watching her grow from a determined teenager into a focused and mature leader had been thrilling to watch over the years. Here she was in her greatness, making room for all the other guides to be in theirs. Together they rowed the rest of us into discovering parts of our own.

The passengers brought these women guides the remarkability of Woman in all her guises, with a fierce desire to overcome fear, experience the wildness of self-acceptance, the unknown, and taste the wilderness of the Earth's bounty. We would share community, drums, silk veils, eager hands, silvery voices, and a circle of being that encompassed us all as related. In our hearts we stood witness for all women, everywhere, in all times, longing to bring humankind to its sensibilities and sanctity. We wove a textured vessel that held initiate and initiator as reflections of each other in newness. Each of us came with as much of ourselves as we knew, committed.

The first morning that we awoke on the river was a poignant

ceremonial opening. It began in the slim light of dawn, the hiss and flare of propane stoves striking the bottoms of porcelain coffee and tea pots. Our camp became an anthill of activity. Women in the Canyon for the first time scrambled and looked. We all ate breakfast, sorted gear for both hot weather and cold water, and packed everything else in a waterproof dry bag. Waking up in the morning, listening to the call of the Canyon Wren, feeling soft sand shift beneath me, and watching sunlight creep down the rock walls, is ecstacy closest to my soul. We gathered on the beach for morning announcements and our trip blessing ceremony. Standing in a circle, holding hands and looking at each other, it was quiet. We could almost hear the pounding of hearts.

Four women's prayers sang out, calling and welcoming the directions, the winds and their Keepers. Each of us bathed, one by one, in the rolling smoke of smouldering sage, fanned in a small abalone shell. Those of us familiar with this ceremony welcomed with grins and tears those who trusted themselves enough to enter this ceremony for the first time. We all were standing at different gates of beginning, vulnerability, and challenge. With the smudge, we stepped in to face our danger and our ecstacy with resolve, tenacity, joy and humor. After our prayer circle we moved as an undulating wave down to the boats. Each boatwoman stood on the seat of her ship and faced us. Susan walked to the water like one having walked to the Euphrates many times long ago, and knelt, her fingers gently skimming the skin of the river. She gave thanks for our safety, offering our respect, honor, and gratitude for being there. Each boat was welcomed, her boatwoman acknowledged and thanked. We sang our closing prayers, emotionally bonded through ceremony, feeling prepared. The final tear-blurred silence was broken by "Let's load 'em up!"

That day brought a deepening bond that would serve as the foundation for our way of discovery as a community. Just below mile 20 we beached the boats above North Canyon rapids. Ann, who was my partner in the vision and production of this trip, Ruthie, and I, had decided North Canyon would be a phenomenal first hike. Before launching, we had asked for group agreement in trusting decisions that might have to be made without group discussion, based on expertise and knowledge, or necessity of timing. Functioning in expedition behavior, this was one of those decisions.

Billie, one of our Crones, an elder sister who has gone through menopause, had never done any serious hiking and was fearful about heights and her ability to complete the hike. As Keeper of the Drum for her women's community Drum Circle, she felt it imperative that she do this hike. Graceful, feminine, with salt and pepper hair tucked under a hat, she marked the rise of the Goddess for many of us. Everyone supported Billie's decision, and agreed to help.

Our destination of desire was a small rock amphitheater that framed a smooth, womb-like rock wash, over which water had trickled endlessly, carving a deep standing pool. Being there provides the feeling of Source, of woman's part in creation, and the femaleness of the Earth.

Witnessing and participating in this jaunt brought recognitions and realizations. We watched each other trust decisions made on our behalf. We addressed our fear with a desire to step into it, and found the support we needed. We took turns leading and following, offering hands and taking them. We walked in silence and erupted in laughter. We shared what we noticed about the canyon and took in what others shared. Some of us bounded quickly up the canyon, then waited to give a hand at tough corners. Some of us sat down, letting others disappear around the bend, drinking in the momentary expanse of being alone in an overwhelming setting. It was as though we were becoming our original selves, the consciousness that is alive to the moment, acting upon what only that moment calls out to be done. We were slowing down into ancient rhythms.

At the pool we gathered, facing the rock wash. The last footsteps crunching on gravel faded away, our breathing became filled with deep sighs, our nostrils with the scent of water and moist earth. Diana's sweet, high voice began drifting through our theatre in song, Sarah's deeper one joined in like the drone of a drum. One by one everyone's voices opened up. We became a choir. Those of us new to each other began to feel familiar. It was a long while before we rose to go. The return was a pilgrimage from a holy shrine.

Each day brought an unfolding of challenges and discoveries. Together, we encouraged each other to try something new, break a taboo, let go of a belief, lighten up, learn, face a danger, be honest, laugh at ourselves, be fierce, and have humility. We marvelled at each other's beauty and strength, coupled with vulnerability and shadow. Whatever dogma each of us might have carried to the Canyon was gracefully hoisted aside for the sake of possibility, and given up to the best of our abilities. Other than what we chose to share in brief biographies before the trip, two-thirds of the women knew little or nothing about each other, and for the most part it didn't matter. We were choosing to come together as women, as human beings, finding the common denominators of connection and celebrating our diversity. We called out to each other in ways unimaginable in other circumstances, marking what I call the wilderness of the soul, the place of original and authentic being.

Every bend in the river unfolded a plethora of experiences and stories. Being in a different boat with different women kept our learning and exploring always alive with newness. Being in a boat with an old friend carried our comfort forward into unknown territory. With each mile of water, more of the next layer of rock formation revealed itself, as did our inner being. We were reminded that down in the bedrock, carved deeply by flash floods, relentless scorching heat, gnawing winds, timeless water and waiting, bounty grew, adapting itself to circumstance.

Two weeks of living in the moment, in community, provides a wealth of images and layering of experiences. In the Canyon, unlike any other place I've been, there is a rawness of soft sensuality mixed with the hardness of endurance. It is nature's mix. Simultaneously we responded to the river, rocks, animals, elements, other women, our bodies, emotions, and perceptions. It was life on the edge, feeling like a hollow reed, with nature somehow cleaning house and building nests at the same time inside our individual reeds. Each day flinted another chip from our emerging soul jewels.

On day hikes in side canyons we would scramble over rocks, our hands and feet searching for holds. Standing under pounding waterfalls, scalps and skin came alive all the way to the tips of nipples, goosebumps erupting in the cold all along our limbs. Some of us would cram together on ledges underneath the falls, shouting and laughing, our bodies electric with cold water and the warmth of each other. When we could, we would leap into pools below, completely letting go in those airborne seconds. When we couldn't, we would swim, float, splash and play, like sea otters momentarily discovering new water.

We bathed in the river, naked and adventuresome. We serenaded those in the camp kitchen with drums and singing. Gathering in small groups, lounging on the sand or our bedrolls, we told stories of the day. There were back rub lines in the evening, and hair-braiding ones in the morning. Kem and Betty gave back adjustments and energy alignments. Muffy would appear and disappear, photographing poignant moments of each of us. At night, near and on the full moon, we wrapped sarongs and veils around us, slipped into a skirt or leggings, and called the moon up. We made music with drums, rattles, water jugs, sticks, and tambourines. We sang rounds and solos, Katie and Diana melting our ears with harmonies. We danced with bells on our ankles and drums strapped between our legs. It was undeniably the rites of all women. It was auspicious to the remembering of Woman.

Not drinking enough water created disorientation and weakness. Wanting to stay in one place for a while, instead of being daily gypsies, pressed in at moments of deep conversation over coffee and tea, lying in a warm shallow streambed, or snuggling in a quiet nook journaling. On days of the big rapids, we approached morning prayers differently. Each of us stepped into the largest and most powerful place we had available inside. Many had to stretch farther, pushing through terror.

Standing on ledges and hillsides, we often spent long hours studying rapids, water levels, currents, holes, snags, and eddies. Under intense sun, we listened to the pounding of massive rolls of water grinding; we felt fear mingled with unprecedented surges of anticipation and excitement.

As we floated into the rapids, hunkered down and holding on, everything became sharply focused. Each time we crossed the edges of the v-wave at the top into the frothy churning, everything surrendered to the river and its forces. Nothing existed except the roar of the river, the shifting of our weight into waves breaking over the boat, split second instinct, and trust in the benevolence of Spirit. The power of being in "the zone" is unsurpassable.

To all of this, we brought the mark of our humanness into the realm of the sublime with our ceremonies. We spoke our hearts in circle below the Anasazi ruins at Nankoweap. We acknowledged our blood mysteries above Salt Creek. The full moon was celebrated near Blacktail Canyon, and we journeyed with the animals at Stone Creek. The passing of beloved friends Georgie, Sandy, and Fred were honored below Lava Falls. Our last night together as full crew, dressed in our river-exotic best, we did a giveaway ceremony. Each of us came away with a treasure from someone else to remind us of the depth of our connections. We drummed and danced ourselves to empty that night. The full moon had passed. We came home changed. At takeout, Diamond Creek, we unstrapped frames, washed, carried, and deflated our river ships. Our joy and pleasure ran abreast sorrow at our completion and parting. We closed the doors of our vans, and were gone from the river.

A New Generation of Women
in the Wilderness

China Galland

SUMMARY. This article presents the author's personal account of
her experience as a mentor for several young women who participated in a group independent study entitled "Women in the Wilderness." The young women's difficulty re-entering society after their
profoundly transformational experience in the Sierra backcountry is
told from the point of view of China Galland, a seasoned wilderness
educator and guide. This article is excerpted from a non-fiction
work-in-progress, *Running Wild.*

I warmed with the steepness of the ascent up the trail. It was
September, 1992. I was hiking alone through forest up to Wawona
Falls in Yosemite National Park, California. When I first set out at
6:30 a.m., the sun was still coming up, the sky was a clear manga-
nese blue and the air crisp and cold. It was a trail I'd never been on
before. My red wool hat was too hot to wear now. I jammed it in my

China Galland is the author of *Women in the Wilderness* and *Longing for
Darkness: Tara and the Black Madonna,* as well as Research Associate at the
Center for Women and Religion, the Graduate Images of Divinity Research
Project. She has worked as a university lecturer and wilderness guide and is a
long-time student of Buddhism, Christianity, and other comparative religions. She
organized the first adult women's Outward Bound course in 1974, and co-founded
the organization Women in the Wilderness in 1975. Her fiction has won awards
from the California Arts Council.

[Haworth co-indexing entry note]: "A New Generation of Women in the Wilderness." Galland,
China. Co-published simultaneously in *Women & Therapy* (The Haworth Press, Inc.) Vol. 15, No. 3/4,
1994, pp. 243-258; and: *Wilderness Therapy for Women: The Power of Adventure* (ed: Ellen Cole, Eve
Erdman, and Esther D. Rothblum) The Haworth Press, Inc., 1994, pp. 243-258. Multiple copies of this
article/chapter may be purchased from The Haworth Document Delivery Center [1-800-3-HAWORTH;
9:00 a.m. - 5:00 p.m. (EST)].

243

pocket, then began pulling off my blue neck scarf. Next came the green sweatshirt, leaving only a light turquoise capilene cold-weather shell underneath. For the moment I was finally comfortable and walked on, tying the t-shirt around my waist, the neck scarf and hat skewered into the knot, walking faster now, feeling calmed by the exertion, the smell of the pine forest and the sight of manzanita, its gray bark curling, the dull red silky wood glowing underneath. Greetings! I thought as I walked past the manzanita, its presence in the Sierra landscape as familiar as an old friend. But soon the capilene was damp with perspiration from the climb and I took it off, too, adding it to the growing pile around my waist. I was finally down to my bra. Taking a look around, still not seeing a soul in sight, I unsnapped it, pulled it off and stuffed it into my waist pile. The prayer beads around my neck rolled free now, swinging gently back and forth across my breasts and set my nipples softly abuzz as I walked on, the air soft and cool on my warm, damp skin.

Just as I started up the trail again, the sun came up above the granite ridge in front of me, bathing me in a stream of warmth and in the fullness of early morning sunlight. Instinctively my voice rose up to greet the light and called out aloud, "Yes!" Then again, "Yes!" saying it to the sun, to the dusty trail, to the ponderosa pine, to the manzanita, to the mountain, to myself, and to Claudine Perrault, Denise Cavitt, Marlene Krouk, Terry Ellis, Didi Tergesen, and Andrea Luchese, the six young women in the camp below from Prescott College in Arizona who were completing a course of independent study, Women in the Wilderness, in the Sierra backcountry. The course culminated in the completion of a three-week wilderness expedition together and an ascent of Mount Whitney, a 14,400 foot peak.

The warmth of the sun grew and widened across the dry, dusty trail. Suddenly I remembered why I had driven 250 miles to be with these young women. I broke into a run, calling out silently now to myself, "Yes!" Their request that I be their mentor for the independent study course they created had been an enormous gift. I had written the book *Women in the Wilderness* in 1980, but I resigned from running wilderness trips in 1985 to write full time. I thought I'd left that part of my life behind. Now, in the exertion of running up the trail, I saw that in answering their call back to the subject of women and wildness, these young women were giving me back a part of myself that I had left behind so gradually that I hadn't noticed that it was gone–a sense of confidence and physical well-being. This morning in the mountains running, hot and wild, was giving me the chance to acknowledge once again that I have a body, a woman's body, an opportunity to remember that I can have confidence in this body, and that I can find joy in this woman's body that for so long I had feared, hated, rejected, that I had sought to escape, to disguise, to forget, to leave behind, or to ignore.

I had arrived at Yosemite and found the Wawona campground the night before. I had agreed to meet the Women in the Wilderness group from Prescott for dinner at the cabin of a friend of Denise Cavitt's. Mealtime came and went. About 10 p.m. the phone finally rang. It was Denise.

"Is everyone all right?" I asked immediately.

"No," Denise said. "I mean yes, we're all right."

"Did you make it to the top of Whitney?"

"No, we didn't climb Whitney," she replied. "Plans changed. Tell you about it later. We've just had a hard day coming out of the mountains doing things like getting in cars–what are these things?–being in traffic, going grocery shopping, being around other people. It's like landing on Mars. Everything seems very strange. We've got a lot of processing to do. We're in a kind of shock. Don't feel like you have to wait up for us. We'll talk tomorrow. It may be closer to midnight before we get to Wawona. I'm not sure where we are."

Karl, Denise's friend, and I looked at each other, puzzled, shrugged our shoulders and helped ourselves to the spaghetti dinner he'd been keeping warm. It was drying out despite the tin foil over the top. We laughed when I told him how I'd been imagining the group making it to the top of Mt. Whitney on my drive to Yosemite. I had envisioned them on a snowy peak yelling into the wind, all six of them, wild with exhilaration, jumping up and down, hugging each other, nearly breathless in an exhausted, raucous joy after the last push to the top. They looked sunburned and strong. Karl had simply expected half a dozen or so people for dinner at 6 p.m. and cooked accordingly.

Within an hour of Denise's call, the group rolled into the campground. I was happy to see them safe, no matter what their state of mind. We hugged and chatted briefly. There was mention of something about Andrea's foot, about her having an injury, as we dragged our sleeping bags and gear into the nearby empty cabin Karl had saved for our group.

Now it's after my morning run up the trail to the Falls and I'm sitting outside writing in my journal at a chipped, green painted table. A pickup truck at the other end of the campground takes off in a growl of backfires and sputters. The noise fades. Quiet settles in again. My thighs and calfs are twitching softly from the unaccustomed exertion of hiking and running at 7,000 feet. I live at sea level. I bask in this bright morning, happy to sit and wait for the group to gather, and look forward to finding out what happened.

The breakfast crew calls out the back screen door of our cabin with a shout, "breakfast in ten minutes." Terry's just back from her morning run; Didi, from her first bike ride in weeks. Marlene gets off the pay phone outside, having finally gotten through to her boyfriend in Arizona. Andrea and Claudine are on breakfast duty. Denise sits quietly on the floor of the cabin writing in her journal. I line up behind Terry for the shower, washing and changing quickly into clean clothes. The sleeping bags we'd laid out across the living room floor in single file last night have been put away and the space cleared. Claudine slices fresh fruit for breakfast and the hot water comes to a boil with a loud whistle in the kettle as we line up to take our dishes.

"There's soy milk and three kinds of cereal on the table. Help yourself," Andrea announces as Claudine pulls a second basket of fresh strawberries out of the refrigerator to add to the table and kicks the refrigerator door shut with her foot. I stop to dig the bananas out of the bottom of a groceries bag and add them to the feast laid out before us on the checkered table cloth. We help ourselves to the food and then gather in a circle on the floor to sit in silence momentarily, bless the food, and then begin our meal.

After eating, dishes are put to the side, and cups of hot tea, cocoa or coffee are refilled. Then we go around in a circle, giving each woman a chance to speak without interruption. Claudine grabs a pillow, stuffs it under her chin, and stretches out across the rug propped up on her elbows, her face in her hands. Marna, the name

Marlene prefers, sits on a foam pad with her back against an outside door. Everyone makes themselves comfortable on the floor with the various foam pads and pillows around. As we begin to speak, the warm enthusiasm I had felt on the trail earlier begins to dissipate. Terry sits cross-legged on the floor next to me, pulled back slightly from the rest of the circle.

"We broke up our life in the mountains for this?" she wonders aloud, running her hands through her short brown hair, her hazel eyes troubled, as she speaks. Terry is tall, quiet, intense and very self-sufficient. Her brow furrows, her eyes moisten. "Cars, traffic, grocery stores, bars and Burger Kings? School? I have to talk about what happened in the wilderness? What happened is so much bigger than an independent study project. It wasn't about school. It was about life . . . I don't *begin* to have the words to talk about it. I just want to go back. That's all I know. The mountains are where I can be myself. Saying goodbye to the mountains was the hardest thing I can remember doing in a long time. Coming out. I didn't want to do it. I wasn't ready. It was the first time in so long that I felt safe, like the child inside me could come out. Leaving the mountains meant leaving her there. I don't know how to bring her, that part of myself, into this reality. It's not safe here," she said in a low voice, her eyes downcast, staring at the carpet.

At the beginning of the summer when Terry was working as an instructor at the North Carolina Outward Bound School, her final course was a group of teenage boys, ages 14-16. Terry was the only woman on the trip and she was the lead instructor. The first night in camp the boys informed Terry that since she was the only girl around, they were going to have to rape her. "Just a joke," they said. Terry blew up. There were no more such remarks made. But her experience in this all-women's group over the past three weeks was all the more healing in contrast to teenage male company she'd had on her last Outward Bound course. It had been a balm on the wounds a woman's body had cost her.

We continue around the circle. Didi sits across from me in a red t-shirt and black cotton shorts. A disarmingly small, white-blonde haired, blue-eyed woman of 5'3", it's as though Didi's size makes her all the more determined to be a strong outdoors woman. She seems to be in a state of mourning or shock similar to Terry's. Didi had come to the women's expedition straight from a summer job with a rafting company in the midwest. She had her fill of being periodically harassed by male guides and beer-drinking passengers. She had spent a lot of time rebuffing uninvited male approaches, so much so that she had nearly quit the job altogether. She was consistently having to stand her ground single-handedly. Finally, she was able to establish a few friendships with understanding people, men included, that allowed her to finish out the summer. The contrast with her summer job made her experience of this all-women's group that much stronger. Though Didi is a senior due to graduate in June, 1993, she, too, questions returning from the wilderness. To what is she returning? Why not live in the mountains? The world she saw when the group began their drive out of the mountains to Wawona yesterday made no sense.

Re-entry, coming back into "the world," was proving to be a painful experience. As we continue around in the circle, it becomes clear that Terry's and Didi's feelings are shared to varying degrees of intensity by others.

I remind them about Alexandra David-Neel, the remarkable early twentieth century French traveler and Buddhist scholar, whom I feature in a chapter in the *Women in the Wilderness* book. David-Neel had mentioned stories of nomadic bands of women living high up in the Himalayas. It was not unheard of for women to live together as mountain nomads, at least in other countries, especially if they were nuns or yoginis living in spiritual communities. Buddhist cultures would be one place to look. Undoubtedly there were others. We have documents of women travelers that go as far back to the fourth century of the common era (Robinson, 1990).

"Quit school if you want. It's your choice," I am surprised to hear myself saying. I'm not sure that Prescott College would consider this good mentoring on my part. "Please remember that you don't have to go back to school. Maybe it is too soon, maybe you're not ready. Only you know. It's up to you."

I back up and stop. I try to approach their sense of loss from another direction.

"If you choose to go back to school, please make it a conscious choice to do so and don't return only because it was planned or expected. We are not prisoners of our own lives. This is a choice to be made."

The mythic journey tells us that the return to the community is fraught with difficulties. From his life-long study of world mythologies, Joseph Campbell put it well: it's easy enough to go off on a quest, to have adventures, but to return—well, that's another story. What has been gained can still be lost at this point. In the mythic journey of the hero, the purpose of answering the call to adventure is to win the elixir of life, the Grail Cup, for example. But the purpose of such an elixir is to renew the life of the community, to save it, thereby regenerating and renewing the Great Round of Life. The return is the final test in the mythic quest, I assure them. In mythology, there is often a battle at the threshold before one can return to the world of the larger community. Many who depart on a quest never return. But for those who are able to return, the reward can be the enlightening experience of discovering that the human and the divine, the conscious and the unconscious, the wilderness and civilization, are but forgotten dimensions of one another. They are not separate spheres, but each is contained within the other. In mythology, the hero's reward is to be able to go back and forth between the worlds and know them as one.

Everyone listened politely and respectfully to my words. After all, they had asked me to be their mentor. They could hardly object, but suddenly I feel foolish, my words sound hollow and abstract, even to myself. I had lapsed into a lecture. Their polite silence tells me that my lecture isn't working. They are still on the other side of the threshold.

Increasingly uncomfortable, I struggle for words to assuage the sorrow that I can see they feel. I tell them about a time of sleeping alone high on a ledge on the side of a butte inside the Grand Canyon and being called back to my group the next morning, far below. I did not want to go, I dreaded it. I wanted only coyotes and cactus for companions, not people. I want to convince them that I understand, but do I? Other moments come back as they resume talking.

I recall for them my first trip to Nepal as a single mother of three young children. The Nepalese people were astonishingly gentle and gracious. They included their children in their way of life. I found the contrast with American life startling and painful. Yet I was relieved to discover a culture where children were genuinely valued, despite the terrible poverty and diseases prevalent there. I had experienced first-hand how vicious, hostile, and impoverished American culture can be for children despite our affluence and all the talk about "family values." I, too, had asked the question these young women are now facing: Why go back into American society?

I stop talking. I am at a loss as to how much to support their feelings about not returning to school. If I take a position and advocate going back to school as planned, I sense that I might be betraying them as their mentor. Perhaps Didi's and Terry's instinct to stay in the mountains is precisely what's called for now. This is not what I thought mentoring was about. I am discovering my place in this group by what it is not, the *via negativa*. Though I have experiences to share, and though they might be similar, what's most important is their experience, not mine. Rather than try to convince them that my experiences are similar, I need to listen for the ways in which our experiences are different.

Suddenly I see that I am the student, the one who needs to learn. The task, no matter what my role might be called, is simply to be present and to listen. I have no answers. Further, I can trust these women's own wisdom. It brought them this far, so much further than I was at their age. They will find their own answers. We continue around the circle.

"Can you see it?" Denise asks me with a shy smile now, pulling back her curly blond hair from her forehead, pointing to a pale crescent moon still faintly visible. She explains that she read *The Mists of Avalon* (Bradley, 1982) over the summer and had been captivated by hearing the Grail legend and stories of Guinevere and King Arthur from a woman's perspective. Didi read it over the summer, too. Terry had read the book years prior, in fact, almost everyone in the group had read it. I had never finished it and didn't remember much about it, it was so long ago, so I couldn't understand the connection Denise was trying to make for me in pointing to the moon on her forehead.

Denise explains that all the priestesses of Avalon wore crescent moons on their foreheads, from the Lady of the Lake, to Morgaine, down to the prophet Raven. In honor of September's vernal equinox and the sense of sacredness the Women in the Wilderness group was experiencing together, they painted small blue crescent moons on each other's foreheads and hiked that morning of the equinox in silence.

Painting moons on each other's foreheads, marking each other in this way and then walking over the mountain pass that morning in silence, inspired them to continue painting moons on their foreheads every day thereafter. It became a daily ritual. Word traveled up and down the trail. Other hikers good-humoredly called them the High Priestesses of the High Sierras. Depending on the mood and the person they were painting, they experimented with different colors. Some moons were red, some brown, green, yellow or purple, imagination was the only limit. By the time I am meeting with them in Wawona, their moons no longer need to be painted on, the sun has tanned their faces so around their crescents.

Andrea's turn in the circle comes around. She tells the story of how she had sprained her foot on the expedition, the same one that she had injured working at the Voyager Outward Bound School earlier in the summer. Andrea's injury in the first few days of the trip combined with the surprise departure of another woman who had been a seventh member, forced the group to reconnoiter and review their route and goals for the trip. The beginning of their trip had been further complicated by Denise's absence because of a last-minute work conflict. Denise didn't meet up with them until Day 7 of the expedition, when she brought in their resupply and joined them.

The group had originally been composed of eight women when I met with them in April. One dropped out shortly before the expedition started. Another left after the group set out on the trail, Andrea reported without a trace of judgement. Weight had to be redistributed so packs became heavier than planned. Terry accompanied the woman who was leaving back to her car at the trailhead. To allow Terry to move quickly to catch up with the group, some of Terry's pack was redistributed, too. In addition to losing time over the loss of a member, the extra weight slowed the group further.

In the push to meet up with Terry the next day, Andrea sprained her ankle. Then the bulk of Andrea's pack had to be redistributed as well. By the time Terry rejoined the group and Denise arrived with the food for resupply, it was clear that their itinerary had to change.

Andrea did not want to leave the group, despite the pain she was in, nor did anyone want her to leave if she felt she could go on without further hurting herself. Losing one more group member threatened to dissolve the group altogether. Andrea felt that she could continue with a lightened pack and a slower pace, but to make it to Mt. Whitney under the circumstances meant the group would have to hike from dawn to dusk, every day. It became clear that no plan was going to match everyone's needs and goals, individually, or collectively. There were feelings on both sides of the issue–to push on despite the difficulties or to hike fewer miles and give up the goal of reaching the top of Mount Whitney. Whitney was a great symbol to the group, and letting go of reaching it was a difficult conclusion, arrived at with reluctance. Yet it was clear that more people's needs could be met and more of the group goals fulfilled if they let go of Whitney.

Sitting on the back porch of Arlene Blum's house in Berkeley in 1979, after the expedition Arlene had organized, the first American Women's Himalayan Expedition, had made a successful ascent of Annapurna in 1978 and became mountaineering history, I will never forget Arlene's words. Arlene had followed the model of pushing on no matter what the obstacle or how extraordinary the difficulty. The Annapurna expedition reached the peak, and Arlene paid the dearest price, the loss of two of her friends' lives. Arlene was devasted and told me flatly, "no mountain is worth a life."

These young women had made a quieter, less dramatic choice. Their decision gave me a chance to examine and begin to loosen yet another knot in my own psyche, my own drive to go for the peak, regardless of the price. They had chosen each other and the particular set of circumstances they'd been given to deal with, rather than the abstraction of a mountain peak. Didi adds that losing a member and Andrea's injury gave her an opportunity to observe her own tendency to take on extra responsibilities, no matter how large a burden she is already carrying. It was typical of her need to be a superwoman and made her exhausted and sad when she realized it. Once she realized this, she was more able to establish her own pace, to slow down, to not have to carry the biggest burden. Several of the young women struggle with this "superwoman syndrome," as Terry calls it. I share it, too, I realize, in my unconscious longing for them to have made the ascent of Whitney–regardless of the consequences.

Now it's Claudine's turn to talk. She sits up, her thick dark hair bobbing as she starts to talk, but she stops. Her dark eyes flash and moisten. Her smile fades suddenly. Before breakfast she was cheerful, even singing, but now a wave of feelings breaks over her. Suddenly she feels vulnerable, angry, and unfocused, she says. "Not now. Maybe later. I just can't talk now." We move on.

Mama is quiet, too, and not yet ready to talk. I'm not sure what to do next. I have never worked with a group like this. I've come to Wawona with a list of exercises and ideas to help them through this transition, but no one is interested in what I have to offer, at least not this morning. I have brought three and four-foot wide rolls of drawing paper, oil pastels, acrylics, watercolors, and brushes for them to draw maps of their journey. They know that I have some understanding of the power and intensity of a wilderness experience. I want them to have a container for these experiences. I've seen people ignore their own key experiences or dissipate the power of it in small talk upon return to everyday life, thus losing or hiding from what is most valuable in their own experience. Something primitive gets touched in wild places. It's unsettling, can hit a nerve and leave one raw and unprotected. I make another suggestion for a group exercise. They say no. I read from a book on spirituality. More polite reserve.

Finally, Mama reacts and announces that she's about to bolt out the door. Her voice is low and cracks as she tells me that I remind her of her mother. I frighten her.

"I can't see you, China. I know you're not my mother, but I see her face, not yours. I feel like a terrified child. I know this isn't rational, but it's the truth. I just need to be quiet and to concentrate on breathing. I know this will pass. Please understand. I have to say this out loud so that I can stay here and not get up and run out of the room."

She's caught me by complete surprise. I don't know what to say. I can't take her mother's mask off my face. Only she can do that and she knows it. The little I know of Mama's story gives me a willingness to be guided by her through this moment. She is extraordinarily aware of her own process. She's had to be. Though I know something about her struggle, I know little about Mama's relationship with her mother other than the fact that Mama loves her very much. My preparations, earnestness and plans are useless to me now. Someone else begins to talk, but I am distracted. Yet before long, Mama announces that she's ready to talk and to be part of the group again. The projection has passed. I am relieved to hear that she sees me as myself again, not as her mother. My heart goes out to this young woman who's battled demons I've never dreamed of.

Mama celebrated her twenty-second birthday in January, 1992, nine months prior to the trip. At sixteen, Mama had been diagnosed with aplastic anemia and given three to five years to live. Living to this past January of 1992 meant beating the prognosis of her death. She had lived a year beyond all medical predictions and at that 22nd marker, her world began to explode. She gave herself a "re-birthday" party. Suddenly she wasn't going to die, she had a life to live. The doctors concurred, Mama is in remission from aplastic anemia, a rare and remarkable occurrence. There is no cure for this disease. In aplastic anemia, the stem cells in the bone marrow don't produce red blood cells, white cells, or platelets. The disease is chronic, and most often fatal.

Because of her condition, one of the biggest challenges for Mama on the expedition had been discriminating between the symptoms of a relapse of her disease and the normal signs of strenuous physical exertion such as shortness of breath and rapid heartbeat. In her situation, the signs of illness and health mimicked one another. She had been relieved not to hike up to Whitney. Each pass she hiked over had been a Mt. Whitney for her.

We broke for lunch well after noon. The maps I had wanted the group to do would be put off until tomorrow, if they were to be done at all. I walk outside for some time alone under the trees. Three women stay inside organizing lunch. Sitting outside, away from everyone, I realize that everyone in the group has been living in the midst of an intensive group process for the last three weeks. They're asking for time alone with me, one on one. They need to be seen and heard as individuals, to tell their own particular story of the expedition. There is a larger wisdom here to guide me if I will let go of plans. I finally understand. After lunch, we begin the individual meetings to review student's learning contracts. Time stretches out like a cat in the afternoon sun, relaxed.

Evening comes. As I met with women over the afternoon, others had gone off and begun to draw maps of their journey. Now everyone wants to do them. We have tomorrow to continue with interviews and maps.

After supper this evening, they read to me from their group journal, each person taking a different day to read aloud. I read from the intermittent entries in my journal about them, from those moments when I had been thinking about them in the mountains. Images overlap. Once I had wakened at 4 a.m. and gone outside thinking about them sleeping in the mountains. The night was clear enough to find the Pleiades, one of my favorite constellations. They had noted the Pleiades, the Seven Sisters, that same night in the group journal. There are six women in the group. My presence makes the seventh. A sense of synchronicity grows.

Our individual meetings continue throughout the next day. I sit in the sun at the picnic table between our cabin and the next, taking a short break between each student. Though we call our meetings a de-briefing, as the stories unfold it is evident that topics they had thought to focus on and to write about had paled before the magnitude of their experience in the wilderness. Women's spirituality, the uses of ritual, the natural history of Yosemite, the psychology of food, the relationship of various emotional states to body image, the recovery process, just to mention a few of the topics for study, quickly receded as academic subjects in the face of experience. Rituals had arisen spontaneously, the landscape of the Sierras was suffused with spirit, natural history was a source of wonder. An encounter with a deer was an epiphany or kensho experience, depending on what tradition one views it from. How can these moments they share from their journals undergo academic scrutiny and evaluation, they wonder aloud to me. I can see that what's happened between them and the wilderness goes far beyond any academic framework. Their ties are with each other and the mountains.

Witnesses for one another, day after day, they heard each other into being like Aborigines singing up the land down under. Story after story emerged from each person, set off by the intensity of the encounter between wild places and the wildness of the deepest self within. The quiet of the mountains allowed tears to surface. Underground springs began to flow. Memories from childhood, like deer startled out of tall grasses, leapt out unexpectedly into full communal view. They had begun to view their lives from within this tiny community forged in the wilderness. In this moment, they had each become a window from which they could look out upon their lives in solidarity. In the face of the various difficulties, misunderstandings, and conflicts, all of which arose, they continually chose tolerance, love, and acceptance of one another, time after time, making themselves a community of sisters, a shelter for each other. I am honored to see them so revealed.

For each of them, the idea of leaving Yosemite, breaking up this nomadic community, and driving back to school in Prescott, is bittersweet and ironic. I am charged with the complicated task of helping them re-enter a world that is no longer familiar, but there is little I can do. I can only witness their difficulty. I had no idea that being a mentor could be so hard and so simple.

Now comes our third day, and the day we are to leave Wawona. It is also the feast of Rosh Hashana in the Jewish calendar, the head of the year. Rosh Hashana marks the beginning of the Days of Awe until Yom Kippur, the Day of Atonement. It is said that during this liminal time, the Book of Life and the Book of Death are opened. The names of who will die and who will live this year are inscribed. We break a loaf of challah bread that I've brought for the occasion this morning, as is done traditionally, each taking pieces that symbolize what we want to be rid of in this new year. Before leaving, we have to think of what it is in our lives that the bread symbolizes, and then find moving waters to throw it into.

We stuff the bread in our pockets as we go about the rest of the morning packing and singing, off and on. Suddenly someone comes up with the idea of taking over the main room in the camp's community cabin for an exhibit of all their maps. Though time is running out, the room is empty and available. Denise and Marna grab the masking tape and in a matter of minutes, everyone's map is up on the walls of the room we've found in our midst.

We are taken on a visual tour of the expedition from each person's point of view. Terry has drawn the outline of her body as a mountain on her map. Didi, so often cheerful, shows us that she's discovered a mysterious darkness along her path. Claudine is laughing and explains excitedly that in drawing her map, she's rediscovered her love of paint and colors. She had put them away as a child. Now she wants color back. Mama's map outlines her transformation. Andrea's shows a promise of new direction. Denise's shows three mysterious figures: the virgin, the mother, and the crone? we wonder. She doesn't know yet. Each person's map is unique, yet it's clear that they've shared the same journey. Claudine begins the song "Rise Up, Oh Flame," the song they sang the morning they walked out of the mountains three days ago. It is a fitting close.

Outside we take more pictures in the parking lot and hug goodbye again and again. With long drives ahead for all of us, and no moving water nearby, we promise that we will stop at the first moving water we find and toss our bread in then rather than spend time as a group finding a creek or river now. I throw my sleeping bag in the back of my car, get in and pull out of the campground with the six of them waving goodbye in my rear view mirror. Within five miles I come to a river and pull over to stop. Standing alone just off the highway by the water, with high speed cars and trucks whizzing by, I stare at the water for a long time. I think of my work that I'm returning to, the Images of Divinity Research Project,[1] especially the Black Madonnas of European Catholicism, the ancient Earth Mother[2] in contemporary form. There's a way in which Mama captured the essence of my research in a phrase she coined, "the mountain is the mother, the mountain is the mother." It became a mantra that got her through the hardest part of her journey. I say it, too, now as I leave the mountains.

Suddenly I'm chilled. The day is sunny but still cool at 7,000 feet. I pull on a green sweatshirt I got from Denise. "Yosemite" is spelled out over the heart. For a moment I feel very alone, then I think of Mama, Denise, Terry, Claudine, Andrea, and Didi in their three cars going in their own direction back to Prescott. The wind whips through the trees as the morning breeze picks up and the sun blazes overhead. A diesel honks on the highway behind me. It's time to go. Feelings well up–gratitude for our time together, happiness in knowing these women, and sadness as the pang of separation washes over me. I toss my bread into the river, turn back to my car and begin the long drive home.

NOTES

1. Sponsored by the Center for Women and Religion at the Graduate Theological Union, Berkeley, CA. In pre-Indoeuropean Europe, the color black symbolized fertility and the earth, white symbolized death. One of the many sources of the hundreds of European Black Madonnas is the ancient lineage of the great Earth Mother.

2. The project grew out of my last book, Longing For Darkness: Tara and the Black Madonna (New York: Viking, 1990; Penguin, 1991).

REFERENCES

Bradley, M.Z. (1982). *The mists of Avalon*. New York: Ballantine.
Galland, C. (1980). *Women in the wilderness*. New York: Harper and Row.
Robinson, J. (1990). *Wayward women: A guide to women travellers*. New York: Oxford University Press.

Index

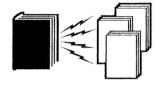

Haworth
DOCUMENT DELIVERY
SERVICE
and Local Photocopying Royalty Payment Form

This new service provides (a) a single-article order form for any article from a Haworth journal and (b) a convenient royalty payment form for local photocopying (not applicable to photocopies intended for resale).

- *Time Saving:* No running around from library to library to find a specific article.
- *Cost Effective:* All costs are kept down to a minimum.
- *Fast Delivery:* Choose from several options, including same-day FAX.
- *No Copyright Hassles:* You will be supplied by the original publisher.
- *Easy Payment:* Choose from several easy payment methods.

Open Accounts Welcome for ...
- Library Interlibrary Loan Departments
- Library Network/Consortia Wishing to Provide Single-Article Services
- Indexing/Abstracting Services with Single Article Provision Services
- Document Provision Brokers and Freelance Information Service Providers

---

MAIL or *FAX* THIS ENTIRE ORDER FORM TO:

Attn: **Marianne Arnold**
Haworth Document Delivery Service
The Haworth Press, Inc.
10 Alice Street
Binghamton, NY 13904-1580

or **FAX**: (607) 722-1424
or **CALL:** 1-800-3-HAWORTH
(1-800-342-9678; 9am-5pm EST)

PLEASE SEND ME PHOTOCOPIES OF THE FOLLOWING SINGLE ARTICLES:
1) Journal Title: _____
   Vol/Issue/Year:_____Starting & Ending Pages:_____
   Article Title:_____
   _____

2) Journal Title: _____
   Vol/Issue/Year:_____Starting & Ending Pages:_____
   Article Title:_____
   _____

3) Journal Title: _____
   Vol/Issue/Year:_____Starting & Ending Pages:_____
   Article Title:_____
   _____

4) Journal Title: _____
   Vol/Issue/Year:_____Starting & Ending Pages:_____
   Article Title:_____
   _____

(See other side for Costs and Payment Information)

COSTS: Please figure your cost to order quality copies of an article.

1. Set-up charge per article: $8.00

                   ($8.00 × number of separate articles) _____

2. Photocopying charge for each article:

                   1-10 pages: $1.00 _____

                   11-19 pages: $3.00 _____

                   20-29 pages: $5.00 _____

                   30+ pages: $2.00/10 pages _____

3. Flexicover (optional): $2.00/article _____

4. Postage & Handling: US: $1.00 for the first article/

                   $.50 each additional article _____

               Federal Express: $25.00 _____

               Outside US: $2.00 for first article/

                   $.50 each additional article _____

5. Same-day FAX service: $.35 per page _____

6. Local Photocopying Royalty Payment: should you wish to copy the article yourself. Not intended for photocopies made for resale. $1.50 per article per copy (i.e. 10 articles x $1.50 each = $15.00) _____

                            GRAND TOTAL: _____

METHOD OF PAYMENT: (please check one)

❑ Check enclosed   ❑ Please ship and bill. PO # _____

                   (sorry we can ship and bill to bookstores only! All others must pre-pay)

❑ Charge to my credit card: ❑ Visa; ❑ MasterCard; ❑ American Express;

Account Number: _____ Expiration date: _____

Signature: **X**_____ Name: _____

Institution: _____ Address: _____

City: _____ State: _____ Zip: _____

Phone Number: _____ FAX Number: _____

MAIL or *FAX* THIS ENTIRE ORDER FORM TO:

Attn: **Marianne Arnold**
Haworth Document Delivery Service
The Haworth Press, Inc.
10 Alice Street
Binghamton, NY 13904-1580

or **FAX:** (607) 722-1424
or **CALL:** 1-800-3-HAWORTH
(1-800-342-9678; 9am-5pm EST)